TICKING CLOCK

ALSO BY IRA ROSEN

The Warning: Accident at Three Mile Island

(with Mike Gray)

TICKING CLOCK

First published in the United States by St. Martin's Press, an imprint of
St. Martin's Publishing Group

TICKING CLOCK. Copyright © 2021 by Ira Rosen. All rights reserved. Printed in
the United States of America. For information, address St. Martin's Publishing
Group, 120 Broadway, New York, NY 10271.

www.stmartins.com

Designed by Omar Chapa

The Library of Congress Cataloging-in-Publication Data is
available upon request.

ISBN 978-1-250-75642-8 (hardcover)
ISBN 978-1-250-75643-5 (ebook)

Our books may be purchased in bulk for promotional, educational, or busi-
ness use. Please contact your local bookseller or the Macmillan Corporate and
Premium Sales Department at 1-800-221-7945, extension 5442, or by email at
MacmillanSpecialMarkets@macmillan.com.

First Edition: 2021

10 9 8 7 6 5 4 3 2 1

To Max, Jake, Johanna, and my wife, Iris.
You light up my life.

CONTENTS

TICKING CLOCK

INTRODUCTION

When I began as a producer on *60 Minutes*, there were no computers and no internet. The phones were rotary, and the newspapers from
around the country came three days late. Stories were often found or
assigned based on what was in *The New York Times*. I and other producers who didn't want *Times* retread stories would play "airport roulette." The way it's played is I would head to the airport and go to the
first plane ticket counter I found. I'd throw my credit card down and
say, "next flight out"; even if the plane was going to Detroit and the one
after it was going to more fun cities like Los Angeles or Las Vegas, I
would go to Detroit. It was part of the karma of the chase.

When I got to Detroit, I would grab all the local newspapers to
see if there was anything interesting going on. If there was, I'd make
a call or two and visit the person who was involved. If there were
no *60 Minutes*-worthy stories, I'd go back to the ticket counter and
once again say, "next plane out," and keep going, sometimes for days.
We had an unlimited budget, so I could travel and stay in any hotel I
wanted. Usually by the time I got back to New York, I'd have a couple
of really interesting ideas to pursue.

Though I would play airport roulette when I was desperately
looking for a story, the most frequent destination I traveled to was

Washington, D.C. The shuttle flights were open seating, and I would always try to board late to have my choice of seatmates. I would pick out politicians, cabinet members, or sometimes businessmen with a cache of interesting documents on their lap. After a fifty-minute airplane ride, even the most closemouthed, discreet bureaucrat would open up and provide me with stories or tips to pursue.

It was on one of those shuttle flights that my career almost ended. In 1982, I was working on my first major investigative story for *60 Minutes*. It was an exposé of how the U.S. government illegally permitted the entry into America of thousands of Nazi war criminals who committed atrocities in World War II, in exchange for their intelligence help in fighting the Soviets. It was an extraordinary smuggling operation conducted by the CIA in defiance of presidential orders.

I had carefully cultivated a source who gave me top secret documents that laid out the details of the operation. I convinced a former member of the Justice Department's unit that prosecuted Nazis to become a whistleblower and go on-camera about the smuggling operations. And I located some of the Nazis, one living a few miles from the *60 Minutes* offices in the Bronx, and another working at Radio Free Europe.

Proud of myself for making all the right moves, I was lost in daydreaming about all the compliments and awards I would receive as I boarded the shuttle flight at LaGuardia Airport, to meet correspondent Mike Wallace for an interview with the whistleblower, John Loftus.

I was less than two years into the job, still on probation, but I hoped this story would get me a permanent position. This was the story that I felt would show everyone at *60 Minutes* that I belonged. On the flight I worked on the interview questions and a script for the story. After the plane landed, I descended the ramp and felt the wonderful warm spring day sun. I relaxed for a moment until I saw the marble obelisk of the Washington Monument. Out of habit, I had flown to Washington, as I had done countless times before. The problem was, I was supposed to be in Boston.

No one had checked my ticket at the New York airport and I had tuned out all the announcements made on the plane. I was in Washington when Mike Wallace was on his way to Boston. Wallace was the show's top correspondent; he didn't have the patience to wait for a urinal to open in a crowded bathroom. I thought, *He will kill me, then fire me, though maybe not in that order.*

I ran back into the terminal, found a flight to Boston, and purchased a ticket at the gate.

Cell phones were not yet invented, so I ran to a phone booth and threw in quarters. I called the cameraman and said I had an emergency and I was running late. "Tell Wallace, but don't start without me," I said. Then I hung up and quickly boarded the plane. I didn't want a cameraman to explain why the twenty-eight-year-old producer just ended up in the wrong airport.

The Eastern flight slowly taxied on the runway.

Faster, faster, I thought.

After a slight delay, the plane took off. In the air it seemed to be flying at half speed.

I couldn't contain myself. I got up and went to the cockpit door. This was way before 9/11; pilots would sometimes leave the door open and even give impromptu tours while the plane was in the air.

I knocked, and a pilot pushed the door open.

"Hi, my name is Ira and I am a *60 Minutes* producer. I boarded the wrong flight this morning and ended up in Washington when I should have been in Boston. Mike Wallace is waiting for me and I am really late. Is there any way you guys could fly faster so I won't lose my job?"

The pilots looked at each other. I think at first they thought I was joking, but they soon realized I was serious.

"You want us to fly faster?" one pilot asked.

"Yes. Even five minutes sooner would make a huge difference. Mike Wallace has no patience and he will fire me."

"We will see what we can do," the pilot said.

I went back to my seat and I heard the engine revving louder. The plane seemed to actually be flying faster.

We landed fifteen minutes early. I ran to a pay phone and called Wallace.

I explained what happened. "You better get your ass here fast," he said, but he didn't fire me. Turns out being late had worked in my favor. Mike spent his time taking pictures and signing autographs for the law firm staff. The adulation from strangers was like a drug for him and put him in a good mood. I survived that day, but there would be many other more precarious days to come.

When our story aired a few weeks later, it made front-page news in nearly every paper in the country and would lead to my first Emmy. But, more important, I had earned my first "Hey, Mildred" compliment from executive producer and *60 Minutes* creator Don Hewitt. Mildred was the name of Hewitt's high school sweetheart. He used her name interchangeably to compliment a story or to say it was too complicated for Mildred to understand. In this case he used the "Hey, Mildred" to say the Nazi story would get a viewer to jump up and shout to his wife or companion a "Hey, Mildred, come over here and watch this story, you won't believe it." That's what Hewitt wanted a TV couch potato to say when *60 Minutes* was on. It was the job of producers like me to find those stories.

Over the ensuing years I would earn quite a few "Hey, Mildred's." I received more awards than almost any producer in TV news, including multiple Peabody and duPont Awards, and twenty-four Emmys. I won six Investigative Reporters and Editors Awards, more than *Washington Post* editor Bob Woodward.

But the pressure involved in ascending that award stage and creating epic TV was insane and unreal. The verbal harassment I experienced from Mike Wallace and other TV big shots was, in a word, criminal.

But I endured all the abuse, in part out of fear, but mostly out of ambition. I loved being a *60 Minutes* producer, and if that meant getting scolded or demeaned, I took the treatment as part of the job description.

At the time it all seemed worth it because being a *60 Minutes* producer was like being a spy with a license to kill. *60 Minutes* was the TV newsmagazine that most Americans relied on to stay informed. Its willingness to challenge authority impacted the public consciousness.

60 Minutes invented TV investigative journalism, including the use of hidden cameras and confrontational interviews to tell its stories. Today there is a dilution of news with thousands of potential news sources, but in its heyday, the only TV newsmagazine was *60 Minutes,* with a viewership each week that rivaled the TV audience of a Super Bowl.

That reach gave me superpowers to convince whistleblowers, con men, and mob bosses to tell their stories. It allowed me to be a part of investigations that changed government policy and helped rescue children and women from life-threatening situations. We exposed the plight of farmworkers, refugees, and the hungry, and we revealed shoddy conditions at VA hospitals, where former vets were neglected and left to die. Our reporting uncovered crooked congressmen, greedy lawyers and businessmen, and doctors adept at ripping off insurance and their patients. We got the wrongfully convicted out of prison and helped to restore justice to those who were screwed. We were crusaders and muckrakers, and appreciatively referred to as the "fifth branch of government" for righting the wrongs of society, during a time when our work was not derisively dismissed as "fake news." It was like being Superman.

During my twenty-five years at *60 Minutes* and my fifteen years as senior producer of ABC's *Primetime Live* and *20/20,* I worked with some remarkable, brilliant journalists and editors who made my work—our work—groundbreaking. But I also worked with some deeply complicated and flawed colleagues.

The late Hunter Thompson of *Rolling Stone* once wrote that the TV business "is normally perceived as some kind of cruel and shallow money trench through the heart of the journalism industry, a long plastic hallway where thieves and pimps run free and good men die like dogs . . ."

Thompson wasn't far off. One top network news executive told me that when he is in the room with all the news anchors from his network, he imagines them as zoo animals—lions, snakes, zebras. "They all exist in TV news," this executive said. "And you can't treat the lions the same way you would treat the snakes. If you do, one of them will bite you."

TV news was certainly not the path I set out to pursue. When I started, I freelanced for *New Age Journal,* a magazine dedicated to spirituality and wellness. One of my assignments was covering the yogis and spiritual leaders in the New Age movement. I went from interviewing Yogi Bhajan, who ran the American Sikh group called Healthy, Happy, Holy Organization (3HO), to reporting on Pir Vilayat Khan, who was head of the international Sufi Order.

I was particularly impressed by Pir Vilayat Khan, who gave me a darshan, a blessing and a meditation to think about for the rest of my life. His darshan to me was "Change your career every seven years. That way you become the ruler of your career and your career doesn't become the ruler of you."

I was twenty-two when he told me this, and I must say I didn't follow this spiritual directive. I have always been motivated by trying to expose injustices and felt journalism provided me with the clearest path to do that. My mission and sense of outrage has been fueled by what happened to my father.

He was a Holocaust survivor who was hidden by a Catholic family in a barn during most of World War II.

The Nazis came into his small Polish town named Kańczuga near the border of Russia and told the townsfolk that for forty-eight hours they could do anything they wanted to the Jews. During this two-day period, the neighbors killed most of the Jewish population.

Given permission to commit crime without consequence, many of those in the town chose to commit murder. At the same time, the Chmura family risked their lives to hide my father for three years. Had they been caught, they surely would have been executed. But the family chose the righteous path.

Having lived through this experience, my father always looked on the bright side of life. He always remembered that humanity consists of those who would risk their lives to save a young teenage boy, to feed and protect him while keeping the secret from their family and friends.

When he left the hayloft, the mother, Mrs. Chmura, gave him a picture of herself. She wrote these words on it: "If you remember, keep it. If you forget, throw it away."

He remembered.

In 2013, my father was in the critical care unit at the Delray Medical Center in Florida. He was eighty-seven and near death. He reassured me that everything was going to be fine, a father to the end. Then in some of the last words he spoke, he said to me: "It's an imperfect world." I wasn't sure what he meant, as he had been an optimist all his life, but I think I knew.

Life consists of a series of choices we make; they are what define us. No matter how imperfect those choices may be, we create this world for ourselves. In my father's case, he remembered what had happened to his family in Poland, and how their neighbors had murdered his mother, father, and twin sisters. Still, he was an optimist, but at the end of his life, he realized that maybe the rest of the world was not.

Like my father, I, too, believe things will work out. But as I learned from him, I still keep one eye open, watching the neighbors.

1

THE PHONE CALL

My path to *60 Minutes* began on June 1980, when the phone rang at my parents' home in Fresh Meadows, Queens. "Is this the home of Ira Rosen?" the caller inquired.

"Yes. Who are you?" my mother replied.

"I am Don Hewitt, executive producer of *60 Minutes*."

"Oh yes, I've read about you," my mother replied. "You have a lovely wife."

"Thank you. What are you doing?"

"I am making a kugel," my mother said.

"A kugel . . . God, I haven't had a good kugel in a long time," Hewitt said.

"You come visit me, I'll give you kugel," my mother offered.

My mother, Ethel, was the quintessential Jewish mother—nagging, judgmental, and someone with all the answers.

"Actually, I am looking for Ira," Hewitt said. "I'd like to see if he'd be interested in being a producer for *60 Minutes*."

"Oh, he's not interested. He's got a good job," my mother said. "Thanks anyway."

I listened from across the room to this conversation and asked my mother who was on the phone.

"Don Hewitt of *60 Minutes*. He wanted to offer you a job, but I told him you already had one," she said. "How many jobs do you need?"

I leaped from the chair and raced to the phone to call Hewitt back. Even though a few minutes had passed, he immediately picked up the phone.

He was laughing. "I don't know about you, but I like your mother. If you don't want the job, tell her it's hers."

I wanted the job. The next day I went to the *60 Minutes* office. It was located on the ninth floor of the 555 West 57th Street building in New York. Its modern offices housed some of the finest journalists in the country—many of whom worked closely with the greatest correspondents of the industry, including Walter Cronkite, Eric Sevareid, and Edward R. Murrow. The offices had a classy and modern feel, recently painted dark gray walls, and on them pictures of the correspondents, Mike Wallace, Morley Safer, Harry Reasoner, and Dan Rather. *60 Minutes* had finished number one for the first time that year. Not only was it popular, it had become a cash cow for the network, making nearly $100 million in profit a year.

I was twenty-six and had already been fired from four different newspaper and magazine jobs. I couldn't make it in Fresno or Long Beach, California, or in Columbus, Ohio. My last firing took place in Pontiac, Michigan. I was living back in the same bedroom I had been in during high school.

Now I found myself at the top of the mountain of American journalism. I was scared, starstruck, and in awe of the place that I didn't think I was ready to join.

When I entered Hewitt's office, it was a beehive of activity. There was constant shouting ("Get me Morley!"), and people were entering and leaving his office as if it were a walk-in medical clinic. To me, it felt like the tumult I had grown up with in the Bronx, on Orchard Street, with the constant banter of bargain hunters looking for a good deal.

I met Don and immediately felt at ease. He regarded himself as a Jewish kid from New York, one who liked to kibitz and tell stories. Above his desk were pictures of him with every president going back to John F. Kennedy. And his windowed corner office faced out over the Hudson River and downtown New York. It was the nicest office I had ever been in.

I had been working in television for only four months as an on-air correspondent for a monthly news show called *What's Happening, America?* that was hosted by Shana Alexander, a former *60 Minutes* contributor. The show was part of a news operation at WOR-TV Channel 9. The Times Square station was known for carrying *The Joe Franklin Show* and *Million Dollar Movie,* and I don't think most people even knew it had a news operation.

But one night, Al Kerins, the *60 Minutes* film projectionist, happened to turn the TV on and catch a story I did. The next morning he was standing next to Don in the office coffee line and told Don about the story, saying that it reminded him of the type of segments the show "used to do."

"What the hell do you mean, used to do?" Don replied. Then he ordered a tape of my story.

The story was on how easy it was to obtain military secrets. I posed as a military contractor and had Norton Air Force Base send me classified films stamped *Secret* without checking my credentials. I then went to the Pentagon and did my best Mike Wallace impression in confronting Arthur Van Cook, a Pentagon official who claimed these were among our most protected secrets. I then pulled the film canisters I had gotten in the mail out of my bag and put them on Cook's lap. He expressed total astonishment and said there would be an investigation into how this happened. Then a female colonel jumped in front of the camera and tried to stop the filming. It was a good story but, because the colonel jumped in front of the camera, it made for great TV.

Hewitt told me he had seen the story and liked it and he wanted to bring stories like that to *60 Minutes.*

Don asked me a question or two about my background, but he

showed no interest in seeing my résumé. As I would later learn, Don operated out of a sense of touch. He didn't need a piece of paper to let him know if he wanted to hire you.

I think he took a liking to me after I told him that I worked as a busboy, a lifeguard, and a tennis pro in various Catskill hotels, jobs that helped pay for college. Don had also worked in the Catskills and understood the life lessons you learned there.

One of those lessons was how to join a conversation with strangers as if you have known them for years. I tried, but this person was Hewitt, the most powerful news producer of the time. I was nervous as I sat on Hewitt's couch, but Don tried to put me at ease. He asked my opinion on potential stories and my advice on where to hang some of his many pictures. Part of me thought, *This can't be real.* I was concerned that all they wanted was to steal my story ideas and show me to the door.

Then Phil Scheffler, the senior producer, walked in.

"Why are you here?" he asked without even saying hello.

"He is here for that producer job we have with Wallace," Hewitt answered.

It was the first I heard that the correspondent they would want me to work with was Wallace.

"He's too young." Scheffler then asked, "How old are you?"

"Twenty-six."

"Twenty-six? I have suits older than you," Scheffler replied.

"Did you see the story he did for WOR? That was terrific," Hewitt said, now looking directly at me to make a point.

"You know what the secret of a *60 Minutes* story is? It's the adventures of Mike, Morley, Harry, and Dan."

At that moment, correspondent Harry Reasoner walked into Don's office.

"Is Don telling you about the adventures of the correspondents who make a story work? It's the story that makes the story," he said. "Hi, I'm Harry Reasoner."

My mouth hung open and I felt it hard to breathe. He looked like he did on TV. Reasoner, along with Mike Wallace, was one of the original *60 Minutes* correspondents and a former co-anchor of *ABC World News Tonight.* For me he represented the legendary history of what CBS was all about, and I also realized how far a leap I was about to make. I had been nervous before, but now I began to visibly sweat. I was hoping not to blow this opportunity.

"He may be Mike's new producer," Hewitt said.

"Poor kid. Did they tell you about him?" Reasoner said as he rolled his eyes.

"Oh, don't listen to Harry," Phil said. "Mike is terrific [pause] every other month."

"Come on," Hewitt said as he stood. "It doesn't matter if I like you, he has to."

We walked about forty feet down the hall to Mike Wallace's office. Each office had a glass wall, which made it easy to see in. All the offices of the correspondents were supposed to be exactly the same size, but the fact is, everyone thought that Mike's was a little bigger.

Mike was one of the giants of TV. His force of personality and his interviews set the style for the show. His aggressive interview techniques and confrontations with confidence men and miscreants are what gave the show its distinctiveness. He was then sixty-two, his black hair combed up off his forehead, and he had a ruddy pockmarked face that made him look like a tough guy.

The meeting with him was much different from the frivolity that had preceded it. There was no joking; it was all serious business. Unlike Don, Mike was not trying to make me feel comfortable. He wanted me to feel uncomfortable.

Mike began by asking me about my professional journalism experience. He read my résumé and seemed genuinely unimpressed. He asked about how much television experience I had.

"Six months," I told him, inflating my experience by two months.

"That's not very much to be a producer on *60 Minutes*," he intoned.

He had watched the story I did for WOR-TV and liked it. "You give us the steak, we will add the sizzle to it," he said. I nodded my head knowingly, though I had no idea at the time what he was talking about.

"Are you okay with going off the air and working behind the scenes?" he asked.

"Oh, I don't think I am all that good on-camera," I said honestly.

"I know what I can do for you," Mike said. "What can you do for me?"

I was stumped. It was a great question, and I didn't have a good answer. But then I noticed that in the corner of his office, Mike had a tennis ball enshrined in a glass case—a ball that had been given to him by columnist Art Buchwald, a longtime friend, after Buchwald tripped on the ball and broke his ankle. "A great tennis career cut short by this ball," the case was inscribed.

"You play tennis?" I asked Wallace.

"What's it to you?" he shot back.

"Well, I play a little," I said with false modesty. "I was on the Cornell tennis team."

Mike would tell me later that my answer clinched the job for me. Mike thought that if I didn't work out as a producer, he could get six months of good tennis out of me before firing me. Hewitt returned to Mike's office. "So, Mike, what do you think?" Hewitt asked. "Let's give the kid a shot."

Mike shrugged.

"Great. How much money do you want?" Hewitt asked me.

I was completely unprepared for the question.

I was making $30,000, so I offered that figure. I realized later I could have gotten more, but I didn't want to lose the job over a few thousand dollars.

Hewitt left the room and came back a few minutes later. "Done," he said. "We will get you a contract."

I walked out of the offices dazed; I had come from covering high school sports in Fresno, California, to becoming Mike Wallace's producer on the hottest show on TV. Not only was Mike the star, but I had become the youngest producer they had ever hired. I called my mother to tell her.

"Mom, I was just hired to be Mike Wallace's producer on *60 Minutes*."

Without missing a beat, my mom said, "Mike Wallace? He is so old. Why can't you work for Dan Rather?"

2

60 MINUTES BEGINS

Don loved telling the story of how he founded *60 Minutes*. He was an executive producer of the *CBS Evening News* with Walter Cronkite when Fred Friendly, then president of CBS News, told him that the show was too small for Don to run. He wanted Hewitt to be in charge of something bigger, creating new projects and documentaries. Delighted, Don told his wife about the promotion. "Don, you haven't been promoted," she told him. "You've been fired."

Before his wife had said that, it had never occurred to Don that he was moved to a job that had a title but no staff. But Don, being Don, never had the attention span to watch long documentaries. So, he said, let's come up with "mini-documentaries," which would be 15-minute segments. He believed that the audience might not like all three stories on a given night, but they were sure to like one of them.

Don wrote a memorandum that outlined his vision: "If we package it attractively as Hollywood packages fiction, split the hour into three stories and make it very personal journalism . . . in that sense it will be the voices of living and breathing reporters and not the corporate voice of CBS Reports, an NBC Whitepaper or an ABC Close-up." He wanted it to be the *Life* magazine of TV.

The show began in 1968, with Mike Wallace and Harry Reasoner as the only anchors. At that time, Wallace was anchoring the CBS morning show and documentaries for CBS Reports. Before joining CBS he fronted TV commercials and entertainment shows, but Mike was still a first-rate journalist. He did a documentary on the civil rights movement, *The Hate That Hate Produced,* before the mainstream media had discovered who the Black Muslims even were. But he also had missteps, like the CBS Reports documentary he narrated titled *The Homosexuals.*

"The average homosexual, if there be such, is promiscuous," Wallace said in the piece. "He is not interested or capable of a lasting relationship like that of a heterosexual marriage. His sex life, his love life, consists of a series of one-chance encounters at the clubs and bars he inhabits. And even on the streets of the city—the pickup, the one-night stand, these are characteristics of the homosexual relationship."

Years later he would come to regret that story as one of his biggest mistakes, as the hour was sloppy, hurtful, and homophobic, but it didn't harm Mike's standing in journalism or in politics, as a few months after it aired, he was offered the job of press secretary for Richard Nixon, who was running for president. But Mike, who was fifty at that point, felt he would be more comfortable as a correspondent than as a press secretary and wisely chose to join *60 Minutes.*

Don wanted to make films. He believed that news stories should have the look of movies, with the stories built around great characters. Back then *60 Minutes* was shooting the segments on 16-millimeter film, about eleven minutes per roll. The show edited the stories on Steenbecks, where each edit had to be hand-spliced and taped together, adding hours to the editing process.

But Don resisted changing to tape, as he wanted to maintain the film quality look. He also stressed the importance of good writing, as he believed that a story has to first work on the ear rather than the eye. Don remembered the CBS News radio reports from London during World War II, the sounds of bombs dropping that painted pictures in the listeners' minds.

Though movies were his template, he retained the CBS News

standard of no music in stories, unless it appeared naturally in a concert or on radio. And Don never believed in staff meetings. He felt they were a waste of time.

Don's biggest inspiration was that the stories should become the adventures of the correspondents. He wanted to see Mike in Iran with the ayatollah, or Harry Reasoner eating the world's most expensive meal. When he approached the correspondents to join the show, he promised them they could cover whatever stories they wished, anywhere in the world. Hewitt believed that the audience would care about the correspondent and therefore care about the story. As in a movie, the correspondent became the lead actor.

And it seemed to work. The viewership grew and grew, eventually making *60 Minutes* the number one show in the country.

Hewitt wanted his operation to be separate from CBS News, so he moved it to the ninth floor of a building across the street from the broadcast center in New York. We could still take advantage of the cafeteria, but our jobs and worlds were far removed from the daily operations of the news division.

At the time, *60 Minutes* didn't concern itself much with budgets to shoot stories. The staff of about a hundred people had generous vacations, with everyone from secretaries to correspondents taking the month of July off, fully paid. We also had almost unlimited expense accounts to fete sources, and nice offices overlooking the Hudson River. But don't think for a second that it was a joyful place to work. It was cutthroat, though a casual visitor would not have noticed it.

You couldn't tell how competitive the environment was if you walked past the correspondents' offices. Most afternoons, everyone seemed to enjoy a nap. Mike would fall asleep on his couch around four in the afternoon, with a blanket covering him. Morley would sleep in his chair, usually with a lit cigarette dangling from his mouth. Ed Bradley would try to sleep but would complain about the noise in the hallways. He would often play some jazz to drown out the noise.

Yet at any given time, the correspondents wouldn't be talking with one another. Usually they fought over a story or a producer that had been stolen from them. Mike, of course, given his aggressive nature, was the biggest culprit.

After each TV season he would usually get rid of one of his five producers. It kept the remaining producers on their toes but created bitter rivalries among us. One of his producers, Marion Goldin, once misplaced her tapes for a story and falsely accused me of stealing them. She also wrote a letter to Hewitt that the font size of my name on the story jacket, seen in the storyboard behind the correspondent, was bigger than hers, which also wasn't true. She would end up leaving *60 Minutes* over the font size issue.

The other producers would happily gossip if one of them had a bad screening. One producer, Martin Phillips, shot an entire story in California with Wallace. At the end of the shoot, the cameraman went to the airport to ship the 16-millimeter film canisters. He took them out of his car and put them on the road, and before he knew it, another car came and ran over them. All the film was exposed, and the entire shoot was ruined. There were producers who were happy to hear about Martin's misfortune. Though he reshot the story, it wasn't quite the same. Phillips would be one of those whom Mike would later dump.

The rivalry also extended to the correspondents. Wallace would often poach stories from Bradley or Safer, and Hewitt would acquiesce, either out of fear or greater loyalty to Wallace. Mike would send his producers out to steal a source or a character who was key to a story, and then he would quickly film it before the other correspondent found out. He did this most often to Safer. Months would go by in which Safer would not speak to Wallace, even though their offices were next door to each other. During those periods, *60 Minutes* did not feel like a special place to work.

Don believed in the importance of the producers and tried to build a show with the best in TV. And in those days, the early 1980s, the producers on the show were some real characters.

First, there was the legendary Joe Wershba, who was one of the original producers of *See It Now,* which investigated the red-baiting hearings of Senator Joseph McCarthy. The show would launch the career of anchor Edward R. Murrow and future CBS News president Fred Friendly, who would be portrayed in a movie directed by George Cloo-ney·titled *Good Night, and Good Luck*. Wershba's role would be played by actor Robert Downey Jr.

Joe was a tall, bald man, who enjoyed freelancing for *The Forward*, a newspaper that covered issues of importance to American Jews, as much as he did working at *60 Minutes*. Joe would serve me whiskey on Friday afternoons, while regaling me with stories of the days when radio ruled the airwaves. He told me about how they began one episode of *See It Now*, "Christmas in Korea," during the Korean War. The story was about the frozen tundra of the battlefield, where the troops were trying to dig foxholes.

"We began with the sound of a shovel hitting the ground. . . . *Tat, tat, tat* . . . This is the sound from Korea," Edward R. Murrow would say, "*Tat, tat, tat,* it is the sound of our troops trying to break the frozen ground of Korea, to dig foxholes with their shovels, to protect them from enemy gunfire. . . . *Tat, tat, tat*." The story always ended with Wershba smiling and saying, "That was how it was, Young America," his nickname for me.

Up the hallway from Joe was Al Wasserman, who created the White Papers series for NBC News and then moved over to CBS, where he led coverage of the capture of the U-2 spy plane pilot Francis Gary Powers, one of the most worst crises of the cold war. The backstory of the capture and release of the American pilot, who flew an over-flight mission and was shot down over the Soviet Union, was told in the movie *Bridge of Spies,* with Tom Hanks and directed by Steven Spielberg. Al would fill me with the insights into how he got the Russians and the Americans to reveal details of the swap that brought Powers back to the United States.

Then there was Drew Phillips, Harry Reasoner's lead producer, who did one of the great *60 Minutes* classics on the movie *Casablanca*. Drew, when he wasn't spending his days reading cheap dime-store novels in the office, would scan the paper for esoteric stories. One day he noticed an item in the paper about how a movie studio was auctioning parts of the set from *Casablanca,* one of the greatest movies ever made. He told Harry that covering the sale might be a good idea for a story, as it would provide a way to revisit the movie.

The story Reasoner and Phillips did was romantic and sad, and in the end redemptive, about the importance of movies in our lives. Reasoner was dressed in a tuxedo, talking to the camera. "I remember a piano and a lamp and the lovely girl sitting at the table and both the memory of love and the foreshadowing of despair," Harry wrote. "I don't suppose, then or now, young men wind up for good with the young women with whom they first saw *Casablanca.* I didn't. The story seems to lead to bittersweet endings in real life, too. But you never forget who you first saw it with. I wonder if she remembers. If she does: Here's looking at you, kid."

There was the young investigative reporter George Crile, who would do the story called *The Uncounted Enemy,* about how the U.S. military would fake the levels of enemy troops during the Vietnam War in order to create the impression that the Americans were winning the war. He accused four-star general William Westmoreland of leading the cover-up, an accusation that would lead to a monumental lawsuit that helped launch the career of a young lawyer, David Boies, and nearly destroyed Mike Wallace, who would later fall into a depression that he said was caused by the court case.

George had no concept of time. He would show up for a one P.M. lunch at two, if he showed up at all. I would eat lunch before he arrived. George was fearless and crazy. He once took correspondent Bob Simon to South Waziristan, one of the most forbidden and dangerous parts of Pakistan. Simon would later tell me that the best thing that happened was they got arrested ten minutes into their trip. If they hadn't, they all would have been dead.

Then there was Bill McClure, a former cameraman who lived in London and became a producer for Harry Reasoner and Ed Bradley. He shot one of the most expensive stories in *60 Minutes* history, about monks of Tibet. He stationed his cameramen to get the best sunrise and sunset shots from the country and shot endless hours of monks praying, which needless to say, was not very exciting.

When Hewitt screened the story, with Ed Bradley as the correspondent, Hewitt said, "The monks walk to the left, and then the monks walk to the right, then they walk to the left again. What kind of fuckin' story is that?"

It never made the air.

McClure not only survived that story, he prospered in the laissez-faire *60 Minutes* environment. He would have the camera crews drive his truck to the shoots and then rent his truck to CBS, charging a high fee. This might have been okay if the story was near London, where he lived. But he would have the crews drive the truck to the Middle East and even the far reaches of Asia. No one was quite sure how he was able to pull this off, but he did. When the truck finally broke down in the Himalayas, he had CBS tow it to a nearby town, where he charged them to have it fixed and sold. CBS happily paid to be rid of it.

It was against this backdrop of legends and characters that I tried to establish myself. It was clear that they all played by their own set of rules, rules not taught in journalism school. I needed to figure out how to operate and how to succeed.

My first story was on Teamsters violence. A California judge ruled that it was okay to commit acts of vandalism, harassment, physical coercion, even arson, if they were part of union organizing activities. If the ruling stood, it would open the way for union organizers, who maintained they were trying to grow their membership ranks, to be excused from felonies. Our main character, a man who worked for the Los Angeles organized crime strike force, gave us proof of how the mafia was behind the union-organizing activity.

He desperately wanted us to do the story, so I wore him down until he allowed me into the Federal strike force offices, around three in the morning. I felt like a cat burglar let into a big mansion by the house butler. As soon as I was in, I began to rifle through the files, looking for any document stamped *Secret*. I then copied what I needed on their

Xerox machine. I don't remember much about those files, except for one that discussed the attempts of the mafia to infiltrate the movie business. I remember the exhilaration I felt after my successful seduction of a federal agent in order to get classified files. The information was not critical to the story, but just the fact that I was able to get it made me feel world-class.

I was co-producing the story with Allan Maraynes. He was not that much older than me, but he had more experience, having produced about five stories with Mike. Allan didn't regard me as a rival and prided himself on remaining calm despite what was going on around him. The day Mike Wallace was to arrive in Los Angeles, our main character, the labor investigator, had a change of heart and dropped out. It was one thing to let me take files, quite another to go on *60 Minutes* and show your face. Even though he was nearing retirement, he didn't want to get fired, which is what he thought would happen if he went public. We had other interviews scheduled, but his decision not to appear was a blow to the story. We picked Mike up at Los Angeles airport. He took the front seat and I sat in the back.

Allan was driving the car and told Mike how the investigator bailed on us. Mike went crazy. He took documents out of Allan's briefcase and threw them at him. Wallace cursed Allan, told him that he was a failure as a producer, and that he would be demoted as soon as we returned to New York. It was the most astonishing verbal abuse I had ever witnessed. I was soon to learn that in the world of Wallace this kind of verbal abuse was common. But I had never seen anything like this before. I was scared; maybe I was to be Mike's next victim. I sat in the back of the car, and Mike turned around. "Hey, kid, how are you? Bring your racket? Maybe we can get a little tennis in."

I learned the first rule of *60 Minutes*: the producer gets blamed for all failures, while the junior producer usually skates by.

After we checked into the hotel and Mike settled into his room, Allan and I went to get a drink.

"How can you take that?" I asked.

"Take what?" he asked, puzzled.

"Take that abuse, the shouting, yelling, name-calling."

"I don't know what you are talking about."

"What just happened in the car? All that stuff Mike was saying," I said.

Allan looked at me like I was crazy. "I tuned him out. I didn't hear any of it. If you are going to listen to everything he says, you will go crazy, so I figured out a way to go into a cone of silence."

Allan was a talented filmmaker and had married Mike's former secretary. He appeared calm on the outside, but he lost most of his hair in his twenties.

Mike's abuse, I was to learn, affected people in different ways.

The least harmful way was that your back went out. Allan walked around with a back brace. The tension of the job led other producers to develop heart disease or cancer at an early age. One lucky producer "only" got ulcers, which he nicknamed Myron, Mike's real name. For me, my back would go into spasms during my entire time working with Wallace. I would end up sleeping on many hotel room floors to reduce the pain, including years later, during my honeymoon.

I realized that the real trick of being a successful producer was to save a story that was going to hell. Producing was easy when subjects showed up on time, the correspondents got a good night's sleep and prepared for the interview, and the subject was full of wit and energy.

That rarely happened. Usually correspondents showed up pissed off, angry that they actually had to work; the main interview subject decided to bring his lawyer, who interrupted constantly; and the cameraman got distracted and doesn't notice that the subject was moving around in his chair and was going out of frame.

So, to save this story, since we didn't have a whistleblower, we needed to find someone Mike Wallace could aggressively confront. Fortunately for us, the judge who made this crazy ruling that it was okay for Teamsters to commit violence for union organizing purposes decided to go on-camera. Mike at this point was suitably pissed off, and he showed no mercy to the judge. After we put the story together, the screening with Hewitt went well. I began to learn that the most important part of a Mike Wallace story was the confrontation. He had to have someone to hold accountable. Without that someone, the story likely wouldn't work.

That lesson became apparent when I solo-produced my next story, a few months later, on school violence in Los Angeles. Several parents were suing the state, claiming it was cruel and unusual punishment to send kids to the schools in Los Angeles because there was so much violence. Parents wanted to take their kids out of public schools and send them to private schools, with the state paying the bill. In order to tell the story, we had to establish the violence. The first person we interviewed was a fifteen-year-old girl who claimed that someone tried to assault her in school. We interviewed her and she appeared not particularly angry about what happened.

Mike was livid over the interview. I drove down I-5 with Mike and he ripped open my briefcase and threw papers at me. Suddenly I was getting treated like his whipping boy. I kept telling myself not to lose my cool, uttering "Nam-myoho-renge-kyo," a Buddhist chant, quietly to myself, saying it over and over as he screamed at me. Like Allan, I discovered my own cone of silence. The documents he threw at me had little to do with the story, but that didn't matter. "Why didn't I see this?" he would yell as papers would cover the car window, making it tough to drive. My stomach turned and I told him that the next interview would be better.

This interview was with a sixteen-year-old Chicano girl who had been stabbed inside a school. She lived in a Los Angeles barrio in a neighborhood below all the rich homes of Beverly Hills. The girl was slight of build, shy, and was scared of talking about what happened in school, so her mother insisted on sitting next to her. Mike began by asking the girl where she got stabbed. She pointed to the side of her belly. "Can I see?" Mike asked and tried to lift her shirt. Her mother slapped Mike's hand away. This only empowered Mike to try again. Once again, the mother slapped his hand away.

The interview had gone on for only a few minutes, but it was effectively over. I bummed a cigarette from one of the cameramen and walked out while Mike continued to ask questions. I didn't smoke, but that day I did. I began to wonder what I would do next in my career, when I noticed a group of kids standing outside the house where we were filming.

I played a hunch. "How many of you have gotten stabbed in school?" I asked. A couple of hands were raised. "How many of you did the stabbing?" I asked. One hand went up.

I gathered the group of kids together. At this point Mike emerged from the interview looking like he wanted to fire me on the spot. I told Mike to interview the kids.

"What do I ask them?" he asked, looking at me with a combination of amusement and anger.

"Ask them who got stabbed in school, who did the stabbing, and follow your instincts," I said.

Mike spoke first to the victims about how they got attacked in school. He then turned to the one kid who said he had stabbed someone in school.

"You think you are a big man to put a knife in someone's belly," Mike asked. "How old are you?"

"Sixteen," came the reply.

"Did that make you feel strong? Did it make you feel important? You are nothing but a punk," Mike scolded. It was signature Mike, but it made for great TV.

Mike and I got back in the car and drove up to the Beverly Hills Hotel, where we were staying. A few minutes went by in silence.

Mike spoke first.

"You know you saved your ass tonight," he said.

"I know," I said. And that was it. We said nothing else for the rest of the car ride. We didn't have to. We both understood I had survived my first real test of producing.

3

MIKE AND DON

Don's decision to build the show around the personality of the correspondents made them rich and famous. And no correspondent enjoyed the fame as much as Mike Wallace. Each Sunday's broadcast after the ticking clock would often begin with his introduction. In the early 1980s, Wallace was making $7 million a year, more than even CBS anchor Walter Cronkite. He was one of the only people I knew who enjoyed walking through airports. People would shout, "Go get them, Mike!" or "You're the best." Those walks were intoxicating ego massages, in which he basked in the recognition of being the public face of *60 Minutes*. He was a star and he knew it.

At the time, Mike was married to his third wife, painter Lorraine Périgord, whom he had met on a vacation in Haiti. He said that he first liked her because she showed him the proper deference more commonly exhibited by European women. When I joined the show in 1980, they had already been married for twenty years, and there were signs living with Mike was wearing on her.

Morley Safer told me that she would eat only certain things like sardines, and then eat them every day. She was always very quiet when she was with Mike, almost afraid to say the wrong thing. Mike told me she was medicated. Mike, who was notoriously cheap, would scrutinize every bill she paid and every dollar she spent. He would sit down with his accountant and go over them one by one. I think he drove her crazy. A year after I began working with Mike, they separated and eventually divorced.

Newly single, Mike began to date openly. He enjoyed the attention of women, and he discovered many women had a secret crush on him and let him know it.

Around this time, we were in Los Angeles, staying at the Beverly Hills Hotel, one of Mike's favorite places. The hotel had two tennis courts and the great Pancho Segura as its tennis pro. And they always had a court available for Mike. We played a little tennis and he then asked if I would join him for dinner with a friend.

It turned out his friend was a rich Texas widow who was following Mike around the country as he filmed his stories. She was a petite blonde in her fifties and came to dinner in a see-through blouse. The two of them flirted through dinner. At one point she slipped her hand between his legs under the table and then made strong eye contact with me.

I think she was misinterpreting the relationship of a network producer and a correspondent and wanted a threesome. I didn't belong at the dinner; this was Mike playing the mad hatter. He wanted to watch reactions of people close to him for his amusement. He never cared how awkward it made me feel. But I said nothing, as we had a story to shoot and he could be vindictive if he felt I had crossed him.

After dinner, I drove the two back to the hotel. I excused myself, as I had to write the questions for the next day's interview. Mike told me in front of his date that he wanted to see the questions that night. *As if he would ever read them,* I thought.

I wrote the questions and went up to his room. I knocked. No answer. I knocked again. This time, the door opened, and standing before me was Wallace, completely naked. Looking in, I saw his girlfriend in the room.

"What the hell do you want?" he asked.

"I have your questions."

He grabbed them out of my hand and slammed the door.

The next morning, I waited for Mike outside the hotel entrance. I was driving and I wondered what kind of day we were going to have. Mike got into the car and didn't speak.

I simply asked, "So?" He turned to me, no smile, looked me straight in the eye, and said, "I enjoyed your questions very much last night."

I pretended to care about his exploits to fill up the emptiness inside the car. Mike rarely listened to the radio when driving, but he acted as if I was too inconsequential to even have a conversation with.

A few weeks later after we edited and screened the story, I asked Mike whatever happened to the Texas widow.

"I gave her to Harry," Mike said, referring to Harry Reasoner.

Mike was constantly needling Harry, who was trying to get back in the game after a divorce. Harry was linked with actress Angie Dickinson, who was one of the most glamorous and beautiful women in Hollywood. Dickinson was quoted as saying that Harry "was the love of her life."

One day after Harry took a nap on his couch and emerged from his office looking particularly disheveled, Mike grabbed a mail deliveryman in the hallway and said, "Sir, do you know who this man is?"

The deliveryman said no. Then Mike asked, "Do you know who Angie Dickinson is?" Yes, came the reply.

"Would it surprise you to learn that this is the sort of man that Angie Dickinson can't keep her hands off?" Mike said. I began to realize that he was as mean to his fellow correspondents as he was to the producers.

Mike was part of the *Mad Men* culture: he thought women were there for his amusement. He would snap a secretary's bra straps like a rambunctious teenager and would think nothing about grabbing the ass of any woman who walked by.

One very elegant and sophisticated female producer happened to have made the mistake of walking by Mike's office when he was bored. As she passed, he smacked her ass.

Without missing a beat, she turned and slapped Mike and told him never to do that again.

"What the hell is her problem?" Mike said out loud.

Mike had a sense of entitlement when it came to women. The women on the staff regarded him as a chauvinist pig, but few complained, because they feared their careers would be adversely impacted.

Once, I was going over a script with Mike when one of the female managers of the show came in. Mike motioned for her to sit on his lap and she did. He began to touch her breasts.

"I'll come back later," I said, shocked at what I was seeing. "Why don't you two just get a hotel room?"

I understood Mike's sense of playfulness and entitlement, but to grope a female staffer in front of me crossed the line.

Mike insisted I stay and work on the script. I didn't.

Another female producer repeatedly harassed by Mike told me he grabbed her breasts and squeezed them. "That time of month," he said to her. He once made up a trip to get her to travel to Washington for a nonexistent meeting so he could get her alone in a hotel. Eventually she left Mike to work with another correspondent.

There was an effort to protect the franchise by suppressing anything that might damage its image. Once, in the 1980s, a producer and editor were editing a controversial story on a publicly traded company that, when aired, would no doubt affect the stock price. The producer and editor shorted the company stock while editing the story. When it aired, they made a sizable amount of money. Hewitt found out about what they did and wanted to fire them. But he became convinced it would be bad for the show's image; instead he suspended them for two weeks and then allowed them to return.

None of these stories were ever made public. I know of several cases where women chose to leave the business rather than endure the harassment and humiliation by Mike and other senior managers. Mike defined himself as a troublemaker and he regarded his hazing of women as no big deal. But such treatment was a big deal to those who were his victims. And sadly, he was allowed to do what he wanted.

Meanwhile the esteem in which Mike was held and the show's

ratings continued to grow, and he felt he could continue to say and do anything he pleased. Those were traits that Hewitt admired and hated.

Don Hewitt's role model was Hildy Johnson, the cocky star tabloid reporter from the movie *The Front Page,* about a reporter covering an execution while always looking for the scoop. And he would talk like a New York tabloid editor, inspiring the staff with his boundless energy, humor, and ideas. His editing of stories always included great theatrics. Once he told me to remove a grandmother of the main character by saying, "Take that yutz out of the piece. She has nothing to do with your story."

Another time he said of a character, "She is a lox. You don't need her."

Don believed "you should never underestimate the public's intelligence and never overestimate its knowledge. You never want a husband to turn to his wife during a story and ask, 'Do you know what this guy is talking about? No? Then hand me the remote.'"

Though Don was a brilliant editor, he also had a keen understanding of his own shortcomings. Mike would tell me that Don had no moral compass and preferred personality over substance in stories. When I did the investigation into how Nazis were smuggled into the United States after World War II to help in intelligence efforts against the Soviet Union, I was leaked top secret documents that supported the thesis of the story. The source told me to protect their identity, but said I could reveal their identity to my boss.

"Don, as editor, you are entitled to know who my source is," I said.

"Don't tell me, don't tell me," he said. "I can't keep a secret."

What Don *did* do was come up with brilliant ideas for stories. In 1986, he famously told Ed Bradley to do a profile of Muhammad Ali. Bradley argued that Ali couldn't speak. Don's reply was "If he could speak, it wouldn't be a story."

Ali had Parkinson's disease, and at one point in the interview Ali pretended to fall asleep.

His wife, Lonnie, told Bradley, "Ever since the Frazier fight in

Manila, Muhammad will . . . it's sort of like—like narcolepsy. He'll just start sleeping, but he'll have these flashbacks.

"And he'll have . . . it's like nightmares. And his face will twist up, like he's boxing, and he'll throw punches at people. And he does it at night sometimes. . . . Whenever he starts snoring heavily, I have to get out of the bed because I know it's going to start."

He then uncontrollably threw a punch at Ed. It was all a joke, and it was done without Ali's saying a word. The Ali story would go down as one of Bradley's best stories, made possible by Don's great story sense.

Don rarely hired from the super elite schools because he felt those people came from lives of privilege. Hewitt preferred producers who had to overcome hardships in their lives or those with a little hustle to their step.

We all hated to disappoint him. The goal was always for him to jump up from his chair after screening a story and utter one word: *sensational.*

Story screenings at *60 Minutes* determined your success as a producer. They took place in a small windowless room, with twenty chairs lining the wall. Don and Phil Scheffler, his deputy, sat up front with the other senior producers or fact-checkers. The room was painted battleship gray and sometimes smelled like sweat. Some of the top producers in the world would show their work there, tiptoeing into the room, trying to make small talk with Don, giving him some gossip or a cheap compliment. But none of that mattered if your story wasn't good.

You could disappear for weeks at a time or do three gym workouts a day, but no one cared if your screening went well. On the other hand, you could work eighteen-hour days, but if your screening went badly, you could be fired, a reason Mike was often very tense when Don screened his pieces. Mike's pieces were rarely cut for time and usually led the show. Yet Mike still felt a need to embarrass Hewitt whenever he could, and that led to some memorable clashes.

The Don Hewitt and Mike Wallace face-offs at the office would make a great reality show today. The two of them yelled and fought and teased each other endlessly. I asked Mike why he was always picking a fight with Don and he said, "It gets your blood moving. It makes you feel alive."

Mike and Don needed each other, and the success of the show depended on them. Don told the story of how Mike once blacked out at an airport and was lying on the floor. "Get up," Don said. "Don't die on me. We haven't beaten *Cheers* [in the ratings] yet."

Early in my tenure as a producer I had just completed a story on Marine corporal Arnold Bracy, who was a security guard at the American embassy in Moscow. He was accused of having an affair with a Soviet woman and providing the Soviets with access to the U.S. embassy, which they used to place electronic bugs. The story wasn't bad, but Bracy wasn't a good TV character—and bad characters often lead to bad screenings.

Mike knew this. He said, "Stay near me during the screening and do as I say." When the screening ended, Don began to speak. "I don't understand why—" That was all Don got a chance to say.

"There you go again, Don. We traveled all over the world for this story and you don't understand this or that," Mike said loudly. "You diminish our work. I have had enough of you." Then, looking at me, he said, "Let's go, kid."

I walked out with Mike. "That went pretty well," Mike said.

"What are you talking about? You didn't let Don say one thing."

"He was going to fuck up the piece," Mike said.

"How do you know? You didn't let him say anything," I said.

They didn't talk for days. My piece was in limbo. I finally sneaked into Don's office and asked him what he wanted to say in the screening.

"I just wanted to know why Bracy decided to go on-camera," Don said.

"Because he is participating in a book that is coming out."

"That's it. Say it," Don replied.

I slipped the language into the story, and a few days later I screened it again. The screening ended and Don got up to leave, saying nothing. But Mike couldn't help himself.

Pointing at me he said, "The kid worked his ass off on this story and you can't even say *nice job*. Come on, Don," Mike said disingenuously. He really didn't care about my getting complimented. His request was intended to break Don's balls.

At this point, everyone including me was against Mike, but senior producer Phil Scheffler was the one who spoke. "Mike, sometimes you are just a prick."

No one argued with Phil.

Scheffler kept Don from going too Hollywood. He also tried to rein Mike in when he was abusing producers or stealing stories from other correspondents. Phil was a bald, grumpy fellow who enjoyed playing backgammon in his office. He, Morley Safer, and Don would also play poker in Don's office. Morley usually won. Phil kept a watchful eye on me and would at times accompany us on stories. Unlike Don and Mike, he remembered how young I was.

In the first two years I was at the show I had done some decent stories but I needed a big interview and at the time there was no bigger "get" than Robert Vesco, the world's most wanted fugitive. Vesco had carried out one of the biggest securities frauds ever—worth more than a billion dollars in today's dollars. He was widely regarded as the undisputed king of fugitive financiers. He used his stolen money to bribe presidents and prime ministers who protected him as he fled to Costa Rica, Antigua, Nicaragua, Paradise Island, and ultimately Cuba. Vesco was trying to negotiate a deal with Senator Orrin Hatch to get back into the United States, and his staff encouraged Vesco to speak with me.

Vesco agreed to meet on Paradise Island, in the Bahamas, to discuss the possibility of appearing on *60 Minutes*. When I told Scheffler, he said that this was a big story and he was going to come along.

When we arrived in the Bahamas, we went to the Paradise Island Beach Club overlooking the waterway. Vesco, wearing dark sunglasses, greeted us at the bar. He was much taller than I thought, with long sideburns and a thin mustache. He had the face of a person who rarely smiled, a face that looked like it held many secrets. He told us how the FBI assigned agents to track his every move. But he had a cooperative arrangement with the FBI agents assigned to follow him. He said he would tell them what his plans were for the day, and they would be able to collect daily photos of him for their bosses in Washington. Then they spent the rest of the day relaxing and tanning, though a few agents still kept tabs on him.

He pointed to a boat in the harbor. "They are the FBI," he said. "They are taking surveillance pictures of us, and then [the boat] will turn around at that bridge and come back and they will take more photos." Sure enough, that's what happened.

Vesco was mysterious and paranoid, and delighted in thumbing his nose at those trying to catch him. In his life on the run he had befriended and been protected by the president of Costa Rica, the Sandinistas of Nicaragua, the Colombian cartel, and the government of Libya. During our seafood lunch, he said that every politician from Richard Nixon on down has been bought. He made Nixon a partner with him in a bridge in the Bahamas, in the hope of having the Justice Department drop charges against him. The Justice Department never dropped the charges, but they did come up with the idea of suspending a rope from a helicopter to lasso him up and take him back to the United States. They were about to put the plan into action until an FBI agent pointed out that if the rope slipped, it might end up hanging Vesco. In the end, Vesco decided he didn't want to go on-camera, as he worried about further raising his profile.

A short time after our visit, he went to Cuba, where he was welcomed by the Castro government. Seven years after he arrived, the Cuban government would turn against him and put him in jail, where he would die in 2007.

Mike made it clear that Vesco-type stories were what he wanted. He was getting more and more obsessed with his image, and this was reflected in his story choices.

"Kid, the public knows me by what I put on the air. So if I do twenty stories a year, I want five to be investigative, five to be profiles, five to be issues—pro-gun, anti-gun—and five to be foreign. That way I will be seen as well-rounded, and I won't be typecast."

Mike had always been a celebrity, but the show's success made him think he was bigger and more important than those he was interviewing, a very dangerous trait for correspondents.

I had seen this play out when we tried to get legendary actor Marlon Brando to sit for an interview.

Earlier, I had done a profile of former organized crime boss Joe Bonanno and wanted to use some video from the movie *The Godfather*. Normally this request would be handled through the Hollywood studios, but one day the phone rang in my office and it was Marlon Brando.

"I understand you would like to use some of the *Godfather* film," he asked without introducing himself.

I nearly fell off my chair. At first I thought it was one of my friends playing a joke on me, but the more Brando talked, with special knowledge of the story I was working on, I realized it was him. Brando was a recluse and almost never talked to the press.

Brando said he called me because the studio asked him about the use of the video, and he decided to find out for himself what the story was about. He wanted to make sure the piece would not offend Bonanno. I explained this was a cooperative piece and that Bonanno and his family had already sat for an interview. Brando agreed to let us use the movie clip, but what I really wanted was to do a profile of him with Mike Wallace.

We began to talk regularly, conversations that would last for hours. He would speak Yiddish to me on the phone, regaling me with stories about his acting coach Stella Adler. He would ask me what stories I was working on and had strong opinions on then-president Ronald Reagan. "Reagan was a lousy actor," Brando said. "Becoming president was his fallback plan."

It turned out that Brando and I were born on the same day, April 3, so I called him up on our birthday to extend my best wishes.

"Trees don't celebrate birthdays, animals don't celebrate birthdays, only humans do. Why do you think we are more special?" he said. "I won't do anything special."

He told me how he once found his neighbor Jack Nicholson's underwear in his freezer. He said Nicholson used Brando's house for his romantic escapades. "Jack left it for me as a souvenir," he said.

Another time, I was leaving my house to go meet a date at a bar when the phone rang. Brando started talking without even a hello. "Do you ever realize that some great artists with great reputations are really assholes? Charlie Chaplin, film genius—asshole. William Saroyan, brilliant writer, an asshole."

I told Brando that I had a date waiting for me at a Georgetown bar and I had to go. He didn't care. He began to read from the writings of William Saroyan.

"'I am an estranged man, said the liar: estranged from myself, from my family, my fellow man, my country, my world, my time, and my culture. I am not estranged from God, although I am a disbeliever in everything about God excepting God indefinable, inside all and careless of all.'"

So now I had a choice. Hear Brando read Saroyan or hang up on him and meet my date.

Brando's reading of Saroyan was hypnotic. I stayed on the phone. He read on in that Brando voice as he and I enjoyed the writing and the language. His reading lasted a half hour. And just as suddenly as he began, he stopped and simply hung up.

There were no cell phones then, so I drove to the bar. My date was gone. Later I explained to her what happened. "Marlon Brando called me and was reading me Saroyan. I didn't want to leave as it was incredibly special," I said. She thought it was a poor excuse for standing her up. We never went out again.

But at the time, my career came first. I was trying to land one of the biggest interviews of the time. A few weeks later Mike and I were in Los Angeles and Brando agreed to have dinner with us. I told Mike to behave himself, that he needed to show that he would treat Brando with respect. Mike did not appreciate being lectured by someone he regarded as a young upstart. He merely gave me a glance that made me feel like I was a fly in his soup.

We stayed at our usual hotel, the Beverly Hills, and Brando picked us up in a white Rolls-Royce. He was wearing a white suit. Brando was driving, and his huge body filled up most of the front seat. Wallace sat next to him and I slipped into the back.

They shook hands and Brando said that he was a little nervous. "I am, too," Wallace admitted.

I thought it was going great. Brando, however, was driving up Mulholland Drive and was running every single red light.

"Marlon, you are going to get us killed," I said.

"You are a human being. You are going to let a machine tell you what to do? Be a man," he said from the front seat. Wallace remained silent.

We somehow managed to get to a small Italian restaurant in the Valley that Brando had picked. They were ready for us and led us to the table. When the menus were delivered, Brando studied the waiter's hands. They were shaking.

"I want to look at the way you deliver the menus, because someday I might have to play a waiter in a movie, and I want to see how you do it," he said, making the waiter even more nervous.

Mike and I ordered some food, but Brando said he wanted nothing.

"Why aren't you eating?" Mike asked.

"I have a movie I am about to do. I will be playing Superman's father again. And I need to lose some weight," Brando explained.

Mike couldn't help himself. He looked at the grossly overweight Brando and asked, "How did you get so fat?"

"I go to Baskin-Robbins, and you know they have thirty-six flavors and I can't decide what to order, so I order a quart of each one and take them home and eat them all," he said.

Brando then complimented Mike on being a great actor.

"I am a journalist, not an actor," Mike said somewhat defiantly.

"Oh, Mike, I have watched your acting abilities for a long time—

the raised eyebrow, the look of fake surprise. You are a master," Brando said.

Mike decided to change the subject. "How many kids do you have?" he asked.

There was a full minute of silence. Mike and I continued to eat as we waited.

"Four," Brando finally uttered.

"What took you so long to answer?" Wallace said.

"I was trying to figure out which ones are my kids and which ones women *say* are my kids," Brando replied.

At this point Mike leaned over the table and extended his hand. "Marlon, I am sixty-five years old. . . . I don't need to make my reputation by showing America what an asshole you are. . . . Let's just be friends."

"That's great," Brando said. "Now I can relax."

I gave Mike a swift kick under the table and a look of complete bewilderment.

I don't think I said more than a few words the rest of the night. When we got back to the hotel, I asked Mike what he was thinking.

"We have to wait for Brando to come to us. . . . We can't be begging him for an interview," Mike said.

"You said you would make him look like an asshole. Why in the world would he do an interview?"

"I know what I am doing, kid," Mike replied, though I could tell he realized he might have screwed up.

After that dinner, Brando and I rarely talked. I kept trying, but he was either not picking up or was busy. In my final conversation with him, we somehow began to talk about stocks.

"I put all my money in one company," Brando said.

"What's the name of it?" I asked.

"Apple," Brando said.

"I never heard of it."

"You will. Listen to what I am saying," Brando said.

Brando had learned about Apple from founder Steve Jobs, who

wanted him to do a commercial for the products. I told Mike about the conversation.

"Are you going to buy the stock?" Mike asked.

"Are you crazy?" I said. "Why would I take a stock tip from someone who can't decide what flavor ice cream he wants?"

4

SETTING OUT

I am not quite sure when I first realized I wanted to be a reporter. Always full of curiosity, I found being a journalist gave me a license to ask the nosiest questions of a total stranger.

Being a reporter has been a job that fits my personality. I was a Jewish kid raised in the Bronx and Queens, intellectually curious but with tendencies toward attention deficit disorder. The perfect job for me was one that would let me go from subject to subject without having to specialize in any one.

I attended Cornell, which even in 1972 was very expensive. My parents had some money, but they felt as a matter of principle that I should pay for a large part of my education. I was pretty good at tennis—first singles on my high school team—and thus was able to get a job as tennis pro.

I would spend my summers and some weekends traveling to the Catskills to teach tennis at the Homowack Lodge, and the money I earned went to pay for part of my college tuition.

During that period the resorts in the Catskills were still a popular vacation destination and a great training ground for young comics and musicians.

As tennis pro I learned to cajole people into taking lessons when they really didn't want them. Hustling lessons turned out to be a great skill for being a journalist. Most of the time, as journalists, we get people to do what every instinct in their bones is telling them not to do—to talk to the press. What I discovered is that everyone wants to find a reason to say yes. Hustling lessons honed my skills in the art of persuasion.

I learned the art of storytelling by working the spotlights in the hotel's nightclub. I watched the comic acts and realized that telling a good joke is very similar to telling a good story. There is an arc to each joke. The simplest one, made famous by Henny Youngman, is "Take my wife . . . please." That joke, meant as a putdown to his wife, has a beginning, a middle, and an end. It has a subject, a conflict, and certainly a punch line . . . all in a few words.

I absorbed the rhythm of the jokes, which later helped me write and edit scripts. Viewers remember a story that has some humor if it makes a point. Diane Sawyer would later dub my stories "investigative comedies," an art form to which I owe the Catskills a big debt.

After my summer in the Catskills, I returned to Cornell and began working as a sports reporter for the *Cornell Daily Sun,* covering the basketball team. One night, while I was out drinking with one of the team players, he told me that they had their pregame meals at McDonald's. It made no sense to me, as I always thought basketball players ate well, especially before games.

The player said that their road per diem was only $15 a day, and that was all they could afford. So I went to the school's bursar's office and got the paperwork for the team's meals. One sheet I found had each player's signature under a line stating that they had received $55 in cash for their per diem. That seemed like plenty of money for the players to get a good meal. When I showed the sheet to some of the players, they were dumbfounded. They had been given $15, not $55, and when they signed the sheet, it was blank. Only later was the amount typed in.

Though I was only nineteen, I still felt I was onto a big story. The Watergate reporting by the *Washington Post*'s team of Bob Woodward and Carl Bernstein had lit a desire in me to be an investigative reporter. The potential thievery of the coach was not like exposing Richard Nixon, but for Ithaca, New York, it could be a big-deal story.

We discovered that the coaches were using the money they took from the players to pay application fees for incoming recruits, a violation of National Collegiate Athletic Association (NCAA) rules. Even with fees accounted for, there was an additional $600 still missing. We also reported how the coach would show up at games smelling of liquor and slurring his words.

The coach was eventually fired, and the school was put on NCAA probation. I was voted the Ivy League writer of the year, beating out Buzz Bissinger, who would later go on to a brilliant journalistic career, and write the book *Friday Night Lights*.

After the story's publication, I was introduced to Peter Maas, who wrote *The Valachi Papers* and *Serpico,* two bestselling biographical books, about the mafia and corrupt cops. Maas chain-smoked cigarettes, dropped names, and told stories that placed him at the center of major newsmaking events. I was entranced. Even though Maas had an outsize ego, I admired his dedication to detail. I told him about my Cornell exposé and his face brightened. "I did a big exposé of sports when I was a student at Duke," he said. Suddenly we had a common bond.

I became his protégé, and Peter invited me to parties in New York with Tom Wolfe, Nora Ephron, Gay Talese, Jimmy Breslin, Pete Hamill, and E. L. Doctorow. When these writers gathered, they would drink and tell stories and jokes. The conversations were provocative and revelatory, as if they were trying out early drafts of manuscripts on one another. As journalists, they were observers of how the planet operated and shared their opinions liberally. To me, they were rock stars. I never wanted to be like them, as I thought I never could be like them. They worked hard at their professions, but you couldn't tell based on how they drank.

In the summers I was a guest at Maas's Hampton house. My one obligation was to be his weekend tennis doubles partner. That's where

I first met *60 Minutes* correspondent Morley Safer. Peter arranged a game against Safer and writer Kurt Vonnegut, who wrote the magical book *Slaughterhouse-Five*. Morley and Kurt were good friends, and neither went anywhere without a lit cigarette, even while playing tennis. Between every odd game changeover, they would take a cigarette break, but then they got tired of putting the cigarettes out and began smoking while playing. They were not good players, and I didn't want to hit the ball at them, as I feared they would choke. I remember how much fun we had. It was old-man tennis the way old-man tennis was meant to be played—slow, with lots of banter and no one caring about the final score. That is, no one except Maas, who yelled at me for playing "soft."

On those weekends Peter would teach me about how to conduct an interview. He said that you should always try to establish commonalities with the subject—schools, cities lived in, shared friends. If that didn't work, figure out a joke to open a conversation. He said this created the right atmosphere.

When Peter interviewed someone, he seemed to do all the talking. I began to wonder how Peter ever got *any* information from his subjects. But soon the subjects forgot they were being interviewed and began to have conversations with him. And if the conversations were interesting or fun, the person would want to spend more time with Peter and help him out.

With Peter's recommendation, assisted by my Cornell basketball exposé, I became an intern with the famed Washington muckraker Jack Anderson. At the time, Anderson was considered the creator of modern investigative journalism. His exposés of government waste, political conflict of interests, and crooked politicians would be the template for Washington exposés for the next forty years.

When I arrived in Jack Anderson's office, I was ushered in to see his top deputy, Les Whitten. I sat in a chair next to Whitten's desk.

Les was on the phone, and as he spoke, he was fidgeting with a letter in his hand, which he finally managed to open.

"Oh, shit, it's a letter bomb!" he screamed. He threw the envelope at me. It landed on my lap. I sat frozen in my chair, waiting for the explosion.

It turned out that the person he was speaking to on the phone was Jack Anderson. They had planned the prank together, right down to the fake phone call. Les picked up the phone. "The kid fell for the old letter bomb trick," he told Jack. "You should see him; I think he wet his pants."

This was my introduction to Les Whitten, and over the next several months there would be many more pranks.

Paranoia ruled. One day a man who believed that the CIA had planted an eavesdropping bug in his body showed up at the office. No one could get him to leave, and no one could dissuade him it wasn't true, except for Les.

Les came out of his office and listened to the guy's story. Whitten left for a moment and came back with a clothes hanger. He had unbent it so it was one long piece of wire with a hook at the end. "Here, attach this to the belt on your pants," Les told the man. "This short-circuits the system. It fucks them up bad."

The man, grateful to Les, left with a clothes hanger wire dragging behind him. I often wondered what became of that guy.

Jack Anderson's office was an amazing training ground for investigative journalism. I did one story on Helen Bentley, the chairman of the Federal Maritime Commission. We had information that she was accepting expensive gifts from shipping companies that she regulated. Les told me to visit her and act like a student. Let her underestimate you, he said. He also instructed me to bluff her, if the opportunity arose, to get her to admit that she accepted a diamond and ruby brooch from Avondale Shipyards. I went to her office around six at night and carried a backpack. I wore jeans and a sweatshirt. I began asking her about her job and her travels, and after about an hour, I asked if I could see the brooch that had been given to her. She claimed it was in the office and was not in her personal possession.

She got up, ostensibly to go look for it. After a minute she came back and said that she forgot that she had sent it out for cleaning.

At that point I decided to bluff her, as Whitten instructed. I said stridently, "We have documents that show you were given this brooch and kept it as your own."

"I would like to see those documents," she calmly said.

I left and called Les.

"Oh my, oh my. You are in trouble," he said. "You got the clap. You got syphilis. Why did you say you have a document?"

"You told me to bluff," I said.

"You bluff by saying you have sources, not documents," Whitten scolded.

I felt horrible. I was scared and disappointed in myself. I had over-played my hand.

The next morning Bentley called Whitten. "He didn't have docu-ments, did he?" she asked him.

"No, he didn't," Les said.

Bentley had known it all along. Hustling Washington required more game than hustling for tennis lessons in the Catskills. But that day in her office she told Whitten that she had seen the raw talent of someone who had the potential to be a good reporter.

"If I was starting a newspaper, he would be the first person I would hire," she told Whitten. Though I didn't get the story, she was impressed, and Whitten let me stay on as an intern.

Bentley would later serve five terms in the U.S. Congress.

After Watergate, every reporter envisioned themselves as the next Woodward and Bernstein. Or the next Sy Hersh, the *New York Times* reporter who broke the story of the My Lai massacre, the horrifying mass murder of unarmed Vietnamese men, women, and children, car-ried out by U.S. troops during the Vietnam war.

In Washington, I practiced tennis at the courts at 16th and Kennedy Street. One day, Hersh was there, practicing his serve by himself. I asked if he wanted me to return the serve to him.

"You any good?" he asked.

"Not bad," I said.

Soon I started belting the ball back. It was 1975, and Hersh was a star reporter covering Watergate for *The New York Times*. He would get up at six-thirty in the morning and catch sources on the way to work to ask them questions. At night he would knock on their doors when they got home. He was rude, pushy, and relentless, and boy, did I admire him.

We developed a casual friendship based mostly on tennis. That didn't stop me from asking him for advice.

Since I was worried about not getting a professional reporting job, I decided to become a lawyer. The day before I was to take the law boards, I called Hersh. He asked why I was taking them if I wanted to go into journalism.

"I figure being a lawyer would make me a better journalist," I said.

"Dummy, if you need a lawyer, you can call a lawyer. You don't have to become one. If you want to be a journalist, be a journalist," he said.

The next day I took the law boards. About forty-five minutes into them, I began to think about what Hersh said. I got up and left. I still remember the bewildered looks of those taking the test as I got up to leave.

After graduating from Cornell in 1976, I sent my résumés to over a hundred newspapers and received ninety-eight rejections. Only C. K. McClatchy, the publisher of *The Sacramento Bee,* and an editor in Hawaii expressed mild interest.

Hawaii was a long way to go for a job interview, so my only prospect was Sacramento. I decided to hitchhike across the United States, see the country and visit newspapers along the way. I was in no hurry, as I really had no other job prospects, and "seeing America" sounded better to future employers than being out of work.

Before I left on my trip, I wrote an unsolicited feature op-ed story on the art of sneaking into the best seats at baseball games and sent it to the *New York Times* sports section. While I was in high school attending games at Shea Stadium, I usually found a seat near the dugout even though I had purchased only a $1.30 general admission ticket. Occasionally I was caught by the ushers and asked to move, but I got quite good at picking seats that would remain empty. The article explored whether sitting in a better seat than the one paid for is ethical.

I didn't have much hope that the *Times* would run an unsolicited sports op-ed piece from a twenty-two-year-old, but I had nothing to lose. I soon forgot about the submission and started hitchhiking at the Throgs Neck Bridge in Queens. My father dropped me off in front of the Clearview Park Golf Course. I crossed the road divider of the expressway and stuck out my thumb. I had constructed a sign to get me to Pittsburgh, as I knew a girl who lived there. By the time my father had completed his U-turn to head back to work, I had been picked up and was gone.

While on the road I would call my parents, collect, once a week, to let them know I was okay. During one call my parents told me that I had received some mail from *The New York Times*.

"Can you open it?"

"I already did," my mother said. "There is a check for $250."

"Anything else?" I asked.

"There is a letter that says your submission has been accepted and they will publish your article. Congratulations, dear."

I screamed. To have something published in the *Times* was to me akin to winning the lottery. I called the paper and they said that they planned to run the story at the end of October.

After I got off the call, I decided to take advantage of this feat by timing my arrival in Sacramento for the Monday after the article appeared, thinking that it might impress the publisher C. K. McClatchy. Looking back, I have to say that was a pretty smart move.

The McClatchy newspapers were not large, but they had a stellar reputation for good, clean, honest journalism. McClatchy had three papers, in Modesto, Sacramento, and Fresno, and they controlled the media in the San Joaquin Valley.

I hitchhiked to the newspaper office. I was a little unshaven and my clothes were rumpled. I went to C.K.'s office and left my backpack near his secretary's desk. I shook hands with C.K. and we chatted a little bit about where I had been hitchhiking. He soon asked if I had any recent writing samples with me.

"Do you have yesterday's *New York Times*?" I asked.

It turned out it was right behind his desk. I directed him to the sports pages, which then had a sports op-ed section.

C.K. read the article and laughed. He wondered aloud how a twenty-two-year-old hitchhiking around the country got a story published in *The New York Times*.

"The cool thing about being the editor is that I can create jobs sometimes when none exist," he said.

He walked me into the newsroom and introduced me to Frank McCulloch, the executive editor of the newspaper, a bald man who resembled Archie from the comics.

C.K. told Frank to give me a job.

"Boss, we don't have one," he said.

"I am authorizing you to create one," C.K. told him.

McCulloch and I chatted about what position would be best. Given my sports background, McCulloch thought I should start in a midsize city like Fresno and cover sports.

"After you get a little experience, we will bring you back to Sacramento," he said.

When I arrived in Fresno, I decided to borrow from my journalism playbook and do an exposé of the college recruiting practices of the Fresno State basketball coach. Unlike what had happened at Cornell, when I was able to find documents that revealed the story, the basketball coach freely admitted to me that he was violating NCAA rules by paying the application fees of incoming recruits.

One night the sports editor was away, and the assistant sports editor read my story, liked it, and ran it in the paper the next day. When the editor got back, he was livid. It turned out the coach was a regular player at his weekly poker game.

I was fired within a month.

I returned to New York and worked for a few months at *Sport* magazine as a researcher, but then a job opportunity came from the most unlikely of sources, *Hustler* publisher Larry Flynt. A friend told me that Flynt was trying to go legit, by starting a new magazine called *Ohio Magazine.*

Flynt had read some freelance stories I wrote for *Penthouse Forum,* a sex magazine. Back then, most serious reporters tried to publish their mainstream work in reputable magazines like *Esquire* or *The New Yorker,* but the articles that paid the bills were published under pseudonyms in sex magazines or in the *National Enquirer,* which paid the most. Les Whitten taught me how to navigate the world of freelancing, but still I tried to not write anything raunchy. But Flynt liked my stories and flew me to Columbus, Ohio, for an interview. The job opening was for Washington bureau chief and columnist of *Ohio Magazine.* My friend at *Penthouse Forum* gave me some issues of *Hustler* to read, so I could get a sense of what interested their editors. I saw that nearly every issue involved stories about the JFK assassination, the mafia, or UFOs.

When I arrived in Columbus, I was told I had to be screened before I met Flynt. They wanted to make sure I would fit in. Bruce David, the editor of *Hustler,* interviewed me. I remember David wore tight-fitting jeans, cowboy boots, and sunglasses in a dark room. But that wasn't what made this interview memorable.

He began it by asking me who killed JFK.

"It was clearly a conspiracy, probably the CIA working with the mafia out of Florida and New Orleans," I said.

"Do you believe in UFOs?" he asked.

"I think it is crazy to think that all those pictures out there of UFOs are faked," I said. "All you need is for one of them to be real and it's the biggest story of our time."

"Do you do drugs?" he asked.

"Of course."

"Great," David said. "You're perfect for us."

David next drove me to Flynt's mansion in Columbus. Flynt was a great character, full of life and laughs and mischief. He told me that the one story he wanted me to investigate was how babies were being made in Massachusetts without belly buttons and without souls.

"Who is making these babies?" I asked.

"The CIA," Flynt whispered.

"I'll make it a priority," I said.

He offered me the Washington bureau chief job for *Ohio Magazine* and said he wanted me to write a column for the *Plains Monitor,* the weekly newspaper in President Jimmy Carter's hometown. Flynt had just purchased the paper.

I told him I'd be delighted, and he asked me how much money I wanted. Hoping I didn't seem too greedy, I said $20,000. He quickly agreed. *That was too easy,* I thought. But before I took the job, I wanted to know if he was serious about becoming legit.

Flynt said he wanted me to meet someone. And he called upstairs and down came Ruth Carter Stapleton, President Jimmy Carter's sister. Flynt maintained that if Stapleton believed his conversion was real, then I should feel comfortable as well. Stapleton, an evangelical, told me that Flynt was born again and was going to run religious articles in *Hustler.* She said that he received the baptism of the Holy Spirit on a private jet, a plane ride he spent speaking in tongues. She advised that I take the job, as he was a changed man.

Flynt said he was now rearranging his life to follow the Lord. He had a vision of the apostle Paul and he was about to announce that he was turning over control of *Hustler* to Paul Krassner, a member of the Merry Pranksters, the cohorts and followers of Ken Kesey. Krassner was a key figure in the counterculture and a founding member of the Yippies.

Within a few hours of my accepting the job, Flynt announced Krassner's promotion at the office Christmas party. Krassner was now my boss.

Krassner and I met later in a hotel room. Flynt's conversion threw the staff into a tizzy. One of the most prolific *Hustler* photographers, Suze Randall, was visibly upset about what would happen to her job. All I remember was how she stood in an open bathrobe, with no underwear, pleading with Krassner to keep the nude pictures in the magazine. Her persuasive approach worked and Krassner agreed to keep her pictures in the magazine.

Many journalists labeled Flynt's move to religion a stunt to avoid getting busted on pornography charges. But he insisted he was moving away from porn, and he hired a number of mainstream editors and reporters from Ohio newspapers to work for the magazine.

But after about a year, Flynt was hemorrhaging money and decided to revert to the formula that got him rich—hard-core porn. One year later, in 1980, Flynt was in Georgia fighting a legal battle over obscenity when he was shot. The bullet left him partially paralyzed and in need of a wheelchair. He recovered but had speech difficulties. He made it a point to tell people, though, he could still have sex.

White supremacist serial killer Joseph Paul Franklin confessed to the attempted killing, saying he was outraged by an interracial photo shoot in the magazine.

As for my time with Flynt, it didn't last long. I took the job in Washington and wrote some stories, but four months after I began, they said they were over budget and I was fired.

After my adventures with Larry Flynt, I worked for a year in Michigan as a reporter with *The Oakland Press*. I was given the assignment to solve the murder of Teamster boss Jimmy Hoffa. I never solved the case, and after about a year was again fired. It was time to return to New York, where, thanks to my friendship with Peter Maas, I was able to get a commission to write a story for *The New York Times Magazine* on the rise and fall of the South Bronx, focusing on the area around Charlotte Street where my grandparents had lived. Urban renewal had not reached the street, and it looked like Dresden after the war. I wanted to tell the history of this one street through the stories of people who lived there.

My grandmother, whom I was very close to, had lived in the Bronx, and every time a fire engine siren passed, she would say, "The Bronx is *brenen* [Yiddish for burning]." At the age of five, I believed it. The sounds of the elevated rail trains were comforting noise at night, a reminder that the beat of the city continues, despite the fires. In the article, I wrote about a legendary Bronx figure, Jake the pickle man, who sold pickles out of a barrel, one at a time. If he liked you, you got pickles. If he didn't, he would throw your jar top into the street and say in Yiddish, *"E hunich a pickle for te"* ("I don't have a pickle for you"). You never wanted to hear that. As the neighborhood changed, crime soared. No one was safe, not even the pickle man. Jake would end up being murdered, his body discovered in an alleyway.

The article publication gave me street cred with other publications, and *Rolling Stone* gave me a chance to freelance for them. The magazine was the trend-setting magazine of its time, at the center of covering the cultural revolution, and my first assignment was to cover the most dangerous nuclear accident in U.S. history—Three Mile Island.

5

ACCIDENT AT THREE MILE ISLAND

On March 28, 1979, a small radiation leak was detected at the nuclear plants at Three Mile Island near Harrisburg, Pennsylvania. Maryanne Vollers, *Rolling Stone*'s associate editor, commissioned Mike Gray, the writer of the just-released movie *The China Syndrome,* a fictional account of a nuclear plant disaster, to write the cover story. She asked if I was interested in collaborating with him. "Of course," I said.

The radiation leak caused widespread panic on the East Coast, especially in the offices of *Rolling Stone.* The publisher, Jann Wenner, fled to his house in the Hamptons, to gain distance from a radiation cloud that was feared to hit Manhattan. It would become our country's closest brush with nuclear catastrophe. So of course *Rolling Stone* decided to send the new guy to cover it. I was selected because I was viewed as expendable.

Maryanne and I drove through a severe rainstorm to get to Harrisburg on the night of March 28, stopping to buy grapefruit along the way because we thought the outer skin would protect the fruit from radiation. Gray was scheduled to arrive the next day. Before leaving, I was able to call some contacts and pick up a couple more freelance assignments, from *The Nation* magazine, *The Sacramento Bee,* and CBC radio.

Shortly after arriving, we ignored the press conferences being run by the utility and headed for the local saloon. I stationed myself at the bar and bought drinks for the control room operators as they came off shift. Soon they started to tell us what happened.

They spoke in hushed tones of how certain control room operators ignored warning lights to close certain valves and how the operators instead shut off important pressure valves that would have cooled the reactor. They simply didn't believe what their instruments were telling them. History has taught us, in this age of machines, to believe our instruments, a lesson that airline pilots know by heart. When you begin to disagree with your measuring devices, it is the first sign of panic.

After spending a few hours hanging out at the bar, one of the workers invited me back to his house, where we proceeded to get drunk on beer. This control room operator, a good-looking man in his thirties, kept saying, "It's bad, man, it's really bad."

He told me the details of what happened inside the plant, but the problem was, I didn't understand a word of what he said. I was worried that I had the key information to what caused the accident but that I would get it wrong. Fortunately Mike Gray, an engineer, could figure it all out, I thought.

We picked Mike up at the Harrisburg airport. Mike had long hair, a scraggly beard, and a constant urge to get stoned. After saying hello to me and kissing Maryanne's hand, he asked if I had any pot.

"No."

"Well, I need to be stoned to function," he said. I told him about the control room operators I found. He didn't care. Here we had the scoop on what caused the TMI accident and this Hollywood screenwriter wanted only to get stoned. I read Mike my notes of the conversations I'd had with the workers. Mike immediately realized that the plant had the possibility of exploding. But he still didn't want to talk to any of the control room operators until he was high.

We went to the local Penn State campus in Middletown and I went inside the library. I found a student studying and said the only thing that came into my mind:

"I am a reporter from *Rolling Stone* magazine, and I am covering the nuclear accident. My coauthor needs to be stoned to function and I am looking for some pot to buy so we can tell the world that the plant might explode."

Somewhat shocked, she looked at me, smiled, and said, "Are you really with *Rolling Stone?*"

"Yes," I replied.

"Cool."

She left the library and came back with some pot and some rolling paper, certainly enough to get Mike through the night.

After smoking a joint, he was ready to work. I took him to meet the plant worker whose house I had gone to earlier. I didn't understand very much of the conversation except for "holy shit" that Mike kept repeating.

"When I wrote *The China Syndrome,* I made it up. I never imagined that it might happen," Gray said.

Back at the hotel, I filed my freelance stories for the CBC, *The Sacramento Bee,* and others. As I was writing, Maryanne came rushing into my room. She had heard a report that the plant was about to explode, and she said that our time could be better spent getting to know each other better.

But I was oblivious to the potential danger. Jimmy Carter was set to arrive in the morning, and I didn't think the nuclear industry would allow their plant to blow up before a presidential visit. I kept writing. The next morning, my story in *The Sacramento Bee* laid out how operator errors nearly caused the plant to melt down. Since no other journalism outfit had it, many other newspapers in the *Bee* syndicate didn't pick it up. But my article was copied and distributed to the collective masses of reporters who waited for the presidential visit. This was my first big national scoop.

Meanwhile, Gray was back on the prowl for some pot. Eventually he made some new friends who took care of him. Together we formed an unlikely Woodward and Bernstein duo of nuclear power reporting. I got the sources, and he translated the intricate engineering details into layman's terms.

The danger began to wind down by the fourth day, when President Jimmy Carter came to the plant. It wouldn't be until years after the accident that we would learn that the Nuclear Regulatory Commission (NRC) experts were worried almost until Carter came inside the control room that the plant could still explode.

Our story made the cover of *Rolling Stone*, and I became a minor celebrity in the antinuke world. I spoke at a few colleges, gave interviews on TV and radio, and was assigned by *Rolling Stone* to cover the antinuke rally in Washington. An estimated crowd of 125,000 stood in front of the Capitol Rotunda to hear Joni Mitchell, Jackson Browne, and Graham Nash perform.

After the rally, the singers gathered at the Tabard Inn. I sat at the bar next to one of the most beautiful women I had ever seen. It turned out she was dating Nash. Suddenly I felt a tap on my shoulder. "You are in my seat," Nash said.

"I don't see your name on it," I replied. The girl laughed. "I will give you my seat if you introduce me to Joni Mitchell. I am a writer from *Rolling Stone*."

He told me to follow him. Mitchell was in the corner of the restaurant talking to a few people. Nash made the introductions. After all, they had once been a couple.

"I would love to chat with you, if you have a few minutes," I said.

And then, in a line I will always remember, Joni Mitchell replied, "Let me get a cognac and a cigarette, and I will be right with you."

In 1979, she was arguably the most successful and dazzling singer-songwriter of her time. She was liberated, elegant, and utterly beautiful. I was smitten. We ended up talking for hours, leaving the Tabard and going to another bar. At one point, she grabbed a waiter's guitar and began to sing "Big Yellow Taxi" to demonstrate her old music and then began to play from her recent collaboration with the great jazz musician Charles Mingus. "I am now playing between the beats," she explained.

She told me about her adventures like hitchhiking across the country by herself. She would show up at a bar and simply enjoy the freedom of being a vagabond, until someone recognized her and she would have to split. When she arrived in New York from California, she realized that she had such a good time being a free spirit, she simply turned around and hitched back to California. It was a great interview. The next day I excitedly called New York and *Rolling Stone* and told them that I got Joni's first interview in over a decade.

"You're too late. Cameron Crowe interviewed her last month. It's running in the July issue."

I was devastated. I wrote the story about the rally, but the quotes I got from Mitchell were removed. As for Mitchell, I never saw her again.

Meanwhile, Mike and I agreed to write a book together about the accident. Over the next few months in the summer of 1979, I traveled between Washington and Topanga Canyon, where Mike lived. I did the research at NRC headquarters, going through the tapes and transcripts of the event and getting to know some of the commissioners. I sifted through more than two hundred hours of transcripts and brought the reporting back to California, where I entered the mountain of facts into the computer memory of a Wang system word processor.

The book, titled *The Warning,* was a selection of the Book of the Month Club. The *Los Angeles Times* called it a must-read and wrote: "If you read no other book in the next five years, by all means read *The Warning.*"

But with all the good press and positive reviews, Mike and I made only about $50,000 each for nearly two years of work.

At that point I was nearly broke and borrowing money from my parents. I needed to find a full-time job. Feeling desperate, I began to think of applying to law school. One day I read in Page Six of the *New York Post* about news director Frank Anthony at WOR-TV in New York, who had been passed over for a promotion. He said he was more interested in starting a newsmagazine like *60 Minutes.* When I read that, I realized that he could be hiring and that he might be so angry at not getting promoted, he would do something crazy and hire a person without any television experience.

Luckily, I was right on both counts. Anthony hired me as an on-air correspondent and producer of a show called *What's Happening, America?* Anthony believed TV can be taught to any idiot in a few days. Thank God.

But I did not come to him empty-handed. One of the control room operators from Three Mile Island, who was a source for our book, agreed to go public. Anthony liked the idea that I brought an exclusive to the first show, an appearance by a TMI control room operator, Hal Hartman.

I found Hartman by reading all the depositions taken by the two NRC committees that investigated the accident. One deposition stood out. A control room operator laid out in precise detail how the accident happened and how it could have been avoided. But he was a confidential source, and any reference to his name was blacked out, his identity hidden. But I read the full deposition, which was over three hundred pages, and one of the references to him remained. An investigator referred to him as "Hal." So I got the list of all the control room operators who were working at the time at the plant, and there was only one Harold.

I looked his address up and went to see him. I brought a copy of the deposition and to convince him to go on-camera, told him I would be okay with his just repeating what he told the NRC. He agreed.

Hartman told us that Three Mile Island was a disaster waiting to happen and that before the 1979 accident, the operators at the nuclear installation falsified data on leak rates to the Nuclear Regulatory Commission in order to avoid shutting down the plant for repairs.

The story would lead to a grand jury investigation and an indictment of Metropolitan Edison, who ran the plant at the time of the accident. Four years later, the company would plead guilty to document falsification. It was my breakthrough story and led to front-page coverage and a congressional hearing.

I did a couple more stories before I came upon the idea to test the national security system by trying to obtain secret military films through the mail, the story that led to my interview with *60 Minutes*.

Looking back, I often think how lucky I was. If the film projectionist Al Kerins who saw that story hadn't had a fight with his wife the night it aired, he said he would not have been watching TV. And if he hadn't spoken to Don on the coffee line the next morning, I doubt Don would ever have known about me. But they did talk and my life changed forever.

6

HITTING MY STRIDE

By 1982, I had worked at *60 Minutes* for two years in New York. But then Mike asked me to move to Washington to take the place of his top producer Barry Lando, who wanted to work out of Paris. For me, Washington was a dream assignment. I had lived in the city and had developed some friends and contacts. It was a much more livable city than New York and hadn't yet gone through the real estate and population boom that would happen twenty years later. I played golf at public courses on weekends for reasonable prices and a minimum wait. I went white-water canoeing on the Potomac on Friday afternoons, and on weekends, I would hike in the nearby Shenandoah Valley. And it didn't hurt that the ratio of women to men in the city was said to be about three to one.

I rented an apartment in Georgetown at 28th and P Street NW and biked to work, about a seven-minute commute with traffic. For me and my relationship with Mike Wallace, it was the perfect place to be.

The distance also made it harder for him to harass me. At the time, Mike built a reputation as a no-nonsense journalist who held bad guys accountable. As one ad from CBS put it: "The four most feared words in the English language: Mike Wallace is here."

Unfortunately, that applied to those working with him as well. When Mike would phone to discuss stories or yell about something, I would simply put the phone receiver down on the table. As he continued to rant, I would read the paper or look out the window. When I worked in New York, he would come to my office every few hours to see what I was working on, behaving like a factory foreman. "Why are you wasting your time on that?" he would ask, no matter what I was doing. Once he came into my office and asked whom I was talking to on the phone.

I simply got up, gave him the phone, and left the room. It turned out it was my mother. He never did that again.

But in Washington it was different. At the time, I shared office space with Suzanne St. Pierre, who was married to the legendary CBS News commentator Eric Sevareid. He was one of the original Murrow boys and covered World War II for CBS. He would often come into my office and sit on my couch as he waited for his wife to get off the phone. He would always talk about the war, the root of all his memories.

I once asked him for a restaurant recommendation in Bordeaux. He thought for a moment and named a place. He paused for a moment, and then said, "No, I think that was destroyed in the Normandy invasion." I thanked him for the effort.

Suzanne began working at CBS when it was an old boys' network; almost all the producers were men. Suzanne remembered how the executive producer of the documentary unit made a pass at her, and when she turned him down, she found herself being demoted to the research desk at CBS News. Soon, because of her drive and talent, she became a producer on *60 Minutes*.

Some weekends Suzanne and Eric would invite me to their country home in Virginia, once owned by CBS anchor Edward R. Murrow. It was a simple place but had its own small pond. It was there that Eric tried to teach me how to fly-fish. I was not very good and don't remember ever catching any fish. Sevareid, on the other hand, seemed to catch a fish every time he cast. He made it look easy. While we fished, Suzanne would lay out a lovely picnic with some wine and cheese. It was so old-fashioned and civilized, a welcome respite from the pressures of the job.

In return for their hospitality, I took Suzanne and Eric to a Michael Jackson concert at RFK Stadium. I gave Eric some earplugs to muffle the loud music. The three of us got some stares and some high fives, as I think Eric was the oldest person there, but he thoroughly enjoyed himself and stayed till the end.

In Washington, I no longer needed to play airport roulette to find stories. For less than ten dollars in cab fare, I could make the rounds on Capitol Hill or at the federal agencies. After a day of trolling, I would come back to the office with a nice bounty of ideas.

Being a *60 Minutes* producer in Washington gave me access to people like William Casey. He was a mysterious figure, who went from being Ronald Reagan's campaign manager to heading the CIA. He didn't want to be in the office and would often do the work of his subordinates, including taking secret flights to Rome to brief the Vatican on the U.S.'s cold war efforts against the Soviet Union.

He operated in the shadows, conducting covert actions like the Iran-Contra deal, a political scandal in which senior Reagan officials facilitated the sale of arms to Iran in the hopes of securing the release of U.S. hostages being held at the time in Lebanon, and obtaining money to fund the Contras' war against the Sandinista government of Nicaragua.

Casey never gave interviews, but through conservative Senator Orrin Hatch, I was able to get Casey to agree to a meeting. Wallace and I went to the White House to visit with Casey, to try to convince him to do an interview. It was very helpful that Mike was trusted by the Reagans, or I don't think we would have even gotten a floor pass.

We met Casey in a secret alcove inside the Old Executive Office Building. From the hallways, it could have been mistaken for a janitor's closet. But inside there was enough room for the three of us to sit comfortably.

Mike began by asking a few casual questions about how Casey spent his days, and when he mumbled his answer, neither one of us understood what he was talking about. Casey grew up in Queens and had a definite New York accent. I remember Casey having a bad case of dandruff that covered part of his glasses.

Casey made himself sound very important and was clearly trying to impress Mike. The meeting didn't last very long, as it was clear Casey had serious reservations about going on *60 Minutes*. When we left, Mike said that we had better hope he would turn us down for an interview because no one would understand a word he was saying. Fortunately he did turn us down.

Mike and I also spent an afternoon with Israeli general Ariel Sharon. Sharon spoke with a thick Israeli accent that made him quite hard to understand. He had just written a book on his experiences in fighting wars and terrorism, and though the book was interesting, he wasn't, and this time it was our turn to put the kibosh on the story.

Figuring out whom to put on-camera is a critical part of producing. Correspondent Bob Simon told me that you go for the best talkers, not the most well-known people or the military officer with the highest rank. Viewers forget titles or rank, and remember only the words. I developed a file labeled *Characters in Search of a Story*: original, unforgettable storytellers whom I tried to attach to a story I was doing.

If I was looking for a story, I would often go door to door in congressional and government office buildings, casting for talent. Over the years, that was the way I developed my best sources.

That's how I first met the future vice president Al Gore. In 1982 Gore was an ambitious congressman from Tennessee, but still relatively unknown. I entered his office without an appointment. I told his assistant I was with *60 Minutes,* and Gore immediately agreed to see me. We sat in the central area, which was set up like a small newsroom. Since Gore was a former newspaper reporter, he felt very comfortable with this office layout. Gore was not much older than I was; a handsome man, he stood erect and looked you in the eye when he shook your hand. Even then, he seemed a little too good to be true.

"I am looking for stories that would work for *60 Minutes*. Do you have any ideas?" I asked after I introduced myself.

The unspoken agreement was that if I did one of his story sugges-tions, we would put him on-camera. A wide-eyed look of excitement came across his face, and almost immediately he started pitching me. Gore loved discussing policy, and most of his suggestions that day were ideas like "Is nuclear power safe?" This might be an important subject, but it wouldn't make a very interesting *60 Minutes* story, as it has no central character.

I rejected all his suggestions, and each time I turned one down, his face would twitch slightly. He had a young aide named Peter Knight who would later become his chief of staff in the White House and the treasurer of the Democratic National Committee. Gore enlisted him to help with story idea pitches. The first day we met, Gore and I did no business. But we would develop a long friendship and counsel each other through crises and decisions in the coming years.

While I was making the rounds in Washington, one person Mike had me meet was Washington insider and Democratic Party chairman Robert S. Strauss. Strauss built a swimming pool at his Dallas house, even though he didn't like to swim. Strauss said he would sit by the pool at night with a drink and say, "Bob Strauss, you are one rich son of a bitch."

During our lunches in Washington, Strauss would describe himself as a man who could take fundraising money from the rich and votes from the poor and convince both that he's looking out for their interests.

He loved playing poker, and he said that he might someday invite me to his Washington game, "with senators and judges, and a hooker under the table." He told me the woman would be having oral sex with one of the poker players and they all would bet on who she was enter-taining at that moment. I was left wondering if he was making this up, as he never did invite me to that game.

But Strauss did put in a good word for me with President Jimmy Carter. In 1984 Carter wrote his first book since leaving the White

House. He agreed to his first major interview and profile since Reagan had become president. I flew to Plains, Georgia, to spend a little time with him and see what I could get him to say. The trick of these pre-interviews is to negotiate sound bites from the subjects. You need to mine them for things they haven't said. In Carter's case, this meant policies of the then-president Ronald Reagan that he disagreed with and would talk about.

Negotiating sound bites is one of the keys to a good interview. Often the subject will try to stay on safe topics in order to not be controversial. The trick is to always push the subject for more, to get them to say something they have never uttered, to go deep into their psyche. That was something I was trying for in the Carter interview.

After Reagan defeated him, Carter didn't stay in Washington to make money, but instead returned to Plains after the election and began setting up the Carter Center, which would be dedicated to human rights and the alleviation of human suffering. At the time, Plains was a one-street town with a diner, a cut-rate department store, and a gas station run at that time by Carter's crazy brother Billy, who was known for his nutty comments and bizarre behavior, including urinating in front of the press. He also took money from Libyan leader Muammar Gaddafi, who was attempting to influence Jimmy Carter at the same time the United States was working to depose him.

The Carters' Plains home reminded me of my grandmother's Bronx apartment. The Carters put plastic on the couch and chairs so they would last longer and wouldn't get dirty. It felt like a museum. Fortunately, we had our discussions at a cabin near his home, where he did most of his writing.

For me, it was a bit scary to be talking to a former president, in his first extensive interview since losing the election. I prepared by reading article clips produced by the CBS research department. There was no internet to look up and collate material, so information had to be gathered by sitting in the library and going through indexes. Carter was an interesting man, a former peanut farmer who won in 1976 by running as a Washington outsider. He famously posed for the cover of *Rolling Stone* magazine wearing jeans and sitting on his back porch.

He had an unlucky presidency, coming into the White House during an Arab oil boycott, with high inflation that saw interest rates climb above 15 percent. But what most damaged his term was the failure to bring back the American hostages taken by Iran. The hostages would be freed on the day Ronald Reagan was sworn in as president.

Carter was ready to talk about all this and looked at our interview as a bit of a therapy session. In the time I was alone with Carter, I asked about foreign policy and domestic issues, probing to see what questions would help carry the best conversation. I even brought up his belief in UFOs.

"You said in an interview with *Rolling Stone* that if you became president you would release the UFO file. What happened?"

"I tried," Carter said. "But they told me that I didn't have the right security clearance to get the information."

"That makes no sense. You are the president. . . ."

"That's what they told me," he said.

The person who told him that, I was later to discover, was CIA director George H. W. Bush, who would himself become president.

I tried to get Mike to ask the UFO question during the interview, but he refused, dismissing it as a bunch of BS. Mike was in the Reagan camp, having been a friend since the 1950s with Nancy Reagan. This worried me. I wrote a series of questions that would get Carter criticizing the Reagans, but I feared that Mike might not want to go there.

Mike fought me on this interview at every turn. He was worried about what the Reagans would think and was feeling ambivalent about the story. He was giving me only one day to shoot the entire segment, something that is practically unheard of for a *60 Minutes* story.

If that was the case, I told Mike, he had to stay overnight in Plains. The nearest available lodging was a cheap roadside motel, where the cars parked outside your room. All night, cars were coming and going, with their lights beaming into our bedrooms. Mike was a light sleeper, and I stayed up that night thinking where I could get him the strongest coffee in the morning. I knew this was not going to be an easy day.

Mike liked to do the big interview first, rather than build up to it by getting to know the subject. He thought the first interview is when people have the most energy and most tension, and for Mike, that was a good thing.

The interview took place in Carter's home, and after thirty minutes, it was not going well. Mike seemed to have very little respect for Carter. He decided the best way to get a rise out of him was to mention Ronald Reagan's name every chance he could.

"You must be very jealous, in a sense, of Ronald Reagan," Mike asked.

"Not really," Carter replied.

"Jealous of the fact that he is, I mean, if his is the 'Teflon presidency,' nothing sticks—"

"Mine was the opposite," Carter said, cutting Mike off.

"Yours was the flypaper presidency," Mike said.

"I think that is true . . . When I was there . . . I was responsible. And now there is a great deal of doubt about who is responsible, and Reagan has been very successful, more than any of his thirty-nine predecessors, in not being responsible for anything that's unpleasant or not completely successful," Carter said.

There was a real tension in the room. Mike was a friend and defender of the Reagans, while Carter hated everything they stood for. Mike was right to bring up the Reagans, but I was getting the sense that he was worried that Carter would launch into an all-out assault on the Reagan presidency.

Between change of tapes, I suggested Mike ask Carter about human rights under Ronald Reagan, and how Reagan was dismantling the Carter foreign policy achievements in that area. Mike had heard enough criticism of Reagan and wanted to move on.

"I am not going to ask that question," Mike said.

"Mike, this man [Carter] stood for human rights, ask him the question."

"No."

I turned to Carter. "Mr. President, will you tell Mike to ask you about human rights?"

"Ira, don't get me involved in your silly little questions," Carter replied defiantly.

"Mike, you are embarrassing me. Ask him about human rights under Ronald Reagan," I practically screamed.

Wallace picked up the fact that Carter wasn't keen on answering the question, so he asked. "Human rights under Ronald Reagan," Wallace said. It wasn't even a question.

Carter had cleverly conned Mike by acting as if he didn't want the question asked. At that point Carter took the ball and ran with it.

"Well, Reagan has basically abandoned our nation's commitment to the human rights policy that we espoused."

Wallace then asked, "Why, because he [Reagan] is a callous man?"

Carter replied, "I don't know what his motivations are, but the result has been that the world now sees our country as not being a champion of human rights, but as being dormant, at best, in the face of persecution."

Mike looked down at his notepad. "Pretty good," Mike said.

Carter couldn't resist. "How did I do, Ira?" he asked.

I signaled with a thumbs-up.

"Asshole," Mike said, looking at me. I didn't care about the insults, the embarrassment, or the humiliation. I got the sound bite I was after, and in my mind, that was all that mattered.

Carter's remarks on Reagan would make front-page news in *The New York Times*. But at that moment, Mike had no idea how significant his interview would be, and he was unhappy. He had no rapport with Carter and didn't enjoy his company. I arranged for Mike and the president and his wife, Rosalynn, to eat lunch together. I went outside to set up the next location shot, which would be a walk with the Carters through the town of Plains. When I returned to the restaurant, the three of them were sitting in complete silence.

I was stunned. "Why aren't you talking to them?" I whispered.

Mike replied but didn't whisper. "I have nothing in common with this man," he said.

"Ask about the nuclear codes, make conversation. He was the president," I said angrily, upset at Mike's arrogant and embarrassing behavior. Rosalynn heard Mike's remark to me. She would be the next interview that we would do at their lake house.

I pulled her aside. Sometimes a producer must act like a coach, revving his subjects up for the game, or in this case, their interview. "Mike loves Nancy Reagan," I said. "That's why he is acting this way. I want you to come out with both guns blazing."

"I will do my best," she said simply.

Mike asked Rosalynn about Reagan. What she said would become one of the most defining and quoted remarks the Carters ever made. "This president makes us comfortable with our prejudices," she said.

Mike was stunned. All he could say was "That's not very nice, what you are saying."

"But it's the way I feel, and I think it's true," she quickly replied. Then she paused for a moment and said, "I think [Reagan] has been devastating to the country."

At this point Wallace was reeling. "How? How has he devastated the country?" he shot back.

"Well, I wouldn't trade places with him in history, with Jimmy and Ronald Reagan, for anything in the world."

Rosalynn, as Mike would later say, was pure steel. "The magnolia facade had disappeared," he would later tell me. "She hated me."

During the car ride back to Atlanta, Mike fretted how the Reagans would react. I told him they wouldn't even watch the story. He thought otherwise.

The story, which was given the title "Plain Talk from Plains," would make national headlines and put Mike in the doghouse with the Reagans.

But Mike would win them back. He eventually did an interview with Ronald Reagan, an interview that would end with Nancy's jumping on Mike's lap while he was interviewing Reagan, a reaction very different from that exhibited by the previous first lady of the White House.

Looking back on Rosalynn's characterization of Reagan, from more than thirty-five years ago, I thought her description also perfectly fits Donald Trump: "This president makes us comfortable with our prejudices."

7

CIVIL RIGHTS LEADERS: JACKSON AND SHARPTON

In 1983, Jesse Jackson decided to become the first black man to run for president. What better place to announce his decision than on *60 Minutes*, and Hewitt asked me to produce the segment.

Our show had done several stories on Jackson that documented his Chicago civil rights organizations, Rainbow Coalition and Operation PUSH, organizations whose mission was to improve economic opportunities and voting rights for minorities and the disadvantaged.

Hewitt always liked Jackson, in part because he was controversial, a good talker, and Don thought a Jackson profile would present an opportunity for *60 Minutes* to bring more minority viewers to the program.

Hewitt wanted Jackson to announce his run for president exclusively on *60 Minutes* but that was not going to be easy. Jackson had rented out the Washington Convention Center for his announcement and he was reluctant to give *60 Minutes* the exclusive as he felt it would detract from other media covering the event. I met Jackson at the Jefferson, a hotel in Washington, D.C., where he was staying with his staff and family. When I entered his hotel room in November 1983, it was a beehive of activity. His staff was in a tizzy as they fielded calls from assorted media, who wanted the first announcement interview. He had five advisers in his room, some of whom were trying to steer Jackson to do the interview with a black correspondent. Jackson raised that as an idea.

"Cut the black rap stuff," I said. "If you believe in a rainbow coalition you have to include white in that mix."

He came over and put his arm around me. "I could really use you as an adviser on the campaign," he said in a low voice, as not to have all his other advisers hear what he was saying.

"Jesse, you don't need a white Jew who was born in Brooklyn telling you what to do. Cut the shit," I said.

"You tough stuff, aren't you?" he replied.

"Jesse, forty million people will watch you for thirteen minutes on *60 Minutes* say you want to be president. You are going to use us, and we are going to use you, because we will also get the headlines. Do you want to do this or not?" I asked.

"What about the Washington Convention Center?" he asked.

"Fuck the Washington Convention Center. Do we have a deal?" I asked.

"Deal," he said.

Jackson agreed to announce his run on *60 Minutes* and hold a press conference immediately after the story aired. I told him that my approach was to have Mike Wallace ask the same tough policy questions he would a senator running for president. Jackson had never held elected office but had an enormous following in the black community. He also became active in the international scene. He traveled to Syria that year and that helped secure the release of a captured American pilot being held by the Syrian government, which got Jackson a surprising White House thank-you from President Ronald Reagan.

Jackson first came into national view on April 4, 1968, the day that Dr. Martin Luther King Jr. was assassinated. Jackson was talking to King from the street when the bullet hit. Witnesses saw Jackson take some of Dr. King's blood and smear it on the front of his shirt. He then did interviews on TV, claiming he was the last person King spoke to before he was shot. Wearing the bloodstained shirt that day was seen by King's associates as a stunt to raise Jackson's national profile, and it drove a wedge at the time between him and members of the civil rights movement, including King's aides Hosea Williams and Rev. Ralph Abernathy. They saw what Jackson did as an attempt to anoint himself as the new leader of the civil rights movement. It seemed to work, as sixteen years later, we were in a Washington hotel room with Jackson set to make history.

Aides walked into his room that day, holding index cards with the names of media stars calling and seeking the first interview. Each time an index card would be shown to Jackson, he would shake his head: Barbara Walters, Ted Koppel—all were noes. But there was one call that he did interrupt our conversation to take.

"Hi, honey, hi, sweetie," Jackson said. "Do you have on that nice dress I like? Are you wearing the perfume I like? Listen, my kids are going back to Chicago in a couple of hours. Why don't you come up and see me then?"

He hung up the phone. Jackson ignored my smile and my look of astonishment. Clearly he didn't understand that he couldn't continue to conduct business in the same way if he was to run for president, especially in front of a reporter.

I made the quick decision not to report or pursue this lead. I remembered Ben Bradlee, the editor of *The Washington Post*, didn't report any of the stories he knew about President John Kennedy's dalliances. Besides, thirty-five years ago, the personal affairs of those running for office were considered off-limits.

A few months after our interview aired, Jackson was able to get over three million votes and won three primaries, in Louisiana, South Carolina, and the District of Columbia. His surprisingly strong showing empowered him to try again in 1988, and once again Don assigned me the story. But this one had a twist. "Everyone knows Jesse Jackson," Don said. "No one knows who Jackson's family is."

Jackson had five children, one named Jesse Jackson Jr., who would later become a congressman. Jesse was still trying to run for president, be a father, and carry on extramarital affairs, but now in 1988 there were too many women to ignore.

This time I decided to confront the issue head on. His wife, Jackie, the rock of the family and the one most responsible for raising the kids, certainly was aware of the stories. One day we found ourselves alone in an airport, waiting for a flight, when I asked about her husband's cheating.

"When Jesse is with me, he is with me. When he is not, he is not. If it doesn't matter to me, it shouldn't matter to you. And it is none of your business. We love each other and we have a strong relationship."

She would later repeat that line almost word for word on-camera to Mike Wallace.

When the story aired, it was not the womanizing allegation that people remembered. Instead it was an offhand comment Jackson made to Wallace while they rode around in a convertible. With the microphone on and the cameras rolling, Wallace asked Jackson if he would ever live in New York.

"No, I wouldn't even try it," he said.

"Why?"

"Because people steal. There's no sense of neighborhood consciousness and stuff," he said. This was not a comment a presidential candidate should make, even if he or she believes it, and he took a beating in New York's tabloid press.

Jackson had already called New York "Hymietown," which was taken as a slur against Jews. After our story aired, Jackson would call then-mayor Ed Koch and apologize for all his remarks.

The story would be the first national exposure for Jackson's then-eighteen-year-old son Jesse Jr. During the interview, he said he would take an assassin's bullet for his father, because he felt his father's work was that important. Junior would go on to achieve something his father never did, getting elected to a national office. He became a congressman and helped run Barack Obama's first presidential election. But young Jesse had his own office dalliances; he would also be convicted on federal charges of misusing campaign funds for his own personal use and sent to prison.

The son learned the wrong lessons from the father. Jesse Sr. was not defined by his vices, but by a desire to be admired and loved. Junior saw the vices as a way to get admiration, but in his case, they led to his downfall.

As for his father, Jesse Jackson Sr. was years later caught on an open mic disparaging Obama and saying he wanted "to cut Obama's nuts out." Jesse had always thought he would be the first black president, and his resentment toward Obama slipped out. He was banned from the administration, and the Reverend Al Sharpton stepped in.

Sharpton would become a regular at the Obama White House, visiting the president in the Oval Office more than any sitting U.S. senator.

Sharpton and I developed a friendly relationship after I profiled him on the show. The story focused on his extraordinary weight loss, which happened after he traded a diet of fried chicken and doughnuts for dinners of unbuttered wheat bread. We covered his friendship with Obama and some of the controversies in his life, in particular his continued defense of his actions in the Tawana Brawley case—a fraud that led the public to falsely believe that Brawley, a black teenager, was raped by a group of white men.

"I believed the girl," he said, and resisted the need to apologize.

A while after our Sharpton profile aired and as the "Me Too" movement was making its way into the public consciousness, Sharpton asked a reporter who had done stories on sexual harassment if they always believe a woman who makes a complaint against a man.

"Yes," she said.

"Well, I did as well. Her name was Tawana Brawley."

This was as close as Sharpton came to saying he had made a mistake in that case. Remarkably, Sharpton transformed himself from a belligerent, overweight man in a jumpsuit to a black leader whom every presidential candidate consulted with and visited.

When his mother died, I wrote him a note about what we learn about ourselves when parents die. A week later, I went to his annual

National Action Network fundraiser. He spotted me off to the side of the dais. He left the stage, with a couple of thousand people in the audience, and came over and gave me a warm embrace. "That note meant a lot to me," he said. "Let's get together soon."

And we did. We would meet at the Grand Havana Room in Midtown Manhattan, a cigar bar for mostly moneyed white men, where Rudy Giuliani is a member.

One night, I tried to persuade him about the dangers of the expansion of gambling and casinos, especially its effect on poor minorities. New York had approved a slot machine casino in the middle of St. Albans, Queens, a mostly black neighborhood. Black leaders supported it, despite its devastating effect on those addicted to slots.

"The casino cashes welfare and social security checks, which one casino operator told me was 'providing a service' to the community," I explained to Sharpton. "The only service they were doing is making it quicker and easier for people to lose their money.

"The few jobs casinos create paid near minimum wage," I continued. "And many of those are cleaning toilets."

I think he understood my point but was unwilling to get involved. He had gained a new stature during the Obama administration and was not going to waste his special access on opposing gambling.

He would travel to Washington and quietly offer the president counsel. He wanted Obama to reach across the aisle to Republicans, to invite them over for dinner or to play golf, as a way to help advance his administration's agenda. But Obama refused.

"'You see where I am sitting [the Oval Office]. I didn't get here by kissing anyone's ass, and I am not about to start now,'" Sharpton recalled Obama saying. "It was one of Obama's biggest failings that he kept a very close group of advisers and none of them were able to get him to change."

As we smoked cigars (he likes Ashtons), he told me a story about Donald Trump and boxing promoter Don King. The three of them flew in Trump's helicopter one day to promote a coming boxing match. "It was the longest hour of my life," Sharpton said. "All they did was talk and promote each other; they weren't listening to one word either of them said." It must have been doubly frustrating for Sharpton, who also liked to talk about himself.

In 2016 during a trip to Chicago, Sharpton visited Jackson unannounced at his offices—the student visiting the mentor. Jackson was in a three-piece suit, watching daytime soap operas. They spent an hour together and the phone never rang once. Jackson was now alone, his hands shaking from Parkinson's disease, his lifestyle and hustles finally having caught up to him. Sharpton told me the sad scene will stay with him forever.

Sharpton often thought about Jackson's fall from grace and changed his act. His original belligerent confrontational style toward the "white ruling class" disappeared as he became an important national leader. He decided to take control of his life's narrative, and every major Democratic candidate for president in 2020 sought his endorsement. They wanted to be photographed with him and traveled great distances to speak at his National Action Network convention. Sharpton was able to reinvent himself by broadening his appeal to a wider audience, becoming a leading figure in the "Black Lives Matter" movement, and the chief eulogist for George Floyd, who was strangled to death by the police. Obama said Sharpton was "the voice of the voiceless," while critics still called him a "racial arsonist." I found him to be straightforward and committed to trying to help minorities and the downtrodden elevate themselves. In media circles, few people have this opinion of Sharpton. But I was never one to cultivate friends whom all the other journalists collected—which is one of the reasons I liked hoodlums.

8

GANGSTERS

When I first came to Washington, I was overly impressed by congressmen and senators. But after a while I found most of them to lack au-
thenticity. Many of the legislators would say and do whatever it took
to get on *60 Minutes,* which made their beliefs and motives suspect. I
discovered that the more you know about politicians, the worse they
appear. Which is one reason I decided to report on criminals.

My favorite subjects for stories have always been gangsters and
con men. I have found that when they are ready to go on-camera, they
are, in their own odd way, very honest. One of the most memorable
characters I met was Herbie Sperling, a New York heroin dealer and
street muscleman for the mob.

A Jewish gangster from the Bronx, Sperling was about five-ten and
spoke like a character from a Raymond Chandler crime story, with a
thick New York wiseguy accent. He always looked like he was ready
for a fight.

When Sperling was arrested at the Long Island home that he shared
with his mother, he was offered a deal by the cops. If he cooperated, his
mother would not be charged with a felony.

"If you guys have a beef with her, that's her problem. Don't lay it on me. The old lady has to carry her own weight," Sperling told the police.

She ended up going to prison.

After being found guilty of heroin trafficking, Sperling was sentenced to life plus thirty years and fined $200,000. Without missing a beat, he told the judge, "What are you going to do if I don't pay the fine, send me to jail?"

Sperling was ratted out by Leroy "Nicky" Barnes, who was at one time Harlem's and perhaps the country's biggest drug dealer. Between 1973 and 1977, Barnes was arrested variously for homicide, drug dealing, and gun possession, but none of the charges stuck. He became a Harlem legend and very rich. He sported fur coats and Rolls-Royces and flaunted his success by being interviewed for an article published under the title "Mr. Untouchable" in *The New York Times Magazine* and posing for the magazine cover. This of course put a big law enforcement target on his back.

In 1977, Barnes was finally convicted and sent away to life without parole. Then four years later Barnes turned government informant, and his testimony would lead to the conviction of fifty other people, including Sperling and Sperling's son. In return for his testimony, Barnes was given a reduced sentence and better living conditions in jail.

Sperling wanted revenge and agreed to go on-camera to talk about Barnes's heroin operations. Sperling, who was at Lewisburg federal prison, gave us a great interview, but I wanted Barnes. Unfortunately, he was in the witness protection program and had little desire to sit down with Mike Wallace. I needed to find a way to convince him.

I had gotten to know the young New York U.S. attorney, Rudy Giuliani, when he was the associate attorney general working for the Reagan administration. At that time, we were investigating why hundreds of Cuban refugees captured during the Cuban boat lift of the 1980s were being held in the notorious Atlanta federal prison, without any of them having been convicted of committing any crimes. A federal judge in Atlanta thought that was unconstitutional and was freeing them, while the Reagan administration wanted to keep them in prison for fear they might commit a crime.

The judge wanted to be interviewed, but he didn't want his appearance to be used as an excuse to be removed from the case. Enter Giuliani. I went to his Justice Department office and asked if he would write a letter that would hold the judge harmless for appearing on *60 Minutes*. I expected the process to take months. Instead, Rudy swiveled his chair, and on a typewriter behind him, banged out a letter that said the federal government would not ask for the judge's removal if he did *60 Minutes*. The young Rudy just assumed responsibility for the decision and handed me the letter the judge asked for to appear on-camera.

Now one year later, Giuliani was a hard-driving, ambitious, no-nonsense New York U.S. attorney. He understood the power of *60 Minutes,* and if he got Barnes to go on-camera, Giuliani would also appear as the man who nailed Barnes. In Giuliani's mind, it would validate him as a law-and-order prosecutor.

Barnes, now in the witness protection program, was brought to Giuliani's office by the U.S. marshals, and I was allowed to speak with him. He was no longer the dapper fur-coat-wearing street gangster who rode around Harlem in fancy cars. Dressed in an orange prison jumpsuit, Barnes wore black glasses and sported a mustache. He had the look of a man who had been beaten down by life. Barnes had no interest in doing an interview; he told me that if he did, his life would be in jeopardy.

Discouraged, I entered Giuliani's office while he was in a meeting with his top deputy, Bill Tendy, an old-time prosecutor. I told them Barnes didn't want to do the interview.

"Let me talk with him," Tendy said. "I might be able to convince him to change his mind."

About three minutes later Tendy came back into the office. "Okay, Barnes agreed to do the interview," Tendy said.

Even Giuliani was amazed. "What did you say to him?" Giuliani asked.

"I threw him up against the wall and told him that the only choice he had was what color shirt he would wear for the interview. So sit down and stop fuckin' around."

When I went to see Barnes this time, he was very cooperative. Barnes told us that initially he decided to become an informant because he was overwhelmed by guilt from his drug dealing, but then he actually agreed to become an informant when he learned that a member of his crime council, the leadership of the drug operation, had been sleeping with his girlfriend. "I told them when I went to prison that there were three or four million women in New York, so now you can sleep with any of them, but not with my women. So as soon as I get in, they started sleeping with my women."

One former associate would drive around Harlem with Barnes's former girlfriend in Barnes's white Mercedes-Benz. "Tito never had a foreign car. He was a Buick, Oldsmobile man," Barnes recalled bitterly.

And that began to eat away at him and led to his decision to become a state witness. In return for Giuliani's making Barnes available to us, we did a street interview with Giuliani in Harlem, positioning him as the prosecutor who put Barnes away. Giuliani got the airtime, and we had a terrific *60 Minutes* story.

But most of the time chasing gangsters is a losing proposition. The trick was to figure out a way to gain their trust. When I worked in Pontiac, Michigan, as a newspaper reporter for *The Oakland Press* and assigned to solving Jimmy Hoffa's murder, I once decided to visit the home of a mafia capo in the ritzy suburb of Dearborn Heights. I asked another reporter to go with me for protection. Before I got to the house, I stopped to pick up a pizza.

I went up to the gangster's door and knocked. His wife answered and she was visibly frightened. The gangster then came to the door and asked me what I wanted.

I introduced myself and said I was a reporter and I wanted to talk with him.

"Get out of here," he said, and was closing the door.

"Listen, I have a hot pizza here. It's half mushroom and half pepperoni. I personally like mushroom, but if you insist, I will eat the pepperoni."

I opened the box so he could see the pizza, but more important, so he could get a whiff of it. There is something about the smell of a fresh pizza that can drive people crazy.

He invited me in for a talk and a little pizza. "I know you won't tell me anything about your [crime] family. I am interested in what the other [crime] family is doing," I said.

He listened and didn't respond to my offer. "Are you finished with your pizza?" he asked.

With that, he showed me to the door but asked for a business card. A week later he called to ask me to come back to his home.

"You got balls," he said to me at the door. He then escorted me inside his car and turned on the radio. He thought his house was wired by the FBI, so he conducted his meetings in the car.

He gave me some information on the rival mafia faction operating in Detroit, details that led to stories. Now it was my turn to go to the rival mobster, Anthony Giacalone, known as Tony Jack, to see if he wanted to talk.

At that point, in 1978, there was a murder wave happening in Detroit, with two warring mob factions fighting it out. One of the leaders at the time was Giacalone, who, the FBI said, was probably involved in the Hoffa murder.

He ate lunch on Tuesdays at the Southfield Athletic Club, so I went there one day to stake him out. I sat in the lunchroom about ten feet away. As I strained to hear what he was saying to his lunch partner, my name was paged over the loudspeaker.

I didn't understand how they knew I was there, and I heard my name paged again. This time I got up and went to the manager's office. "Mr. Giacalone does not like anyone listening to his conversations," the manager said.

"How did you know it was me?" I asked.

He didn't answer. He merely told me to go back and enjoy my meal.

When I returned to my table, I was scared. The mafia have shot people in restaurants and barbershops, why not a health club? I could see Giacalone staring at me. I decided I couldn't leave or stare back, so I went over and introduced myself. There is no manual to read on how to survive a potential gangland hit. I felt I needed to follow my instincts.

"Hi, I am with *The Oakland Press* and wanted to see if I could interview you," I said, without any sales pitch. I was simply trying to survive the next minute. He said nothing and gave a side glance at his lunch companion, who looked like a weightlifter who had eaten too much pasta.

"Go back and enjoy your meal," he said.

At that point I couldn't enjoy anything. I paid the check and walked out before my food came. One of Giacalone's bodyguards was in the parking lot. He smiled at me and recited my license plate number.

"Drive carefully," he said with a laugh.

I was thinking about these efforts when I went to the federal courthouse in New York during the mafia commission trials in the 1980s to try to convince one of the mafia bosses to appear on *60 Minutes*.

I first approached Genovese crime boss Anthony "Fat Tony" Salerno, at the courthouse. As soon as I introduced myself, he spat at me. I took that as a no. Next I was able to get a seat in the courtroom next to Gambino boss Paul Castellano, who would later be assassinated in front of Sparks Steak House by men in the employ of John Gotti Sr. I introduced myself to Castellano, gave him my business card, and told him we would like him to be on *60 Minutes*. He said nothing and stared at the card I handed him. I got excited that he was even thinking about doing the show. But then he folded my card a few times and began to pick his teeth with it.

I went back and told Don. His response was typical Hewitt.

"You should have given the guy a toothpick," Don said.

It is rare that you get to talk to a mafia boss, but in 1984, that's exactly what happened when I flew to Tucson, Arizona, to interview Joe Bonanno. He had decided to abandon his oath of omertà and write a book titled *A Man of Honor.* I used that to try to convince him to go on-camera.

I first met with his attorney, who told me that there would be certain subjects that were off-limits.

"He won't discuss murder," the attorney said. "There is no statute of limitations on that."

"What about extortion?" I asked.

"No," the attorney replied. "But you can ask him about bootlegging."

"Come on, you are not giving me anything," I said. I think this was the strangest negotiation I had ever been part of.

"Okay, okay, you can ask him about the control of the garment center," the lawyer said.

"That's nothing," I said. "He has got to talk about the Commission."

The Commission was the secret leadership group of the mob, comprised of the heads of the five New York families. They ruled on disputes between families and ordered contract hits. No mafia chief had ever acknowledged that it existed, much less discussed how it operated.

But the attorney and Bonanno agreed to talk about the Commission. Bonanno would even draw a family tree of the leaders of the five families. The drawing is now on my office wall.

He did the interview at his home in Tucson surrounded by his sons and daughter. It would be his only television interview. He called himself a "man of honor" and said that he was a part of a tradition that came from Sicily at the turn of the century. Wallace asked him about the lavish mafia wedding he threw for his son Bill, who married Rosalie, the daughter of Joe Profaci, another mafia boss.

Wallace said that every mafia boss in the United States showed up. Joe responded with pride.

"All United States was there. Congressmen was there, judges was there, Frank Sinatra got sick, he couldn't come, but Tony Bennett sang all night with a nice voice."

And his son Bill Bonanno quickly added, "There were three thousand people there, and I venture to say, according to FBI statistics, that there are not more than four thousand quote mafia members unquote in the whole United States."

And then Wallace said, pointing at Joe, "Out of respect for you."

"Yes, out of respect for me."

That wedding became the inspiration for the opening scene for the movie *The Godfather*. And it was widely believed that Bonanno was the model for the Marlon Brando character.

Bonanno talked about how the mob controlled the garment union and how one of his former business partners in bootlegging during prohibition was Joe Kennedy, the father of John and Robert Kennedy. He also said that if a man sleeps with another man's wife, the "cuckolded man" has the right to kill for revenge, according to mafia tradition.

The story would be a rare double segment spread across two different Sundays. One interested viewer was U.S. Attorney Giuliani, who used the story as the basis to bring a RICO case against the heads of the five New York families. Bonanno's interview gave Giuliani the idea because it was the first time a mafia head acknowledged the existence of a gangster commission to commit crimes.

Giuliani flew to Arizona to try to compel Bonanno to testify. But Bonanno would end up getting "sick" through the duration of the trial.

Bonanno justified his decision to talk about mafia secrets (thus violating omertà, the code of silence) by claiming that he was doing it on his terms and no one was being hurt by his stories. That flimsy argument enraged the gangsters operating the families in New York.

Joe Massino, who took over the Bonanno crime family, was caught on tape saying that Bonanno had "disrespected the family by ratting." But as is typical of today's mafia guy, Massino would himself later become a government informant and be placed in the witness protection program.

As often happens, the best stories were never told on-camera. One had to do with Meyer Lansky.

After the filming was completed and Mike and the crew left Tucson, I returned to Joe's house and had a cognac with him, watching the sunset in his backyard. The pressure of the interview was over, and Joe had his guard down. I don't think he had ever told anyone outside of his immediate family any of the stories of his livelihood and now felt a burden was lifted. While we were sipping cognac, I asked him about the man known as the "mob's accountant," Meyer Lansky.

"Joe, growing up in New York, I was fascinated by Meyer Lansky," I said.

Lansky was the tough Jewish gangster from New York who helped expand the mafia's investments into Las Vegas and the Cuban casinos. He, along with Lucky Luciano, helped create the National Crime Syndicate in the United States. I was interested in how Lansky was so readily accepted into the Italian mafia. I assume it had to do with his acumen as an investor.

Joe didn't see Lansky the way I did. "His value to us was that he had the picture," Joe told me.

"What picture?" I asked.

Joe gave me a look like I was an idiot. "His value to us was that he had the picture," Joe told me. "The picture of [FBI Director] Hoover and his deputy Clyde Tolson having sex."

The picture has been spoken about over the years, but many thought it was apocryphal. Lansky somehow was able to get it.

Joe said that because of the picture, which Lansky informed Hoover he had, Hoover told his agents that organized crime didn't exist. It was Lansky's blackmail chip to keep the FBI at bay, and according to Bonanno, it worked for quite a few years.

"That was his value to us," Bonanno said. "The picture."

As for the assassination of President John F. Kennedy, Bonanno said that when he heard the news of the shooting, he sent his consigliere to Miami to talk with Florida mafia boss Santos Trafficante, who told his emissary that the mob tried first to kill Kennedy in Miami using Cubans, but didn't get the right opportunity. Instead, they brought in a team of Corsican hit men who carried out the murder from the famous grassy knoll. The Corsicans were themselves later killed. He said Kennedy was shot because the Justice Department, under his brother

Robert Kennedy, decided to prosecute the mob, which he said violated the deal they made with Kennedy's father to help elect JFK in the 1960 election. "New Orleans and Miami will take the heat for this," Bonanno remembers Trafficante saying, "New York [crime families] are clear of responsibility." Bonanno says he never asked about it again.

Bonanno refused to say any of this on-camera. His English wasn't great, and his son Bill, who himself rose to a high leadership position in the crime family, acted as interpreter and commentator through the story.

Bill went with Mike Wallace back to Brooklyn, to the old neighborhood that Bonanno controlled before he was forced into retirement. His father opposed the mafia's expansion into drugs, the reason his dad gave for retiring to Arizona. But law enforcement believed that Bonanno lost a power grab to be head of the Commission, and so he was "asked" to retire, or else.

Bill's trip back to Brooklyn was the first time he had returned since he was involved in a war with a rival faction from his own family. Wallace liked Bill, and in typical Wallace fashion asked him, "Something I don't understand—you are intelligent, articulate, you have the gift of command, and yet you are a hoodlum. Why?"

It was raining that day, so the interview was conducted in a car. Bill looked outside the car window and said, "You know how many times I have asked myself that question, Mike? It comes down to two things: a love of tradition and a love for my father."

At Joe Bonanno's ninetieth birthday party, he was celebrated by three hundred people, including some retired FBI agents who at one time had tried to put him away. He would die at ninety-seven.

The last time I saw Bill, at a New York breakfast, he said he was now a writer and movie producer, advising and writing on the mob. "Had I known there was this much money to be made going legit, I would never have gone illegit," he said.

Bill Bonanno died of a heart attack at seventy-seven, after completing a book with Joe Pistone, an FBI agent who had infiltrated the mob. I think even Joe would not have approved that collaboration.

9

IN SEARCH OF THE BIG STORY

One morning in 1984, I biked the five-minute ride from my house in Georgetown to the office. When I arrived, I found a brown envelope on my desk. Inside were top-secret documents alleging a vast government conspiracy to hide the truth about the UFO crash in Roswell, New Mexico. The document, written like a bureaucrat composed it, listed twelve men inside the Eisenhower administration with direct knowledge of the 1947 UFO crash in Roswell and the mechanisms that were put in place to investigate the alien spacecraft, to make sure the secret didn't get out.

I read the document twice and then put it back in the envelope. My heart was racing, as I thought I was possibly sitting on the biggest story in history. I allowed myself a moment to think about all the accolades I would receive, but I quickly snapped out of my daydream. Instead, I decided not to tell anyone about this document until I determined if it was real.

There was no internet to quickly check the names and information contained in the file, so I went to the Library of Congress and painstakingly went through each name listed and even matched up the typeface of the document with other typefaces from the Department of Defense and the CIA from that time period.

But while researching, I discovered another version of the "Majestic 12," or MJ-12, the so-called alien documents, inside the archives. After comparing the two files, I determined that in fact the hoax was so elaborate that someone had even planted the document inside the national archives for me to discover.

I wanted the document to be true, but it wasn't. Some of the best work I have done are not stories I did but stories I didn't do. I have a simple formula: if the shit hits the fan, what documents and what individuals will be in my corner as opposed to the documents and people on the other side.

I put the document back in the brown envelope and put the file in my top drawer. A few weeks later I told my neighbor at work, a BBC producer, about the document, and he asked if he could do a feature on it, even though it was false.

I agreed and gave him a copy. It turned out to be a big mistake. The BBC producer wrote the story straight, treating this document as if it were real and the biggest story of our time. Soon I got a call from Wallace and Hewitt asking me to do a story on the file.

"Guys, I had the file for weeks. I was the one who gave it to the BBC. It is a phony," I told them.

Wallace and Hewitt were pissed. I walked through my reporting with them and told them that the last thing we wanted was for *60 Minutes* to be conned by a phony document. They agreed but were disappointed.

The story had legs for a few weeks. It didn't matter that the FBI's own investigation declared the documents "bogus" and that the Air Force said there never was any committee called MJ-12. Many people simply wanted to believe the documents were real.

At times, I felt I was on the journalistic equivalent of *The X-Files*. Somehow I got tagged by ufologists as a sympathetic voice, or maybe an easy mark.

I had dismissed many of their leads, but one seemed too juicy to ignore. Steven Greer, an emergency room doctor in Charlottesville, Virginia, contacted me about a roster of government employees who had been involved in the UFO cover-up. The list he had was long and impressive, and in addition to the individuals, Greer somehow got internal files from inside the government about UFO sightings that were covered up.

I flew down to Charlottesville and drove to his home. I thought that Greer, being a doctor, could not be your typical UFO nut. But I looked through his files and there was something a little off about the documents. They seemed too pat. The old adage "If it looks too good to be true, it usually is," seemed to apply. One of the documents stamped *top secret* was a wiretap report of a conversation between Marilyn Monroe and Dorothy Kilgallen, a gossip columnist, discussing JFK's canceling a visit to Monroe because he said he needed to inspect a crashed UFO that was being kept at Roswell. That document was later determined to be a fake.

But while I was still in Greer's company, I was prepared to suspend my usual state of skepticism—that is, until he volunteered that he often went into the desert of Arizona to shoot lasers in the sky in an effort to contact alien ships. He said he had even started to take tour groups out to the desert with him.

I looked at him and thought to myself, *Why did you have to tell me that?* And then I began to wonder if I still had enough time to catch the last afternoon flight back to Washington.

Why do I even bother to pursue some of these outlandish stories? Because, every so often, they are true.

In 2007, the 693-page "Family Jewels" documents were released by the CIA. They outlined operations the agency had carried out, including experimenting on subjects with LSD, hiring the mafia to kill Fidel Castro, and a massive spying and phone-tapping operation against journalists and the American public. The documents also spelled out how the CIA spied on antiwar and civil rights groups. The documents were created in the 1970s, post-Watergate era, when then–CIA director James Schlesinger asked all CIA departments to submit to him any covert actions that were carried out that were outside of the CIA charter.

The CIA director then put all these revelations into one classified document. Later, when CIA director Mike Hayden agreed to release the "Family Jewels" document, the only item that was fully redacted and was still Secret was item number one. Given that item number two was the assassination attempts against Castro by CIA-hired mafia hit men, item number one must be pretty good.

I talked with six former CIA directors about item one and got a bewildering array of replies from "I don't know" to "I know and can't tell you." Piecing together bits of my conversations with all of them, I figured out that it involved spying on Americans overseas, with the help of the Allies. But it remains one of the stories I wanted but never was able to break.

Along the same lines, one offbeat CIA story I shot was on the Agency hiring the Stanford Research Institute in California to use psychics to spy on the Russians. Senator Claiborne Pell of Rhode Island went on-camera with us to outline how mind control techniques could be used to extract information from captured spies. The CIA was experimenting with "remote viewing," where a psychic could see inside classified Russian installations and extract information from them, all while sitting in a closed room in California. The CIA even once used psychics to try to locate a crashed plane in Africa. But from what I was told, no great secrets were learned from the psychics, and the program was abandoned.

10

LESSONS LEARNED

I was still only a few years removed from college and had a lot to learn. But I had Mike Wallace as my teacher, and I used our dinners on the road as my tutorials. At one of those meals, Mike once asked me, "What is the best question you can ask someone on-camera?"

I thought for a moment and replied, "Why? As in, why did you kill that person?"

No, he said, the best question you can ask someone is "Because?" As in: "You killed that person because?" It will evoke a more thoughtful response, Mike said.

Mike believed that the key to a great interview was to carry on a conversation with a person as if you were talking to them in a bar. Mike liked to get the hard questions out first, because those are the ones the interview subject expected and was guarding against. After those hard questions had been gotten out of the way, Mike believed that the interviewees would be more relaxed and would let their guard down. Then he would pounce.

This was also a power play move. Mike wanted them to know that he was the one in charge and he would not let the subject steer the interview away from the areas he wanted to cover.

He once did an interview with Israeli leader Menachem Begin, who had been a member of the Irgun, the Israeli terrorist group that killed British soldiers before the 1948 partition. He began by asking Begin, "What is the difference between the Yasser Arafat [Palestine Liberation Organization leader] of today and the Menachem Begin of 1946?" It was a question meant to piss Begin off. Begin denied the similarities, of course, but Mike believed if he got a subject to react emotionally, as in anger, it would elicit a more honest response.

Mike also liked to conduct an interview with staccato questions, ones that would elicit yes or no responses. The technique was meant to get the subject to respond quickly and maybe catch him or her off guard.

When Mike did an interview with President Richard M. Nixon's right-hand man, John D. Ehrlichman, during the Watergate scandal, Mike told me he found a damning laundry list of wrongdoings committed by the Nixon administration and then read it to Ehrlichman.

"Perjury. Plans to audit tax returns for political retaliation. Theft of psychiatric records. Spying by undercover agents. Conspiracy to obstruct justice. All of this by the law-and-order administration of Richard Nixon."

Mr. Ehrlichman paused and said, "Is there a question in there somewhere?"

The reply to the non-question by Ehrlichman was better than Mike could ever have hoped for, because Ehrlichman never denied the charges, but merely asked what the question was. Mike was smart enough not to take the bait and reword the question. He merely moved on to another subject.

Mike used different looks and expressions while conducting an interview, and at dinner, he would playfully show me each expression. There was the "you are so full of shit, I can't believe you are saying that" look. The joyous look was when Mike was able to land a particularly enlightening fact from a subject. That look came with a big smile and a vibe that said, "So you finally decided to be honest, eh?"

He would also repeat certain expressions like "come on" or "forgive me," which indicated a nasty question was coming.

But the secret to Mike's energy and drive was his insecurity. "I have always been fascinated by the insecurities in other people, because I am well aware of my own insecurities," he once said.

Mike's insecurity came in part from his looks. Because of his pock-marked face, he dreaded sunny days: the harsh light would make his acne scars more visible. Interviews were filmed away from his bad side, almost shooting him in profile.

He never cared about being liked, nor did he care about being nice. He was trying to skin his subjects alive. He often said to me that there are "no embarrassing questions, only embarrassing answers."

Producers at the office would speak about Mike's genius as the ability to look at strangers and know exactly what button to push to drive them crazy.

Mike preferred to describe this ability as setting up a "chemistry of confidentiality"—giving someone a psychological reason to reveal themselves. Even though there were people around, Mike made it seem as if he were alone with the subject.

Because he was working on several stories at the same time, he re-lied on a producer to carry most of the load of the reporting. When the interviews were under way, if there was a follow-up question I wanted asked, Mike insisted that I give it to him while the interview was under way, not wait for a tape change or bathroom break.

So I would scribble out a question and crawl over to hand him the paper, like a runner passing a baton during a race. Mike would extend his hand backward, while the interview subject continued to talk, and grab the paper from me. If Mike liked the question, he would keep it on his lap and ask it. If he didn't, he crumpled it up and threw it on the floor.

Occasionally, after he had discarded it, he would want to ask the question I suggested, but it would now be a ball of paper somewhere on the ground. I watched in horror as he would lean over his chair and try to find it on the floor, without losing eye contact with his interview subject.

"If you give me the information, I can persuade the person I am interviewing that I may know more than I do. Then they would get comfortable with me," he said.

Before you get the interview, you need to find the story, and the best stories usually come from sources. The secret to developing sources is to make yourself an interesting person, someone whom people want to hang out with or talk to. Your source should be invested in seeing you succeed and in getting their story out.

Mike believed that you should never phone someone only when you wanted something from them. He maintained that you should keep in touch with a source by passing along a story or a joke, or even just to say hello. That way when you want something from them, they will be more receptive to taking your call.

Why would anyone go on-camera with Mike Wallace?

I learned that you need to give the subject an incentive to appear. I figured that the reasons people agreed to go on-camera were revenge, a desire to feel important or to effect change, and self-preservation.

The self-preservation motive is interesting, as many people who sat for an interview with Mike Wallace thought they could outsmart him. They rarely did. They didn't think we would find that one document or source that would reveal the person to be a liar. And since we taped the interviews and edited them later, the best moments that make the correspondent look good are usually included in the story.

If the producer does his job right, the questions are carefully crafted to make the correspondent look as knowledgeable and tough as possible. The scripting process of a story begins when the questions are first written. Constructed properly, they provide important narrative bridges that would help in the storytelling.

Mike told me that if you succeed in persuading the interviewee that you know more than he thinks you know, he will open up more easily. Interview subjects don't want to come off as liars.

According to Mike, the goal of the interviewer was to make a difference in the life of the person they are interviewing. "They need to feel they are doing something useful, that they are either helping somebody out of trouble or righting a wrong, exposing something that is worth exposing."

At these dinners, Mike tried to get a rise out of me. He seemed to define his life by how much trouble he could cause, both in his stories and to those around him. Morley Safer said Mike "had no off switch. If it was in his head, it came out of his mouth."

Every meal seemed to involve at least one impertinent personal question meant to embarrass me.

"Ever sleep with a black woman?" he once asked in a Los Angeles restaurant. When I refused to answer, he wanted to know if I was prejudiced. When I did answer his first question, he called the waiter over and told him what I said. Today, I might call HR, hire an attorney, and threaten a very public lawsuit against Wallace, but in those days the possibility of such actions never even crossed my mind. Nor did any of the other producers he harassed or demeaned consider legal action against him. We were all building careers, doing great stories, and learning the art form from the Picasso of interviewers. And with no one putting a stop to his abusive behavior, he carried on.

11

CATCHING A FUGITIVE

In 1985, I was chasing a former General Dynamics executive named P. Takis Veliotis, the central figure in a complaint that General Dynamics billed the Navy $640 million in fraudulent claims. He was wanted on federal charges in the United States for fraud, and being a Greek national, he fled to Greece for sanctuary. Veliotis was a hard-nosed, arrogant man. But with the help of a recommendation from my friend Patrick Tyler at *The Washington Post,* Veliotis agreed to the interview. However, the day before Mike Wallace and crew were to arrive in Athens, Veliotis canceled. The reason: I had asked to take a picture of him on his yacht. He thought I wanted to portray him as a rich fugitive, living the good life, and he was not entirely wrong.

Having been told by Tyler that Veliotis was an egomaniac and a control freak, I thought of a way we might be able to talk him into doing the interview again. Mike was in Israel with producer Barry Lando, so I called him there.

"Veliotis has canceled the interview because I asked to get a picture of his boat. But I think we can get it back," I said. "I want you to call him and tell him you made a mistake in entrusting such an important interview to a teenager like me. Throw me under the bus. Tell him that you and Veliotis, two grown men, will do this properly."

I was playing to Mike's ego, of course, and to the belief many correspondents have that producers help the stories, but it is the correspondents that are the keys to their succeeding. More important, Veliotis would think that he was so important that the great Mike Wallace would both interview him and produce the story. Mike enjoyed the thought of being given permission to throw me under the bus; he didn't need to be asked twice. He called Veliotis and got the interview back on track.

"I must say I rather enjoyed that conversation," Mike said, referring to the part where he got to belittle me to the subject of our piece. "Try not to do anything to fuck this up again, kid."

Mike flew from Tel Aviv to Athens and I picked him up at the airport. I was surprised to see he had a traveling companion—Mary Yates.

Mike had been dating Mary for a few months but had known her most of his professional life. Her former husband was Ted Yates, an esteemed war correspondent who had been killed while covering the Six-Day War. Mary knew Mike, the good and the bad, and shared stories, friends, and memories with him. She knew what she was getting into.

The next day, Mike and I went to Veliotis's home outside Athens to conduct the interview. Mary, meanwhile, took a trip to the Greek mountain where Mike's son Peter had died.

In 1962, Peter had just graduated from Yale and was an aspiring journalist, having written for the college newspaper. He had taken a summer trip to Greece and wanted to visit an isolated monastery near Corinth. He left late in the day and began the fifteen-mile hike alone. He never made it. He ended up getting lost at night on the trails and fell off a mountain. Mike was back in New York and hadn't heard from his son. After a few weeks, Mike traveled to Greece, rented a donkey and a guide in the town of Kamari, and began to climb the mountain toward the monastery. And when he got to the top, he looked over a ledge and there was Peter's body. It had been there for a couple of weeks.

Mike buried his son near the monastery. After Peter's death, Mike said that he took stock of his life. Before the death Mike had been a successful game show host and a hawker of cigarettes and Fluffo shortening products. He had also done a show called *Night Beat,* on which he interviewed celebrities, politicians, and criminals. But he had not done news reporting. He wanted to do something that had more heft and integrity. He wanted to work for CBS News—as a father, following the path his son might have taken.

So Mike went to CBS and asked to be part of the news division. He gave up a lot of money to switch careers. But he wanted to become a journalist for Peter.

When we returned from the interview with Veliotis, we went to dinner at the hotel with Mary. She told us that she spent the day visiting the monastery where Peter was headed on the fateful day. She began to cry when she told us how the people inside the monastery took care of Peter's gravesite by putting fresh flowers on it every week.

Mike didn't ask her to go; she wanted to visit the gravesite on her own. She recounted the difficult and arduous journey up the mountain and the beautiful views from the top where Peter fell, maybe the last view he saw before he died. Mary talked about the wonderful people at the monastery, and Mike and Mary began to cry almost uncontrollably.

I had not seen Mike so vulnerable and broken. I only experienced the tough, in-your-face, no-nonsense reporter. That night in Greece, seeing the devastation Mike had experienced at the loss of his son, helped explain for me some of the demons he had to overcome to become America's preeminent interviewer. Soon I would see more of those demons emerge.

12

DEPRESSION STRIKES

It seemed that ever since I had begun working with Mike, he had suffered from bouts of depression that he tried to cover up. But five years
after we started together, I saw that something was not right.

The depression would usually surface when we went on the road.
In the winter of 1985, we had interviews at Lewisburg federal prison
near Harrisburg, Pennsylvania. Though relatively close to New York
City, the facility is harder to get to than California. We flew a small
commercial prop plane and then rented a car for the long drive to the
prison.

It was a cold, rainy day and the plane ride was rough and bumpy.
After we got the rental car, we had been driving for half a hour when
Mike suddenly began to slam his fist into the window—no explana-
tion, no warning. He was angry and cursing. Then, just as suddenly, it
stopped.

"You want me to pull over?" I asked, a little scared.

There was no answer. I pulled the car over to the side of the road,
but he told me to keep driving.

I must admit that I cared less about Mike's well-being and more
about the interview. I wasn't particularly sympathetic. He had been

mean to me and selfish, and I was going to be selfish back. These prison interviews had been hard to set up, and I needed Mike in one piece.

Looking back, I realized how young, ambitious, and stupid I was. I should have focused more on caring for him than on worrying about the story. Instead of riding to the prison that day, I should have taken him to a hospital. Not that he would have gone. It turned out Mike had been battling depression since the 1982 Westmoreland libel trial.

Former U.S. Army chief of staff General William Westmoreland sued CBS for $120 million for a CBS Reports documentary Wallace narrated. It said Westmoreland had manipulated intelligence about enemy strength to create the impression that the United States was winning the Vietnam War. The public sympathy was with Westmoreland, a decorated general. Even though it wasn't a *60 Minutes* story, Wallace was the documentary's voice, so he faced public humiliation and questions about his integrity. CBS would eventually win the lawsuit, but the experience, Mike said, made him feel dead inside.

He consulted with one doctor who told him that "he was a tough guy and would get through it." When the depressed feeling would not go away, another doctor told him if it ever came out that he was depressed, it would be bad for his image.

So Mike learned to cover up his condition and continue to function. When we got to Lewisburg federal prison, he was in top form. It was like a switch was turned on and he was able to become Mike Wallace, master interviewer. But after we left the prison and started to drive back to the airport, he suddenly began to cry. This time he asked me to pull the car over. It was raining; he got out, walked around the car, and began to vomit.

I remember feeling helpless, not sure what to do. But he got back in the car and told me he was fine, and we drove on as if nothing had happened. He asked that I not tell anyone in the office what happened.

It turned out depression was something he didn't share at the time with his other producers or even Don Hewitt.

The next interview I did with him was in Washington with a Soviet defector named Arkady Shevchenko. Arkady was secretly working for the United States while he was at the UN and had given then–U.S. representative Daniel Patrick Moynihan valuable insight and information in dealing with his Soviet counterparts.

During Shevchenko's interview, Mike was disengaged. He looked like he had aged ten years and was merely reading the questions I wrote, one after another. Normally Mike was an extraordinary listener, creating sequences out of the answers. But on this day, he had checked out.

When the interview ended, Mike, Mary, and I drove around Washington. Mary pointed out homes in the city where she used to live. Mike was bundled up in a trench coat, sitting slouched down in the car, looking out the window, saying little. At that moment, there was a real sadness to him.

The night the story aired, Mike called. As he always did, he began to talk without saying hello. "Kid, I watched that story. I was there doing the interviews for the story, but I don't remember doing any of it."

Years later, he discussed what had happened later that night. Mike wrote a goodbye note to Mary. He then took a massive amount of sleeping pills and tried to kill himself. Mary, sensing something was wrong, tried to wake him at three in the morning but was unsuccessful. She called the doctor, who came to the house. The doctor called an ambulance, which whisked Mike off to the hospital. His stomach was pumped, and he was resuscitated. No one at work was aware of this. The cover story was that he went to the hospital suffering from "exhaustion."

The next day he began therapy with a psychiatrist and a new regimen of pills to combat his depression. It took about six weeks for the new drugs to kick in, but he became a nicer person, at least to me. At the time, I had no idea what caused his change in mood. I thought he may have been friendlier because we had a good run of stories. One story, on police corruption in Chicago, had recently won the prestigious duPont Award, and that gave me, in his words, "a weekend pass."

At thirty-two, I was considered a seasoned producer. And I continued to occasionally play airport roulette when I needed to find a story. For some crazy reason, 60 Minutes was still delivering newspapers to producers' offices a few days late. So I looked at flying around the country to gain an edge on my colleagues. That's how I discovered the story of FBI spy Richard Miller.

One weekend I aimlessly jumped on a plane to L.A., and when I landed, I grabbed a copy of the *Los Angeles Times*. The report on the front page described how an FBI agent named Richard Miller gave away classified documents to an attractive Soviet female agent, becoming the first FBI agent ever charged with espionage. But what caught my eye was that Miller freely acknowledged his crime and said he was conducting his own investigation by sleeping with the Russian. His lawyers were letting him talk. That Sunday, I called his attorney and set up a meeting.

But first I left a message with New York to "blue-sheet" the story, essentially a quitclaim on an idea so that no one else could take it. At that time there was no internet and the *Los Angeles Times* wouldn't reach New York for a few days, so the story was mine.

Miller was being held in Terminal Island prison near Long Beach, California. Fortunately, I was friends with Norm Carlson, the head of the bureau of prisons, who let me use the prison system as my personal casting company. He got me inside the jail the next day.

Some of the best stories are in prisons, and if you get in, you have a reasonable chance of talking an inmate into going on-camera. After all, they have no place to go and not very much to do.

But very rarely does a story fall completely together as this one did. Miller's attorneys agreed to put their client on-camera with Mike Wallace, even though Miller was facing espionage charges. Their defense was going to be that he was a bumbling idiot, an Inspector Clouseau. The fact that Miller agreed to go on-camera with Mike Wallace no doubt reinforced that legal strategy.

The U.S. attorney in Los Angeles, Robert Bonner, a good guy, greased the wheels to get us someone from the FBI to participate in an ongoing case. I had everything I could ask for, except for Svetlana.

Svetlana Ogorodnikov was the Mata Hari who seduced Miller to give up FBI secrets. She was locked up in a co-ed jail at Pleasanton, outside of San Francisco. Through her attorney, I called her and explained the story we were doing. I said that Miller was going on-camera, and if she didn't, the story would be one-sided and incomplete. To my amazement, she readily agreed to appear.

We interviewed Miller, whose attorneys bizarrely wanted him to look bad and pathetic because they felt that could help their case. One of their investigators described him as *lunchy,* a word I had never heard before, which means someone with food all over them. Miller was a Mormon, married with eight kids. He claimed that he was doing his own investigation and was trying to get himself recruited by the KGB by sleeping with Svetlana. I reviewed the court transcripts, interviewed fellow FBI agents and the prosecutors, and was able to give Mike a memo that had some interesting facts that we could use in the interview.

MILLER:	I was trying to get myself recruited.
WALLACE:	You were getting yourself recruited every night.
MILLER:	No, it wasn't that often.
WALLACE:	Did you keep up-to-date on your FBI reports?
MILLER:	No, I wasn't very good on paperwork.
WALLACE:	When you were told to lose weight, did you lose weight?
MILLER:	No, the rebellious side went against that.
WALLACE:	Did you sell private information to an outside private investigator?
MILLER:	A fact I am not very proud of.
WALLACE:	Did you cadge candy bars from the 7-Eleven?
MILLER:	I would rather not discuss that.

Mike was using humor to make a point that Miller was an idiot, as he admitted to almost everything, but didn't want to talk about shoplifting Hershey bars from the local 7-Eleven. Even his attorneys seemed bewildered by his responses.

The next day, we flew up to San Francisco, rented a car, and drove to see Svetlana. I had alerted Mike that the prison was co-ed, knowing he would get distracted with the idea of male and female prisoners locked up together with time on their hands. I was worried he would scare Svetlana, as he once did with Brando. "I need you to behave yourself with Svetlana, as this interview could go south very quickly," I mildly lectured him.

"I have done this before, kid," he said. "You worry about yourself."

When we met Svetlana, she was fully made up, had a nice dress on, and looked quite pretty.

Mike started talking. "My, my, my, a co-ed prison. Do you have a boyfriend?" Mike asked.

"Yes, I do," she replied.

"And do you have sex with him?" he asked.

"Yes, I do."

"You must show me where," Mike said, and with that, the two of them went off.

I was left to set up for the interview with the crews. When they returned, they both were smoking cigarettes.

"I enjoyed that very much," Mike said.

Svetlana replied, "I did, too."

At this point I was going crazy, thinking Mike had just had sex with a Russian spy he was about to interview.

Then they began to laugh. They had pulled one over on me.

As soon as the cigarette smoke cleared, we began the interview, and boy, what an interview.

SVETLANA:	I am not a spy. . . . I am not a sexual maniac. Do I look like a sexual maniac?
WALLACE:	I wouldn't know.
SVETLANA:	Sexual Mata Hari, they called me.
WALLACE:	Were you and Miller lovers?
SVETLANA:	Yes, but I did not love him.
WALLACE:	I don't know why you kept seeing him.
SVETLANA:	He scared me. You must believe me, Michael.

WALLACE: You worked for the KGB. . . . Is that a shameful
          thing?

SVETLANA: No, nothing shameful.

We returned to New York and I put the segment together. The story ended with Wallace asking Miller if there were many agents like him in the FBI, a question that occurred to me while watching the interview unfold. I had Mike ask it, and the answer became the final line of the story.

"I certainly hope not," Miller replied.

It was Mike Wallace at the top of his game, but I was at the top of my game as well. After six years of producing, I was finally beginning to get the hang of the job.

We showed the story to Hewitt, and when the screening ended, Don leaped to his feet and charged me, as if he was going to throw a punch. But in fact he was elated.

"Don't you dare show me this piece again, because I will want to do something stupid and make changes," he said.

Phil Scheffler, the senior producer, tried to speak, but Hewitt cut him off. "Shut up, Phil," Hewitt said. "Let's get out of here."

The story would become the lead on the season's premiere. For me, it was a time of utter happiness. I had been accepted to Harvard as a Nieman Fellow, and I was on paid leave from 60 Minutes for nine months. I had just met the woman I would later marry. And I was going out on a huge professional high.

But just when I thought I was invulnerable, I tore my Achilles tendon playing basketball and would spend most of my Nieman year in physical rehab. Still, I felt ahead of the game.

13

A YEAR AT HARVARD

By 1986, Mike and I needed to take a break from each other, and I found the opportunity at Harvard in the form of a Nieman Fellowship. The Nieman program allows mid-career journalists a chance to take courses at Harvard or any college in the Boston area, without having to fulfill any course requirements.

The beauty of the Nieman is that you can do anything. On any particular day, I would go to the library and read a book like *Crime and Punishment*. Another day I would cut all my classes and go skiing or go to an all-day movie fest. Sometimes I would simply get in my car and drive somewhere and get lost for the day. It was a time of total freedom. And for this amazing experience I was paid my full salary, thanks to the generosity of Don Hewitt, who wanted me to come back after the nine-month fellowship ended.

More than twenty-five years later, his son-in-law, cameraman Bill Cassara, discovered the note Hewitt wrote on my behalf to Nieman curator Howard Simons, which no doubt played a big part in my acceptance.

> *Dear Howard:*
>
> *This is a letter that both pleases and pains me to write.*
> *To grant Ira Rosen a nine-month leave of absence would be*

a hardship for 60 Minutes, but one that I would gladly go along with because I feel he is a perfect candidate for a Nieman fellowship. He is a first-rate reporter who can hold his own with the best of them.

Sincerely,

Don Hewitt, Executive Producer 60 Minutes

I have that recommendation framed in my living room.

While at Harvard, I took a literature course from the famed writer and doctor Robert Coles, who wrote a series of books on children in crisis in places like Appalachia. Another course I took was from Stephen Jay Gould, a paleontologist and an expert on dinosaurs and the Boston Red Sox. Beside core curriculum courses, I needed a few chill-out courses, so I studied pottery and impressionism.

I also wandered over to Boston University and took a literature course from Elie Wiesel, and on Tuesday afternoons I would attend the Harvard Medical School. When I arrived at Harvard, I spoke to the dean of medical students, Daniel Federman, and said I was a *60 Minutes* producer. "I basically have a very low opinion of doctors," I told him. "You have nine months to change my views."

So Federman enrolled me in a Tuesday-afternoon course with first- and second-year med students, who were beginning their training. Each week we learned about a different disease and then met and examined patients who had it. I did change my opinion of doctors for the better, but I also learned that you should always get a second opinion. While there, I saw doctors who were tired or distracted miss tumors that appeared on mammograms. I also saw other doctors who had not read the most recent relevant articles in, say, *The New England Journal of Medicine,* articles that could have made the difference in how they treated their patients. I discovered that teaching hospitals are best for care, as there are a number of eyes on any given patient and the chances of mistakes diminished.

The Niemans, twenty of us, came mostly from newspapers around the United States but also from journalism institutions based in Poland, Thailand, and Mozambique.

Two of my fellow Niemans later got married. Our curator, Howard Simons, was the former managing editor of *The Washington Post,* who helped guide the paper's Watergate coverage.

Howard was honest, smart, and direct, and helped take some of the rough edges off me. He pointed out something I had never realized about myself—that I was beginning to pick up some of the bad character traits of Mike Wallace—namely, trying to piss people off for sport.

Howard said that I should stop being sarcastic, as what I said could be misinterpreted. "You can get more out of people by making yourself a character," he once said. "But a likable one."

He always gave great advice, and he looked out for my best interests. Sadly, Howard developed pancreatic cancer and died only a couple of years after I left Harvard.

While I was away on the Nieman, *60 Minutes* and CBS News were in a chaotic state. Larry Tisch, who owned CBS at the time, ordered the firing of hundreds of news employees. One day, while I was at Harvard, I got a call from Hewitt. "Kid, we are going to be firing a lot of people at CBS News tomorrow. You are not one of them."

"Thanks, Don."

"Okay, take care," he said. That was the conversation.

Don and Mike were worried that I wouldn't return, and when I graduated from the program, Don sent the senior producer, Phil Scheffler, to attend my diploma ceremony. It was a nice gesture, and I began to think *60 Minutes* would be a great place to hang out for a career.

But when I returned, Mike made it clear that he regarded my Nieman as an "extended vacation" and he expected me to be twice as productive as before. The nicer Mike, post-depression medication, was gone. He was his old self—a prick.

Mike felt a need to punish me. He was merciless in his verbal abuse and asked that I move back to New York from Washington. I agreed. That turned out to be a big mistake, as now he would see me every day and grill me about what I was working on. He hated to be idle.

At my wedding, Mike asked my father-in-law if his daughter was the one marrying me. My father-in-law said yes. Mike sighed deeply and said, "Does she know what she is getting into? I have to tell you about him," Mike said. "Wait, the wedding is starting," and he walked away.

For the rest of the night my future father-in-law, Bernie, was thinking about what Mike was going to tell him. He didn't know that Mike was shticking, fooling around, and he told us later that Mike's brief remark to him cast a pall over the wedding.

Diane Sawyer heard that I was unhappy working with Wallace, and she was looking for a new producer. Sawyer had developed a reputation of taking forever to finish scripts. Even after Hewitt would sign off on her story, she would tinker with it almost until it was on air. Still, anyone was better than Wallace.

One night, when I got home from work, my wife had a curious, angry look on her face because of a message on our answering machine. "Who is Diane?" she asked.

"I don't know. Why?" I said. I was taken off guard by the question.

"Listen to the message on the machine," she said.

I turned it on. A heavy, sexy, flirtatious voice began to speak.

"Hi, this is Diane. Could it be true? Could it be real? You and I together? I hope so. Call me. Love, Diane."

"Oh, that's Diane Sawyer," I said.

"Diane Sawyer doesn't talk like that," she said.

"Yes, that's how she talks."

"I don't believe it."

We played the message again. It did sound strange, but I had heard around the office that when Diane wanted something, usually from men, she turned on the sexy voice.

"Yes, that's Diane," I said again.

My wife was skeptical, but eventually I had her speak to Suzanne St. Pierre, one of Diane's producers, who confirmed that it was Diane's voice on the machine.

I told Diane I wanted to work for her, but Wallace would have none of it.

"You are not going anywhere," he said.

"But we are not getting along."

"Get back to your office," he said dismissively.

I was trapped with Wallace. He was now seventy-one and was worried about getting old. His insecurities—about work, friends, his memory, and his legacy—were all flaring up and I was caught in that web. And that is not a good place for a Wallace producer to be.

14

INTERVIEW WITH DR. STRANGELOVE

Edward Teller was one of the most controversial figures of the twentieth century. The father of the hydrogen bomb, he was principally responsible and vilified for causing the legendary scientist J. Robert Oppenheimer, the main architect of the first atomic bomb, to lose his security clearance.

He also became known in the 1980s as the leading advocate of the missile defense system known as "Star Wars," which was driving a wedge between the United States and the Soviet Union in arms control talks. But he was more popularly compared to the evil Dr. Strangelove of the movies, who "learned to stop worrying and love the bomb."

In 1987 Teller wrote his autobiography, *Better a Shield Than a Sword,* and Mike and I had a chance to interview him. I flew out to Stanford University, where he had been for most of his life, to prepare for the interview, but more important, to get a measure of the man. During the pre-interview, I asked him a series of questions to see which ones would elicit the best answers. Teller said he would give answers only to questions related to what he had written about in his book. I asked a simple question about Albert Einstein and he sat and glared at me. No answer. He stood up. "This meeting is over," he said.

"Dr. Teller, what's wrong?" I asked.

"You asked me a question that I did not write about in my book."

I assured him it wouldn't happen again. I asked him another question.

"What page in my book did I write about that?" he asked in his heavily accented English.

I quickly looked it up. "Page forty-five," I said.

Satisfied, he began the answer. "As I have written in my book . . ."

In response to each question I asked, he mentioned the title of his book and in some cases the page where the answer came from. It was that way all afternoon. I wanted no part of him. Besides, the thought of two strong-minded Jewish men, about the same age, from Hungary and Russia, who are both used to getting their way, made me feel that this story was going to be a disaster.

I went back to New York and told Mike what had occurred.

"I think it will make fascinating TV," Mike said. "If he refuses to answer a question, we will leave it in."

Meanwhile, Mike had agreed to go to Moscow to interview Andrei Sakharov, the father of the Soviet H-bomb. But unlike Teller, Sakharov had renounced the bomb and believed it should be banned. Sakharov, along with his wife, Yelena Bonner, was maligned by the government for much of his life. But when I went to Moscow in the winter of 1988, he had been "rehabilitated" by Soviet leader Gorbachev and was allowed to live in the city. His small Moscow apartment became a gathering place for dissidents who also opposed Soviet authority.

I knew Teller was interested in what Sakharov thought of him, and although Moscow was a long way to go, I felt it would make Teller more manageable, and lead to a better story.

In Moscow, Mike and I went to Dr. Sakharov's apartment. His wife, Yelena Bonner, met us at the door. There were many people inside, and it had the look of a party, but she said that was the way it always was. His apartment was a refuge for dissidents, and the apartment was considered a safe zone, where Soviet authorities, fearing the backlash that would come from taking on the winner of the Nobel Peace Prize—given to him for recognition of his struggles against "the abuses of power and violations of human dignity"—decided to let Sakharov have his gatherings.

Bonner said that they had only one key to their apartment and told us and Sakharov to be back by 3:00 P.M. or she would leave and lock him out. Mike agreed, and with that, Sakharov put on his fur hat and coat and we were off. We did the interview at the CBS Moscow bureau, and Sakharov came ready to play. He gave us a huge scoop on how the Soviets had figured out how to build the atomic bomb. He said the Soviet scientists would go out in the snows of Siberia and wait for the fallout that would pass overhead from the U.S. nuclear tests being conducted in the Pacific. They would then gather the fallout that fell on the snow and analyze it to determine the makeup of the bombs. At first our translator didn't want to translate, as he thought the good doctor was revealing state secrets. So Sakharov told us the story himself in broken English. He told us that it wasn't convicted spies Julius and Ethel Rosenberg who revealed any important secrets about the making of the bomb; it was our own tests that gave the Soviets the formula.

After the interview we went to Red Square for a walking shot of Mike and Sakharov together. Since his return from Gorky, where he was sent into internal exile before being "rehabilitated," Sakharov had not been to Red Square. Mike and Sakharov were having a good time talking to tourists and ignored my pleas to return to the apartment before three.

It was a cold, snowy day in Moscow and traffic slowed our return. We got there at 3:45. The door was locked. Bonner, true to her word, had left the apartment.

He sat on the apartment stairway, the cold air visible with each breath. I told him we would wait, but he insisted we go. It seemed like he had been through this before. After six years spent in the remote town of Gorky, where he was exiled, a few hours of waiting for his wife probably seemed easy. That was the last we saw of Sakharov, who would die the following year.

As for the Dr. Teller interview, including Sakharov in our story did not make him any easier to deal with.

I worried that if he didn't like one of Mike's questions, he would sit in silence or even leave the interview. Teller was ninety and decided to wear an awful plaid jacket with an open-collared shirt that made him look like a nursing home escapee. He was rebelling and being intentionally difficult. I instructed our sound technician to thread the microphone cord under his shirt, instead of simply snapping it on. Then we tacked the wire to the chair, effectively tying him down. That way, if he wanted to leave, he would have to take his shirt off to get out of the chair.

Sure enough, Mike asked a question that Teller didn't like. Teller sat in silence for a minute and then decided to leave. But Teller couldn't get up because he couldn't figure out how to take his microphone off. I waited to see if the inventor of the H-bomb could figure out how to take a microphone off without ripping his shirt. The cameraman shot me a glance, and I signaled for him to keep recording the scene. Mike gently tried to cajole Teller to continue. Part of me wanted him to tear his shirt off, figuring that's what would be remembered. But in the end, Teller completed the interview.

Mike and I were going through an especially bad patch. He had come in one Thanksgiving Day and wrote me a note about "What ever happened to Young America?"—referring to me. I intuitively knew how this would play out. After eight years of producing for him, Mike was laying the groundwork to get rid of me. Whether he was bored of working with me or angry that I took almost a year off for a Nieman Fellowship, I knew the clock was ticking and I would soon be fired.

When I put the Teller story together, Mike decided he wanted to sabotage it and put me in a bad light with Hewitt. Mike insisted that we not include the attempted walk-off. He said it added nothing. I argued against him but lost. Mike also took out all the interesting parts from the Sakharov interview, including how the Soviets built their bomb, which he said was not relevant to a Teller profile. When we showed it to Hewitt, he found the piece boring. "Nice try, kid," he said.

Mike had intentionally tried to destroy his own story, knowing I would get blamed. I asked Don if I could show him a different cut.

Sure, he said. The next day, I played him my cut, with the walk-off and Siberia story included.

"I have never seen this happen here before," Don said. "You took a 2.2 story and made it into a 9.9. Great stuff."

Everyone was happy except for Mike. "You embarrassed me," he said.

"How did I embarrass you? We went to California and Moscow on this trip and we saved the story."

"Some stories aren't worth saving," he said and stormed off angrily.

A few months after the story ran, it won the National Emmy for best interview. I called Mike up after the award presentation and told him we won.

"Fuck you," he said, and hung up the phone.

15

LEAVING *60 MINUTES*

In 1989, after Mike hit seventy, his behavior got worse. His depression medicine was now creating wild mood swings. He was getting angry, as he wanted more time to enjoy the accolades he was receiving from the public. He was not growing old gracefully; in fact he was worried that he was losing some of his mojo. He continued to blame producers when things didn't go perfectly, and from his body language I could read that he was done with me. I was only thirty-four, but I felt he wanted to trade me in for a younger model.

By luck, ABC News was starting a new magazine show with Diane Sawyer and Sam Donaldson, a combination that was later compared to teaming a harp with a jackhammer. The executive producer was Phyllis McGrady, who had produced for everyone from Maury Povich to Ted Koppel. In the tightly wound and insane world of network TV news, she stood out as one of the sane ones.

She was looking for a senior investigative producer to run a small unit on the show, and a mutual friend recommended me for the position. I received a call from McGrady to ask if I was interested. *Damn, if Mike won't let me work with Diane at CBS, I will leave to work with her at ABC,* I thought.

I went to see Phyllis at a small office building that also housed

Penthouse magazine. She asked me what kind of stories I wanted to do, and I told her that *60 Minutes* pioneered the use of hidden cameras and then abandoned them. Don became worried about the potential for overuse and felt that in many cases they were unnecessary to tell a story. "The cameras are getting smaller and smaller, so we can bring them into places that we couldn't go into before. I would make it a signature of the show, a hidden camera investigation."

At the time the use of hidden cameras on television was infrequent. Phyllis, though, liked the idea and offered me a job on the spot.

I was ecstatic. It all felt right. We were expecting our first child, and this would mean a new job, a new beginning, a future away from an angry old man. And there was a delicious irony to it all. I would principally work with Chris Wallace, Mike's son. And I would be his boss.

We secretly negotiated a deal, as I was still under contract with CBS, and I had to negotiate a release. I needed to get Mike's and Don's blessings, which I feared was not going to be easy.

I was in the middle of shooting a story on obstetric malpractice. Mike thought that since we were expecting our first child, I should know everything that could possibly go wrong in a pregnancy. The perversity did not escape me. Mike always believed that producers weren't as good after they got married and were greatly diminished professionally after they had children. And even though Mike and I were at the end of the road, he thought this piece would intimidate me into not wanting any more kids.

Like an idiot, I mentioned that I was working on the story to my wife's OB/GN, and it resulted in the decision to do a C-section being made within minutes of our arriving at the hospital.

A few days later, Mike and I traveled to Garrison, New York, to conduct our final interview for the story. I told Mike about the job offer at ABC. He looked out the window and said nothing, his wrinkled hand resting on his chin. I knew the next few seconds would be life-changing.

"I will be working with your son Chris," I said. "And I want your blessing."

He remained silent, so I decided to speak his language: bluntness. "If you decide to fuck me over, and hold me to a contract, you also fuck over your kid. It's not worth it, to try to destroy me for sport."

He said that I should accept the job. "But first you must tell Don. If he doesn't hear about this first, he will be angry."

The problem was that Don was in China. Somehow I got in touch with him.

"Don, I have been offered a job as senior producer on this new ABC show and I want to do it. I told Mike and he is okay with it," I said.

"Listen, kid, I have always said that I won't stand in the way of anyone who doesn't want to work here. Good luck. Put Phil [Scheffler] on the phone."

And with that, I was let out of my contract. But before I left, Eric Ober, president of CBS News, wanted me to talk to Andy Lack, who was the executive producer of a different CBS magazine show. Ober said Lack had an opening for senior producer. I went to see Andy and he listened to my idea on hidden cameras.

"I'd love to hire you, but two producers have been kissing my ass for a year and I feel I have to give it to one of them. Otherwise, what is the point of ass-kissing," he said with a smile.

After that conversation, I left CBS. There were no goodbye parties, no nice send-offs. Mike never even said goodbye or good luck. The only person who took me out for a drink was Harry Reasoner, who was always looking for a reason to take someone out for a drink.

16

PRIMETIME LIVE

Roone Arledge, who created the *Wide World of Sports* show, thought he could do the same for news. He put together a staff of sports producers and directors who would go around the world to news events to cover them live. It worked in sports, so why couldn't it work in news? he thought.

As I look back on this now, I find it amazing that with all the smart people assigned to the show, no one considered the inherent problem in the show's concept: there is very little news breaking at ten P.M. on a Wednesday. Unlike sporting events, news isn't scheduled. Yet we built a whole show around the concept of live coverage.

Phyllis McGrady, who had hired me, left the show before the launch to take care of her ailing mother, and was succeeded by Rick Kaplan, who executive-produced *Nightline*. Rick stood six-six and at the time weighed north of 325 pounds. He was a brilliant egomaniac who often reduced staffers to tears if they didn't follow his exact wishes.

Nothing he did was small. He insisted on using only Titleist Pro V1 Black Dot golf balls, which cost more than $3.00 each, even though he would often lose a dozen balls a round. One time he hit his first three balls into the woods and his fourth shot 300 yards down the middle of the fairway. In Rick's world, those lost balls were mulligans, shots that don't count.

Rick liked mulligans in TV as well. He never talked about his failures, only about the successes. He was the ultimate optimist and in many ways was the perfect person to launch the show.

It was 1989, and 60 *Minutes* and 20/20 were the only magazine shows on TV. We had very little competition for talent, as those shows had scant turnover. We were able to hire some of the best news producers in the business. Among the first group hired, three would later become presidents of news divisions, four became news vice presidents, and at least half a dozen others would executive-produce their own shows.

Even with such an incredible producing staff, we would barely survive, and it seemed the only two people who were fully aware of how much shit we were in were Chris Wallace and me.

Chris left NBC News to become the chief correspondent of the show. He was hired to do the investigative stories, as his father did on 60 *Minutes*. I now found myself in the weird position of passing along the lessons I learned from his father to his son.

It is hard to describe the relationship Chris Wallace had with Mike. For many years, their communication was limited and strained. One time Chris said that he felt so bitter toward Mike, he wondered what nice things he would say about him when he died. Chris's anger toward his father was due to Mike divorcing his mother Norma and being an absentee father during his teenage years. Mike's career was more important than his family. Chris always considered former CBS News president Bill Leonard, who later married his mother, to be his father. He felt that those times Mike did check in with him, he was intrusive, rude, and annoying—always looking to start trouble with him. The first time I met Chris was at a Washington dinner. I was with Mike and I mistakenly brought a date.

Shortly after we sat down, Chris laced into his father over his age and asked him when he was going to retire. Chris mentioned that his son was about to get confirmed in the church. Mike saw an opportunity and pounced.

"Confirmed? But you are Jewish. What do you mean, confirmed?" Mike asked.

"I am not Jewish," said Chris, who embraced Catholicism when he married his first wife.

"Chris, your mother is Jewish, I am Jewish. So you are Jewish," Mike said.

"I am not Jewish," Chris replied.

For the rest of the dinner they fought about it. Mike felt he had Chris at a point of vulnerability and wouldn't let up. He seemed to forget that the confrontation was with his son.

Afterward, my date left embarrassed and angry. She had never seen a father treat his son that way. I, of course, was used to Mike's behavior. It was part of his character. He took no prisoners, even if it was a member of his own family. Chris would say about Mike that "he had an underdeveloped sense of other people's privacy," and that dinner I certainly saw it.

Chris would later get divorced and remarry. At Chris's second wedding, Mike stood up to deliver the toast. We all expected the worst and weren't disappointed.

"There is a story that went around NBC News of a tape editor working on one of Chris's stories. The editor called Chris *Chris,*" Mike said, with a champagne glass in hand. "'My name is Mr. Wallace, to you,' Chris said to the editor. 'No, Mr. Wallace is at CBS, you are Chris,' the editor replied."

That was Mike's toast at Chris Wallace's wedding. Chris tried to make a joke about it afterward. "Well, that's my father. He never disappoints." It was not easy being the son of Mike Wallace. Chris was a first-rate journalist with years of solid and serious reporting in Washington, covering the Reagan White House and moderating *Meet the Press*. He would have succeeded in the business no matter what his last name was. And yet Chris wanted to follow in his father's footsteps, and it was my job to help him do that. My idea was to do hidden camera investigations, carefully crafted, well-told magazine stories. I hired a couple of talented hidden camera producers, Robbie Gordon and Mark Lukasiewicz, and assigned them to work with Chris.

Meanwhile Sam Donaldson would walk around the hallways asking why the staff needed to be so large. "We are going to be live," he kept saying.

Gordon shot a story with Chris, on assisted living centers in Texas that were neglecting their patients. She brought a camera hidden in a teddy bear into the facility. One image she captured was of a patient crawling out at night on a pile of garbage, looking for food. I showed the completed story to Donaldson.

"Very interesting, Ira," he said. "But that is not our show." And then he got up and left.

Arledge watched the story and was blown away. He wanted it on the premiere, while others argued that we advertised we would be live, so we had to be "live." Arledge allowed the show's producers to have their way, figuring he could come in later with fixes if it didn't work out. The story didn't run on opening night. Instead we sent Chris Wallace to Israel for a three-minute stand-up about a hostage crisis and Diane Sawyer interviewed a guy named Thomas Root, who shot himself in a private plane and landed it successfully. In addition to Root, we had interviews with writer Nora Ephron and actress Roseanne Barr. The show spent five minutes reviewing maps about possible military actions involving a hostage rescue. It was the slowest five minutes I had ever seen. We had a live audience in the studio, and they were bored. The show was a disaster. Director Mike Nichols, Diane Sawyer's husband, was in the control room, and as the show ended, everyone turned to him for his opinion.

In brilliant Hollywood doublespeak, he said, "I have never seen anything quite like that."

The reviews were blistering. One critic said it "was a slick, high-priced abomination, a parody of our worst fears for television." Roone stuck with us and would join us after shows for postmortems at Café

Fiorello, a local restaurant, usually talking about what he liked, as opposed to picking the broadcast apart. I found it an interesting way to criticize. If you keep doing what he liked, what he didn't like disappeared naturally. The next week we ran Chris's hidden camera story. It later won an Emmy for best investigative reporting. Needless to say, there was a lot of second-guessing as to why it didn't run on the premiere.

Moving from one network to another involved a bit of a culture shock. At CBS, producers operated in silos, responsible for their own stories. At ABC we operated more like a kibbutz, with everyone working and contributing to the same product.

At CBS, a mostly male-dominated news division, looks didn't matter as much as being a first-rate reporter. At ABC, looks were important.

At CBS, most correspondents took care of their own hair and did not have stylists on call. ABC was different. When new executive producers joined the show, one of the first expenditures that caught their eye was how much was spent on paying these stylists, who felt they were the difference between success and failure of the correspondent.

Diane's hair was then shaped by Vincent Roppatte, who was commanding thousands of dollars for a few hours' work per week. One magazine at the time described Diane Sawyer's hair this way: "Diane Sawyer's big break came about when she changed her natural ash brown hair color to a glamorous honey blonde and the rest is history."

As much as those who cut hair would like to think they change the course of history, they do not. The other anchor, Sam Donaldson, had no hair stylist because he had no hair. He wore a toupee.

Sam Donaldson once called me up from a shoot on the road to yell at me. "Where did you get this producer?" he asked me about the producer assigned to him to do a story.

"What's wrong?" I asked.

"We are doing stand-up at the pier, at the water."

"Well, your story is about shipping, so that makes sense," I said.

"You know what's at the water?" Sam said, pausing for effect. "Wind."

Sam had worn his hairpiece for many years and it rarely moved. One producer once went into Sam's bathroom and said he saw all the wires that were needed to keep it in place. Our show was taped live, and I dreaded the idea of a gust of wind that might hit Donaldson's hair at the wrong time. But in the first few months of our broadcast, hair was the least of our problems. The show was still trying to be "live" as promised, and it wasn't working. Rick Kaplan was concerned he was going to get fired. One day I saw him outside our building taking a walk with Roger Goodman, the show's director. "What are you guys talking about?" I innocently asked.

"Who we can blame for the failure of the show," Roger answered.

I quickly moved on.

Occasionally the "live" concept would pay off, as when the U.S. military launched a surprise invasion of Panama to overthrow the country's dictator, Manuel Noriega. The invasion occurred on a Wednesday, and we were on the air that night. Rick put Sam Donaldson and Judd Rose on a private jet and sent them to Panama, to feed stories and broadcast live. We had no clearance to land in what was now a war zone, and if their jet approached the country without authorization, it might get shot down.

I called Pete Williams, at that time the press spokesman for the Defense Department, and presented him with a choice. I explained that the jet was on its way and couldn't turn back. "Do you want tomorrow's headline to be that you launched a successful invasion of Panama, or that the military killed Sam Donaldson? What do you want to do?"

He said nothing for a moment, then replied, "Okay, get me the plane's transponder number and I will get them clearance."

Donaldson and Rose landed an hour and a half before we were on the air. With thirty minutes to go before our broadcast, footage started to come into the edit rooms, and later the narration followed. Kaplan lived for these moments; he divided the video among four different edit bays. He had each room compose a different part of the story and created a batting order for their broadcast.

We were now live on the air, and the stories were still being edited.

Rick hovered over the producer of the first section until the editor was done. Then with seconds to go, he took the tape, went to another edit room, and put that on the show, live. He did that with each room, as the stories were cross-rolled one after another, with no one having eyeballed them before they went out on the network.

It was remarkable to watch and terrifying to be part of. But the viewer at home had no idea, and it looked seamless. As for Kaplan, I had never seen him so calm or enjoying himself so much.

But the show did not have an invasion of Panama to cover live every week, and we struggled to find an identity. A few weeks after that story, Rick summoned me to his office. Betsy West, the other senior producer on the show, joined us.

"Ted is off the list," Rick said.

"What happened?" Betsy asked.

Betsy and Rick had worked together at *Nightline* for many years and sometimes spoke in shorthand. I was trying to learn the language.

"What list?" I asked.

"The list of people who are going to speak at my funeral," Rick said.

"Do we really have to discuss this now?" I asked, especially since Rick was healthy and not about to die. "We have no idea what we are putting on TV tomorrow night."

In unison they answered, "Yes."

They told me that the Ted they were talking about was Ted Koppel, their former colleague and anchor of *Nightline*. It seemed that Koppel and Rick had a falling-out when Rick took eight staffers from *Nightline* and brought them to *Primetime Live,* even though Rick had apparently promised Ted he wouldn't raid the staff. Now Koppel refused to speak at Rick's funeral.

"Who is *on* the list?" I asked.

Rick had the list ready. "Peter Jennings, Walter Cronkite, Diane Sawyer . . ."

I interrupted. "Don't you know a normal person? Like a friend?"

"They don't speak very well," Rick said.

"But you are dead. Who cares?" I replied.

He thought I was an idiot, as if that were beside the point. Fortunately, Koppel and Kaplan made up and Ted's name was put back on the list.

To bolster our spirits, Anthony Radziwill, the cousin of Jackie Kennedy Onassis, set up a lunch with his aunt and the senior staff of the show.

We had rented a small private banquet room at the Ritz-Carlton. When we arrived, Diane Sawyer was already there, clearly nervous. She and her husband, Mike Nichols, were friends with Jackie O. For her, this was like bringing your crazy uncle to meet your relatives for the first time.

With the show lurching from week to week, Diane was trying to overthrow Kaplan, but he didn't know it. She was calling some of the senior staff on weekends to ask us to help get rid of him. I wanted no part of it, as Rick was supportive of our investigative work and besides, this was not a Shakespearean drama. Diane could get rid of him on her own with one phone call to Roone Arledge. So with this as a backdrop, we all gathered as "friends" to meet Mrs. Onassis.

At lunch, Jackie O didn't talk much, and when she did, she whispered. She was very thin and shy. She was a book editor and spoke about the books that she was editing. But even with Jackie O there, Rick Kaplan dominated the lunch. He went on and on to Jackie, in the most minute detail, about how well the show was doing in the ratings, which wasn't true.

The five seniors sat around and quietly listened to Rick drone on. The tension was palatable until Diane, acting out of character, raised the temperature in the room. Diane's true feelings toward Rick emerged. "Do you recite that in the shower?" she asked, glaring at him.

I wanted to yell, "Street fight!" The seniors looked at one another in shock. Diane was finally letting her emotions show. Rick paused for a moment and then kept talking. Jackie O looked utterly bored.

Mercifully the lunch came to an end, with Diane the first to leave. She looked pissed. The lunch was a seminal moment, as Diane decided that she didn't want to entrust her career with Kaplan. As for Radziwill, who had set up the lunch, he was too classy a person to say it didn't go well.

I thought it was kinda fun, a welcome break from the daily pressures. But after that lunch, Anthony and Diane kept us apart from their high-society crowd. And Diane continued to ask on weekend calls, "What are we going to do about [Rick]?"

Meanwhile, the show was going live to places just for the sake of going live. We went live to a roller-coaster ride, even though a taped piece would have been better. We even went live, one November night, to a tree in Texas where a treaty with the Indians was once signed. Not much happened.

We did live interviews, even when we were confronting a "bad" guy in the story. The investigative story would set up the interview and then the anchor would confront the bad guy with the facts. But the subjects soon figured out they could "run out the clock" and escape being seriously grilled.

Also, the anchors generally didn't know the subject as well as the correspondent who did the story. There was a small uprising from the correspondents, especially Chris Wallace, who didn't like the idea that he did all the work and Diane or Sam would interview the bad guy in his story. By having the anchors do the confrontation interviews the correspondents' roles were further diminished. Eventually we ended up doing away with anchor confrontations.

Sometimes live interviews worked the way they were intended, creating a surprise spontaneous feel. That happened the night we interviewed sports announcer Brent Musburger, who had just been fired by CBS.

"They conspired to get me out of CBS," Musburger told Sam

Donaldson, referring to his two executive producers at the time. "These two men decided that I was too big for my britches and that they were going to take me down a peg or two, that I was uncontrollable."

That interview generated news, but that was a rarity. As the show evolved, it was only the hidden camera investigations that seemed to be working. Chris Wallace owned that franchise and was not about to give it up. But like his father, Chris would at times piss off his producers and one of those he angered was Robbie Gordon, a brilliant producer who specialized in hidden camera stories.

Robbie refused to work with Chris and was assigned to do her next story with Diane, a hidden camera investigation into abuses at the Cleveland VA hospital. We had heard stories of abuse and neglect, and with a family's cooperation, we placed hidden cameras in the room of a Vietnam veteran who was a quadriplegic. Our cameras captured how he was neglected, with no nurses checking in on him and no food being brought to his room. I told Robbie to intervene, feed him and give him water. I always felt that was something that would be easy to defend and not change the exposé we were shooting.

We tried to show the hospital director the tape of the patient, but he refused to look at it. Our story would lead to major reforms in that hospital and the vet never went hungry in the hospital again. The story would end up winning an Emmy and other big awards.

We began doing groundbreaking TV and we had the hidden camera franchise to ourselves. I went to Diane with a proposition.

"How would you like to do investigations that affect women's lives—day care abuses, deadbeat dads, sex harassment, unequal pay. . . . You can be a modern-day Nellie Bly [a pioneer female undercover journalist of the late 1800s and the early 1900s]."

"I get it," Diane replied. "Yes."

That exchange may have been the most consequential conversation in the first year of the show. Diane agreed on the spot to go from concentrating on celebrity bookings to conducting hard-core hidden camera investigations. I oversaw all of them but had only a few producers to work with. The support of the key anchor meant more resources and producers.

Diane's regular hair stylist was Vincent, but soon she went to another stylist, who cut her hair short. Her long and gorgeous blond hair was gone. She decided that if she was going to be an investigative reporter, she couldn't look like a blond bombshell.

Diane knew that messing with the hair could constitute a firing offense, so she cleverly went to another hair stylist so Vincent wouldn't be blamed by ABC management. Her foresight also protected his lucrative racket. Vincent would later join the chorus of those who hated the look.

Because Diane was now doing investigations, the direction of the show shifted. We now promoted ourselves as us versus them or good versus bad. We tried to do a hidden camera story every week. In fact, when producers pitched story ideas, they had to look for a hidden camera element.

Some of the ideas were stupid, like bringing hidden cameras into movies to catch people who talk during the film. Other stories we did were truly groundbreaking.

Producers Eugenia Harvey and Mark Lukasiewicz went to East St. Louis and shot a story on racial discrimination. We sent a black tester and a white tester, with identical credentials and both about the same age, to shop and to rent housing. We even used the simple act of hailing a cab to explore racism in action. The cabdriver bypassed the black tester to pick up the white tester.

We caught one landlord who told the black tester he had no apartments to rent. A few minutes later, the white tester was offered his choice of several apartments.

The landlord told Diane Sawyer, "No, ma'am, I am not prejudiced. I've got mixed skin."

"How many black people in this apartment building?" she asked.

"There's none," he replied.

The story would later win a Robert F. Kennedy Award, the first of several major awards the show would win for its hidden camera work.

In fact, between 1990–95, we would win six Investigative Reporters and Editors Awards, a record that no other network could match.

Because there was so much pressure to succeed, the lawyers, for the most part, gave us a free hand to operate. We were allowed to set up our own health clinic in Los Angeles called Morgan Medical to expose a lucrative underground economy in the illegal buying and selling of patients by doctors and middlemen. From the outside, the clinic looked no different than the thousand other ones that operated in the city, but this clinic contained hidden cameras and an experienced clinic operator, who was in our employ. Producer Chris Whipple's story caught patient brokers receiving $175 per patient in kickbacks to deliver patients to our clinic. When we later invited those patient brokers back to answer questions on-camera, they usually ran for the door.

In another story, producer Ceil Sutherland went undercover inside health clinics in Florida to expose the fraud of patient buying and bill padding by doctors. We even recruited an elderly Haitian woman who wore hidden cameras for us; she was billed for a heart operation when the doctor only examined her knees.

We exposed a New Orleans day care center where the caretakers smacked children in the face. Another story investigated the misreading of pap smears—mistakes that can mean the difference between life and death in testing for cervical cancer. Producer Robbie Gordon sent six hundred slides to four labs across the country and found one lab with a 70 percent error rate and the other labs routinely missing obvious cancers. That report would win the Peabody Award.

Our producer Robert Campos took a page from Upton Sinclair, who wrote *The Jungle* about the U.S. meatpacking industry, and worked on the assembly line for a week at a meat processing plant. He brought hidden cameras inside and exposed the conditions and treatment of the animals, which could lead to food contamination. His story helped prevent the Agricultural Department from a money-saving plan it had to remove inspectors from the processing lines. In another groundbreaking report, we exposed a slave trade that forced young Haitian boys to cut sugarcane in the Dominican Republic. To do that story, Campos worked in the fields and cut the sugarcane while wearing a hidden camera. All these were groundbreaking reports, but the most talked about one was when we exposed crooked car repairmen.

Producer Mark Lukasiewicz heard that elderly couples along a major interstate in the South were being pulled over and told that there was something wrong with their vans or trailers. We sent an elderly couple to drive up and down the interstate in a van, to see if they would be targeted. The van had numerous hidden cameras to document what might happen.

Luke, as we called him, spent a week on the road and came up with nothing. Dejected, he came into my office.

"Try another week of it," I told him.

"It will cost $25,000," he said.

"So? Just do it," I said. "It's not your money."

Though that was still a lot of money back then, I knew that the show was hemorrhaging money at such a rate that $25,000 would barely be noticed.

The second week we hit pay dirt. A car mechanic pulled over our Winnebago and said that he noticed smoke coming out from the rear. He happened to run a local garage and said he could fix the problem.

When the vehicle was in the garage, our hidden cameras, positioned underneath the main frame, caught him emptying dirt into the oil pan. He then showed us what he found. He said it would cost $1,200 to fix our engine.

We couldn't believe our luck. What are the odds of a crook picking our random Winnebago out from an interstate to rip us off? The next week we had Chris Wallace go back and confront the mechanic. We let the local police know so this crook wouldn't escape. The mechanic couldn't believe we had caught him on hidden camera. He was arrested later that day and was eventually sent to prison.

I felt a bit like a mother hen having to feed all the chicks, also known as correspondents. If Diane was slated to carry out all the consumer investigations in areas that affected women, I had to find suitable stories for

Sam Donaldson and Chris Wallace. And there is no more corrupt city in America than Washington, where they both lived. We began to target stories that exposed waste, fraud, and abuse in the nation's capitol. If money was being wasted or misspent it became a subject for "your tax dollars at work."

One of my favorite Chris Wallace segments was on do-nothing jobs. He found a government employee whose job was to measure the flow rate of ketchup. The bureaucrat took it very seriously, and so did Wallace, as he listened to the man explain the different consistencies of ketchup. It was a true investigative comedy.

We soon became the target of powerful politicians who didn't like our exposing their earmarks and boondoggles. One was Senator Robert Byrd of West Virginia, who took to the floor of the Senate to attack Wallace, after he exposed how Byrd earmarked projects for his home state that were unnecessary. He called Chris a vulture and a buzzard, on the Senate floor. Chris was ecstatic at the recognition.

But the Washington investigation that had the most impact was exposing junkets by members of the powerful House Committee on Appropriations. Producer Rick Nelson got a tip that members of that committee were heading for five days and four nights to the beautiful beaches of Barbados. After a few hours of meetings, the congressmen did lots of swimming, jet skiing, snorkeling, golf, and tennis. We posed as tourists on the beach and shot with hidden cameras as Washington lobbyists, who joined the congressmen on the trip, paid for Jet Skis and other items for the congressmen.

The video caught two congressmen, Marty Russo of Chicago and Tom Downey of New York, accepting the freebies from the lobbyists. I went to Washington to track down the congressmen with Donaldson. We first staked out Russo at his house, and he ran away without saying much. Then we went to the local Democratic club, where we heard Downey was attending a breakfast. He emerged from the club and decided to see if he could talk his way out. He couldn't.

I still remember, nearly thirty years later, his then-wife watching the interview and the look of sadness and disbelief on her face. Downey and Russo would lose their congressional races, mainly as a result of our story.

Another favorite hidden camera story from that time was when I sent my mother undercover. We had been told that it was a common practice that when a person left a diamond ring or necklace to be cleaned, jewelers would switch diamonds out of the setting and put lower grade ones in their place.

We had already found that jewelers lied about the grade of a diamond, but if we could find a switch happening, it would elevate the story to another level. The producer, Ann Sorkowitz, had tried several times and failed, so I suggested she send my mother in undercover, as jewelers tend to prey more on the elderly.

We gave my mother a diamond with infrared markings to track it and sent her into a jewelry shop in Pennsylvania to have her ring cleaned.

When she went to pick it up, our experts verified that it was a different and much lower grade diamond. Diane Sawyer went back to the jeweler and confronted him. He made up an excuse that he must have accidentally dropped it while he was doing the cleaning, and that's how the switch occurred.

Diane interviewed my mother on-camera, and Mom said she was shocked that such a crime could happen "in such a beautiful neighborhood."

My wonderful mother did the interview with Diane while wearing a dress suit from the 1950s and a beret that looked like it had last been worn by a French resistance fighter—not exactly the look for her first appearance on national TV. I was later asked by some producers if "wardrobe" supplied the clothes.

The diamond exposé would be rerun more times than any story in the history of ABC News. When I look back on this period, it is hard to believe the volume of hidden camera stories we were doing. Andrew Heyward, then-president of CBS News, told me that he would watch each week and curse to himself, "Damn, they did it again." Don

Hewitt, who hated competition, said that our hidden cameras "were being used as stunts, in many, many cases." But he was one of the few critics.

We were generally applauded and honored with the top awards in TV. Even the *New York Times* TV critic said that "the undercover stories can deliver close-ups of wrongdoing that interviews and documents can't match. I have seen most of those reports, and they struck me as zesty journalism and inimitable television. And truthful too." After less than five years with ABC, I was being recruited by Barry Diller and Rupert Murdoch to run a newsmagazine show at Fox. CBS asked me to executive-produce a magazine show hosted by Bryant Gumbel. But I decided to stay at ABC because of the commitment that ABC had made to continuing to do serious investigations, as nearly every show *Primetime Live* did had a hidden camera exposé—and the investigations were saving lives. But then we did a story on a grocery store chain called Food Lion, and everything would change.

17

FOOD LION

In 1992, we had received information that the Food Lion grocery store chain was selling old and spoiled food washed with bleach to kill the odors. Workers were instructed not to throw food out, and if they did, to remove it from the garbage and place it back on the shelves. The allegations came from union employees, who were trying to organize the food chain's workers.

Although that didn't automatically discount what they said, I felt we needed another extra layer of proof. Food Lion was one of the country's largest grocery chains, operating mainly in the South. We wanted to expose the culture inside the grocery chain that encouraged workers to take health and safety shortcuts to increase profits.

Producers Lynne Neufer and Susan Barnett wanted to go undercover with hidden cameras to document what the workers were telling us. To do that they needed to get jobs at Food Lion stores to document how the food was being handled.

Our ABC lawyers reviewed their work applications for employment at a Food Lion grocery store and agreed to let the producers include a comment that they had prior experience, which they did not. The embellishment was a small lie, but one that would later have very large ramifications.

The instances of tampering with food warranted going undercover to expose it. There are few more critical areas for the public to know about than food safety. And statements from interviews with employees, who wanted to organize to form a union, would have been easily discounted. We believed the best way to tell the story was to see the reality by using hidden cameras.

Our two producers went to work at two stores and found that the employees were being instructed to bleach food to make it seem fresh and to keep food on the shelves past its sell-by date. Barbecue sauce was smeared on chicken to cover up the smell of spoilage, and the producers documented on-camera how salads in the deli section remained for sale when they should have been pulled. The cameras provided an unprecedented look into how food was prepared at a major grocery chain.

As we were getting our story ready for broadcast, Food Lion was contacted for comment. Interestingly, they said they had no problem with our revealing the comments of the workers who talked about the food practices, but they didn't want the hidden camera video used. They knew pictures don't lie, but whistleblowers could be discredited. They said that if the video we secretly shot was used, they would sue.

As the airdate approached, most of the top lawyers at ABC gathered to review the story. In the group were Alan Braverman, the general counsel; David Westin, a former Supreme Court clerk who was network president; and Stephen Weiswasser, a former general counsel of ABC, who was now executive vice president of ABC News. In addition, four more lawyers reviewed various aspects of the story.

Tom Murphy, who oversaw Capital Cities, the parent company of ABC News, told Westin that he would hold Westin personally responsible if the broadcast was wrong. Westin told Murphy the broadcast was accurate, and he was prepared for that burden, something he proudly repeated to us again and again.

Food Lion believed that their company's survival was at stake and prepared a massive legal and PR offense against us. They hired Mike Sitrick, a shrewd but devious PR expert, to spin the facts their way. Sitrick's strategy was to focus on how our producers lied to get employed and then falsely claimed they manipulated workers to say things that weren't true.

As for a legal strategy, Food Lion chose not to sue us for libel but for violation of a North Carolina statute that prevents companies from sending spies into a competitor's business to learn trade secrets. Because false information had been put on the job applications, the North Carolina court, in the hometown of Food Lion, determined that the statute was valid in this case.

We went through discovery and I was deposed three times. Lawyers try different personalities to unnerve you. One of their lawyers came at me aggressively, a second behaved in a friendly fashion, and a third was more businesslike. The tension these depositions produced was intense, and my lawyers told me to break pencils under the table to relieve some of the stress. I would go through at least a dozen for each deposition.

Food Lion was carefully constructing a PR offensive. Sitrick set an office up near the courthouse and staffed it with PR experts to take and answer all media calls. Each day they sent faxes to hundreds of media outlets nationwide, providing their spin on the court proceedings. And each day they served reporters full buffets for lunch, accompanied by outtakes from our broadcast that they reedited to make their points.

Meanwhile ABC was completely unaware of the coming case. I told Roone Arledge's assistant that the case was about to begin, and Roone was surprised and hurriedly called a meeting. ABC didn't have much of a PR strategy and instead said they would leave the case in the hands of the lawyers. They agreed to send an assistant PR person, who hadn't even seen the Food Lion piece, to be our principal defender.

The ABC lawyers decided they should hire a local counsel whom they felt would bond better with the local jurors, even though he had never tried a case like this before. And they also decided that Rick Kaplan and I, who were named defendants, should not go to North Carolina, much less testify, because we were Jewish and the people in North Carolina would view us with suspicion.

They thought Diane Sawyer should testify because the jurors would like her, given she is from Kentucky, another southern state.

It turned out that nearly every decision they made was wrong. The jurors didn't understand why Kaplan and I weren't there and would later tell us that they viewed our absence as a sign of disrespect. They didn't think much of the local ABC lawyer, and as for PR, Mike Sitrick ran circles around the outmanned and outgunned ABC PR woman, whom I think finally got to see the broadcast as the trial was under way.

Amazingly, the one issue that landed us in court was on the hidden camera footage, and the jury never got a chance to see the broadcast. The judge instructed the jurors that for the purposes of the case, they should assume the story to be true. Later the jurors told us had they seen the story, they wouldn't have given Food Lion a broken nickel.

When the jury returned their verdict, we were hit with a $5.5 million punitive judgment. Food Lion declared itself vindicated.

The morning after the verdict, network president Bob Iger, who later ran Disney, called. "I want you to know that we totally support you and we will win on appeal," he said.

"Bob, that means a lot. Thank you," I said.

"Had you fucked this piece up, I wouldn't be making this call," he said somewhat angrily.

I was taken aback at the sudden change in tone but understood. As an executive he supported us but hated the bad publicity and how much the legal fees were going to run.

Backed by a much smarter legal team, we won the case on appeal, and all the money damages were removed (except for one dollar). Still, the Food Lion case would effectively mark the beginning of the end for the use of our hidden camera investigations.

ABC had libel insurance, but it was expensive. And as is true of most insurance premiums, after the legal costs of the Food Lion case were factored in, the premium increased. So ABC decided to greatly reduce its coverage and thereby decrease the risk that they were willing to take on. The case would lead to a more conservative approach in doing investigative stories.

A couple of years after the Food Lion decision, I had lunch with Mike Sitrick. We were like two former cold war enemies as we discussed the Food Lion litigation. He said he looked at the case as a job, one in which the client hired him to spin the public to think that ABC was the evildoer and not Food Lion, and he succeeded. I thought it would be interesting for students to hear this, so I invited him to do a forum with me at the Columbia Journalism School. He agreed.

The class was moderated by Richard Wald, a former ABC vice president who was then a professor at the school. Sitrick admitted that several of the claims he made against us in a company video that was widely distributed to the press were in fact false and were included at Food Lion's insistence. The students booed. He realized that he had fallen into a trap by coming to a journalism school and speaking candidly. Sitrick never agreed to do another joint seminar again.

Shortly after the Food Lion decision, Roone Arledge would be replaced by David Westin. As the former general counsel of ABC, he had championed our cause and ultimately got the right lawyers for us to win the case on appeal—four years after we lost in a North Carolina court. Westin was a corporate guy, but he was regarded favorably at the time by those in the news division. He carefully developed relationships with the key anchors, and he returned all their calls promptly, something Roone never had an interest in doing.

I once asked Arledge why he rarely returned a call from Barbara Walters or Diane Sawyer, and he said that if he did, he would probably have to take a side in a dispute they were having. This way, he said, it would work itself out on its own.

Westin, however, prided himself on his decisiveness, which, in the world of anchor monsters, can get you into trouble. Still, most people welcomed this earnest young man.

After taking over the news presidency, he summoned me to his office. I thought that since I had gone through Food Lion with him, he would promote me to be one of his vice presidents.

But that was not what he had in mind.

"I don't understand why we have to do investigative stories," he said. "It costs the most money to produce, takes the most time, and gets us into the most trouble."

I was thunderstruck. I thought we would be sharing laughs. I didn't think I would have to fight for my job.

I mumbled about how investigative journalism is a public service, adds prestige and importance to the networks, and wins awards that we can use to promote our brand. He was unimpressed. Westin believed that it didn't make a difference in the ratings, and that the public doesn't differentiate between an investigative story and one that wasn't.

Later he would ask Phyllis McGrady, who was vice president in charge of all magazine content, why we needed to do investigative reporting. She had a simple answer.

"Because Diane wants it."

Fortunately, that was enough to satisfy him.

As the senior producer, I rarely went into the field. But I made an exception after I received a tip about a man named Loyd Jowers, from Memphis, Tennessee. Jowers ran a small luncheonette called Jim's Grill, across the street from the Lorraine Motel, where Martin Luther King Jr. was assassinated. His grill was located on the ground floor next to the rooming house from where prosecutors said James Earl Ray fired the fatal shot.

Lewis Garrison, Jowers's attorney, called me up and said that his client confessed to him that he played a role in the King assassination. Any information on such a high-profile case that comes nearly thirty years after the shooting would have to be highly suspect, but the fact that the man's own attorney was risking disbarment for violating attorney-client privilege was at least intriguing.

I went to Memphis with Lynne Neufer, the Food Lion producer, and met with Garrison and Jowers. We rented a hotel room in town and spent a few hours trying to extract the story from Jowers. We ordered chicken salad sandwiches and drinks. After two hours of trying to convince him to trust us, Jowers told us a story that sucked the air out of the room.

He said that Frank Liberto, a Memphis mafia boss, gave him $100,000 and that he was part of a conspiracy to murder King. He claimed that he hired someone to do the killing.

He never named the accused shooter (later identified as Memphis policeman Earl Clark) at the time, although he told us that the assassin was not Ray. Jowers claimed he hired King's killer as a favor to Liberto and later would help dispose of the murder weapon, which was left in the back of his restaurant by the shooter. The rifle was, according to Jowers, broken up, bundled, and thrown in the Mississippi River.

Jowers alleged a vast conspiracy inside the government. A few months before the assassination, J. Edgar Hoover sent a note to all FBI bureaus saying that we have "to prevent the rise of the black messiah," a clear reference to King. What Jowers was telling us was not that far-fetched.

As I dug deeper, there were a few troubling "coincidences" that happened in the days leading up to and after the assassination. All the black Memphis police officers assigned to protect King were told to take the day off on the day of the assassination. The black firemen, who were headquartered across the street from the motel, were also un-expectedly given the day off. The area under the rooming house, where Jowers said the real killer entered his restaurant to give him the gun to break down after the shooting, was clear-cut by the police the day after the murder. It was trampled and the bushes removed, even though it was still clearly a crime scene. The police would say it was a previously scheduled cleaning.

And the man who was the first person to reach King after the as-sassination was Marrell McCollough, who was working undercover for the police and FBI. Jowers said he met him in the restaurant along with the real shooter, the day before the assassination. McCollough was seen in the famous picture moments after the assassination, with King on the ground and Andrew Young and others pointing to the rooming house where they had heard the shots. McCollough was the only one kneeling, with his hands on King, holding a white towel on his jaw, as he laid there dying.

I wanted to find McCollough, and I was told by a law enforcement source that he now worked for the CIA. I called the main Agency switchboard and was immediately put through to him.

He acknowledged that he knew Loyd Jowers from Memphis. I asked him about the King assassination, and then he hung up. I immediately called back, but his line was already disconnected. Apparently, as I was to later learn, he had been a CIA employee since 1974.

While we were putting the story together, Sam Donaldson and I received a call from Tom Brokaw at NBC, who tried to talk us out of going with the story. He said his producer checked out Jowers and had found that he was lying.

It was unprecedented to have a competitor call before we broadcast to "warn" us. Roone Arledge and Rick Kaplan wanted to promote the story hard, but Sam and I decided that we would underplay it, not act as if we had solved the assassination.

After the story aired, the King family met with Jowers and concluded he was telling the truth. They ended up suing him in civil court and getting a judgment of $100 against him, but more important, they obtained an acknowledgment in a court of law that the King assassination was part of a conspiracy.

Attorney General Janet Reno would later order a Justice Department investigation that unsurprisingly found that Jowers was lying and there was no conspiracy, in large part because of inconsistent statements made by Jowers and other witnesses.

The problem with stories like this is that anyone who would participate in an assassination of a world leader is probably a lying criminal. In the case of Jowers, I decided about a year after our story to give him a lie detector test conducted by the former director of the FBI polygraph department. If the FBI technician claimed Jowers was telling the truth, it would go a long way to having Jowers's story believed. Unfortunately the day we administered the test, Jowers showed up drunk. He ended up failing except for the question about whether he participated in the assassination conspiracy. The verdict on that was inconclusive, meaning it might or might not be true.

Jowers had changed his story during the exam from what he originally told us, but I believe he did this not because he was necessarily lying, but because he simply didn't know how to tell the truth. He had lied all his life, so lying was second nature to him. Thus even though I believe there may have been a conspiracy to kill King, Jowers unfortunately couldn't be trusted to make the case.

He would end up dying alone in Tiptonville, Tennessee, a small town on the Mississippi River, of a heart attack.

But we were successful in opening up another civil rights murder case: the assassination of legendary Mississippi civil rights leader Medgar Evers, a case that had gone unsolved for twenty-six years.

A white supremacist named Byron De La Beckwith had long been suspected of the murder but denied he was in Jackson, Mississippi, when the killing occurred. But correspondent Jay Schadler and producer Ti-Hua Chang found four witnesses who told us that he was not only in town but at the very church rally Evers attended before being murdered.

When we confronted De La Beckwith, he laughed at us and said about Evers: "I didn't kill Medgar Evers, but he's sure dead [laughs] and he ain't coming back."

After our story, De La Beckwith was tried for a third time—and this time he was convicted and sentenced to life in prison.

Chris Wallace also exposed a racist named Gary Lauck, who was the American sponsor of Germany's neo-Nazi army. Wallace found a guidebook on race Lauck distributed that described Jews as "the parasites of mankind and recommends intensive work to eradicate the last traces of this pestilence." Wallace also discovered a dice game that Lauck designed. The object: "to kill the most Jews."

At the time, Chris was doing some stellar work as an investigative correspondent, but he wanted to do some feature stories, and he got his chance when he was scheduled to do a profile on comedian Chris Rock.

Rock was the country's hottest comedian. He had left *Saturday Night Live* and was killing it with HBO comedy specials and lead movie roles. Wallace didn't do many profiles, so when the opportunity came to do one, he jumped at the chance. But then Chris Rock decided that he wanted Mike Wallace, not Chris Wallace. Mike called and told Chris Rock not to do the show with his son, as *60 Minutes* had higher ratings.

Chris was beyond angry. This was a betrayal on so many levels. I felt I had to call Mike. I could never imagine that Mike would steal a story from his own son. I hadn't talked with Mike in a few years, but I didn't forget how there was never any warm-up in the conversation.

"Mike, are you trying to do a profile on Chris Rock?" I asked as soon as he got on the phone.

"What's it to you?" he asked.

"Well, did you know that your son Chris had him booked and you took it away from him?"

"Do you know Chris Rock? He is so good, so funny. Have you heard his material?" Mike said, trying to avoid the subject.

"That's not the point. Why would you rip off your kid?" I asked.

"He'll get over it," Mike replied.

"You have a decision to make. Your choice is simple. You can have Chris speak at your funeral, or you can do the profile of Chris Rock. You can't have both," I said.

Long pause. "Let me think about it and I'll call you back."

Fifteen minutes later, Mike called. "I solved the problem. I gave the story to Ed Bradley."

"How is that solving the problem?" I asked incredulously. "You are still ripping off Chris."

Mike clearly wasn't getting it. "What are you talking about? I won't do it and Bradley will." Mike was using the trade to make nice with Bradley for stealing an interview from him years before, with Panama dictator Manuel Noriega.

Bradley did do the Chris Rock story and Chris Wallace didn't talk to Mike for nearly a year. The ice broke around the time that Chris was getting divorced and Mike, having been divorced three times, began to act more like a father than a competitor.

Chris and I would talk almost daily. Despite the show's groundbreaking success in investigations, I became a sounding board for his complaints about the show's management, what he considered the poor quality of producers, and the problems with the particular story he was working on.

Chris rode his producers hard, and some of them refused to work with him. So I told Chris, "If the best producers don't want to work with you, you won't get to do the best stories. If you don't do the best stories, this place won't pay you the money you deserve. So be nice to them so you can make the most money." It was a direct appeal that he understood immediately and he was, for a time, a nicer correspondent to work with.

We developed a trust and friendship that I didn't have with his father. He always asked me grudgingly to read his scripts before he finalized them. "Not because I like you, but because you make my pieces better," he said. I took that as a compliment.

Interestingly, he never asked me even once, before preparing for an interview, "What would Mike do?" I think he wanted to create his own signature style.

Chris was always trying to hustle his stories to get on TV. He said to me, more than once, "Being on TV is like oxygen for me. If I am not on, I die."

But the problem was that the ABC magazines had a larger and larger contingent of on-air talent. The decision was made in 1998 to merge *Primetime* with *20/20* in order to rival *Dateline*, which was on five nights a week. We were going to be *20/20* Monday, Wednesday, Thursday, Friday, and Sunday. The thinking was that if the two staffs were combined, no one would have to be laid off.

The staff merger meant that there could be only one executive producer. ABC president David Westin asked Diane whom she wanted,

Victor Neufeld or Phyllis McGrady. Phyllis was the popular choice, but Victor kept the show on budget. Phyllis had had some health issues years before but was now fine. McGrady not only created and hired most of the staff of *Primetime Live,* she was a close friend of Diane's. Westin thought she would pick McGrady for the merged shows.

Diane paused for a moment. "David, we can't be selfish. We must look out for Phyllis and make sure she gets healthy. She has given so much to this network," Westin recalled Diane saying.

Meanwhile Westin thought, *Son of a bitch, she just threw her best friend, McGrady, under the bus.* Westin said that Diane felt Victor would produce a more successful show and his "news you can use" consumer bent worked better in prime time. Still, Westin was shocked by Diane's choice.

For the *Primetime* staff, this was a hostile takeover. I was moved to an office on the other side of the building, a small city block away from Victor and his staff. My neighbor at work was the show's accountant. My office location was so bad that the newest correspondents were given offices near me. At the time, in the mid-1990s, they were not well known. One of them was Chris Cuomo, while another was Anderson Cooper.

Victor thought Cooper, who was the son of Gloria Vanderbilt, was a spoiled rich kid. He had him work on Monday's edition of *20/20* called "Downtown," supposedly a hip version of *20/20.* The only thing hip about it was the anchors wore leather instead of suits and ties. Cooper recalled that they sent him to India to do a story about eunuchs, men who were castrated and carried out menial work. It was supposed to be a sympathetic story, but Cooper found that many of the eunuchs were criminals. It never aired.

Cuomo also was assigned to the "Downtown" show. He, like Cooper, came from a life of privilege, as his father had been the governor of New York when he was a teenager. His brother, Andrew, nicknamed Chris "Mansion Boy" because Chris spent his teen years at the governor's Albany mansion. The little on-air experience he had was from his previous job at Fox, where he learned broadcasting from Roger Ailes.

But Cuomo had ambition, charm, and enormous drive, which made it clear he was going to be a big star. He wanted to do stories on global warming before it was in vogue, while Victor Neufeld, the executive producer of 20/20, wanted him to do crime stories. Needless to say, Victor and Cuomo were not on the same page.

The two senior staffs, which were once rivals, now were unequal partners. The 20/20 folks were in charge, and at every turn they reminded us of that. Their correspondents were favored over ours, as were their producers. Diane thought that by discarding Phyllis McGrady, she would be getting an executive producer who knew how to do "news related to people's lives." But she was wrong.

We had two senior staffs screening stories. It was explained to me that there was a batting order for the senior producers who spoke at these screenings. "Victor Neufeld [executive producer] speaks first, [David] Tabacoff, White, then Bob Lange, [David] Sloan, [Carla] De Landri, then you, then Page, and then Jessica Velmans." With nine people in a screening, we barely could fit into the office.

Chris Wallace lived in Washington and usually stayed there when we screened one of his stories. But Victor insisted that Chris fly to New York, so Chris reluctantly came up for a screening. The story was about how temporary maids, hired daily, rummage through a person's belongings and steal money from drawers. We set up hidden cameras throughout the house to see how the thefts occurred.

This story was not going to win a Peabody, but under the world of Victor, it was what he wanted. While the story was playing for the roomful of seniors, Victor closed his eyes and started to snore. Suddenly we all stopped watching the story and began to watch Victor. When the piece ended, Victor's eyes opened and he said, "It felt a little long, take a couple minutes out of it."

Chris answered, "How would you know? You were sleeping."

"I wasn't sleeping. I was listening to it. Don Hewitt said it has to work on the ears before the eyes, so I was listening to it," Victor responded.

"No, you were sleeping, Victor," replied Meredith White, who was at this time his closest confidante. "We heard you snoring."

Chris felt disrespected and left the screening angry. The exercise of screening in New York was a waste of time. "I will never come up again," he told me as he left to fly back to Washington. "That was humiliating."

Victor was making the broadcast much lighter. Instead of investigations into race relations or VA hospitals, he had us doing stories on how some parking meters run fast and expire before their time. We had an experienced producer, Nancy Kramer, timing the meters with a stopwatch; then Chris Wallace would confront the meter maids as they were handing out tickets. This was not what Chris had signed up for.

Meanwhile another correspondent, Cynthia McFadden, was also having a hard time of it. She came from Court TV and had done serious work in the legal area. Now she was being asked to do lowbrow consumer investigations. She was disheartened and came to me with a story idea she got from the human rights organization WITNESS. The story involved abuses that occur inside Mexican centers for people with intellectual disabilities.

"There is no way Victor would ever go for that," she said.

"I think I can get him to do it," I told her.

I pitched Victor the idea of bringing hidden cameras inside the Mexican facilities. He looked at me like I was telling him a joke.

"You are kidding, right? You have a hidden camera on me now?" he asked.

"No, Victor, I'm serious. It's an important story. We can save lives."

"Who would want to watch that?" he asked.

"I will make a deal with you. I will give you a hundred dollars if the story doesn't win a duPont, a Peabody, or an Overseas Press Club Award."

"You are on," he replied.

And that's how we did that story. As a result, the Mexican government inspected the facilities and closed some of them down and transferred the patients to better institutions. Sweeping changes occurred in how those patients were being housed. And yes, the story fortunately won an Overseas Press Club Award, so I didn't have to pay Victor the money.

Victor later told me he approved the story because of my passion, but there weren't many of those victories. The *20/20* management team even marginalized Sam Donaldson, who was desperate to get on the air. Sam's last big investigation at *Primetime Live* was a story in which he found a Nazi who had been responsible for a massacre in Italy during the war living in Argentina.

"I was just following orders," the Nazi, Erich Priebke, told Donaldson. The story made worldwide headlines and dominated the European press for months. After it aired, Priebke was extradited to Italy, tried, and eventually found guilty of war crimes for leading a massacre. He died in Italy, while under house arrest.

But now, Sam was treated like a second-rate correspondent. In one story, Sam went through school textbooks looking for factual errors and then confronted the unsuspecting authors with their mistakes. It was a big comedown for the correspondent who shouted questions at President Ronald Reagan on the White House lawn.

The combined shows opened an old wound that existed between Diane Sawyer and Barbara Walters. Their rivalry went back to booking wars for newsmakers or high-profile celebrities, when their separate shows competed for stories. They would steal interviews from each other, and there were no senior managers who intervened.

So Roone Arledge thought it would be a great idea for them to work together as a team, and co-anchor a broadcast on Sunday night. But problems for Victor managing two giant egos began even before they were on the set.

Victor told me he struggled to get them to come out of their respective dressing rooms. "Barbara would say, 'I am not going out there first to sit there and wait for her to come out.' While Diane would say the same thing, except she would take her time with hair and makeup.

Finally they would emerge from their dressing rooms and act like they loved each other."

Then they fought over who greeted the TV audience and who said good night. When it was agreed Barbara would say the "welcome" and Diane would say "good night," Barbara jumped in after Diane said good night to say her own good night. They even counted the number of words each one had, introducing the stories. It was a total disaster. The ratings were worse than the show that it had replaced on the network. The Sunday broadcast was hurting their individual brands, so they decided to quit anchoring together, claiming "they were both too busy."

But Barbara continued to anchor her regular slot on Friday, while Diane did her regular anchoring on Thursday, the old *Primetime* hour, but she was now sharing the set with Charlie Gibson, instead of Sam Donaldson.

Meanwhile Diane and Barbara continued to act like they were buddies. I was standing with Diane at the elevator once when she bumped into Barbara. "How are you?" Barbara asked Diane.

"I'm fine, and you?"

"People say we don't get along, they should see us now," Barbara said, reaching for Diane's hand.

"I know, I don't understand that," Diane said and laughed. The elevator came and Diane said goodbye to Barbara.

Inside the elevator, Diane looked at me and said, "I hate that woman. Don't believe a word she says. She knifes me any chance she gets." Diane's face was angry. No smile. She had the look of someone who wanted vengeance.

Diane and Barbara were the best at what they did, but they had two completely different styles. Barbara would type out her questions for an interview on index cards. As she whittled her questions down, she would toss the one she didn't like away. Then she would shuffle the keepers and put them in the order she wanted.

Diane would labor over every question before a big interview. She would have committees of people weighing in, suggesting questions;

then she would solicit opinions of every boss, from the senior producer to the president of the news division. Diane would screen her big stories, not only with executive producers, but also with interns, secretaries, and even relatives of those on the staff. This would of course make the executives crazy, as they thought their authority was being usurped. And it was. With Diane, they never got the last word.

Diane insisted on including in her story screenings a twenty-three-year-old production assistant, whom Diane felt represented the typical TV viewer. The production assistant was a loudmouth from Westchester who had an opinion on everything. Diane always solicited her views and gave them more standing than those managing the show.

Eventually the executive producer realized they should have the assistant at all Diane screenings, and she was eventually promoted to the senior staff.

But writing questions was the easy part of the process in working with Diane. When she scripted her stories, they were often three times longer than they should be.

Producer Robbie Gordon and I did a story with Diane on school violence. We brought hidden cameras into classrooms to show the disruption and chaos in schools, which revealed that learning in that environment was impossible. It was a great story, but it was still not completed the day it was to air. Then executive producer Rick Kaplan came into Diane's office and had a basic and simple question: "How many segments are you planning to run tonight?"

I said two, Robbie said three, Diane said four. Though Rick was the boss, Diane was really in charge.

"When you figure it out," he said, "let me know."

The story took over the entire hourlong broadcast, but that still was not enough time for Diane. The segments were completed right before they were to be broadcast, and we were about five minutes heavy. When I arrived in the control room, while we were on the air, Kaplan was crossing off items on the lineup.

"I don't know how we get off the air tonight," he said to me, barely looking up.

"Kill the midbreak."

"I already did," he said.

"Kill the teases."

"Done."

"Kill the tag pages."

"I did."

"How about the coming attractions segment?"

"Gone."

He had a look of concern, and that worried me.

Roger Goodman, the director, spoke next. "We are going to have to dump out of one of the stories," he said.

One of the ABC lawyers was there and wanted a shot of one of the students to be blurred, but we ignored her as we were live.

I looked at what was being broadcast and realized a perfect spot to dump out was coming up.

"Are you ready?" I asked Roger. My hand went to his shoulders.

"Now." Roger cut out perfectly and went directly to Diane.

Diane was watching her piece and was surprised to see that segment end. Kaplan quickly spoke in her ear. "Say, 'We'll be right back.'"

Diane did. We were now in a commercial break and she picked up the phone on the set and called Rick directly. When she spoke on the set, everyone in the building could hear what she would say. She didn't want that.

"What just happened?" she asked Rick.

"The broadcast came in five minutes heavy, and this was the only way we could get off the air."

We all held our breath. I thought, *If she's going to fire us, I just hope she will wait till we are off the air.*

"It was my fault," she said. "I should have paid closer attention to how long the segments were running."

We all exhaled, including Rick. The producer, Robbie Gordon, came into the control room. She had no idea what had just happened; she had taken the long walk from the edit room to the control room and hadn't seen what was broadcast. We would tell her the story a few minutes later at the local bar. That show would end up being memorialized by the staff cartoonist, who drew a picture of us killing each other, along with an audience of over 25 million viewers.

Another time, Diane was told that Fidel Castro had agreed to an interview, so she decided to leave for Cuba only three days before our show. We had a story that was almost complete on nuns who blew the whistle on pedophile priests, but she said it wouldn't air that week, as she had Castro. I asked her to record her voice on the story in case the Castro interview didn't happen, but she refused. She said the interview was a definite.

When she arrived in Cuba, Castro wanted to meet, but he didn't want to do an interview. We had no lead segment. Diane was in Cuba and couldn't record the story, which normally would make it impossible to air. In fact, she would be lucky if she got back in time to anchor the show.

So, working with the lawyers, we figured out a script. I then asked for the transcripts of old stories by Diane and checked her narrative bridges. With scissors, paper, and a stapler, I began to cut out old narrations. I then asked the editors to find the audio that matched what was on the paper cut I made. The editors strung her old narrations together and then edited them into the new story. Fortunately, Diane had certain stock phrases that she would use for transitions in most of her stories, phrases like "And then there was this" or "and there's more"— that could fit in anywhere. So we repurposed her old tracks and made a story that worked.

Diane didn't make it back to New York and ended up anchoring the show from Miami. She watched in horror, anger, and amazement as we were running the story she had never tracked, with her voice in the piece. When it ended, she picked up the phone from the set and called me. "I never tracked that story," she pointed out.

I then explained to her what I did. She listened, waited a beat, and said, "Don't you ever do that again." But she didn't seem angry.

I didn't care. We survived another show.

Diane was a tireless worker, and she taught me the effort you need to put in to be a winner. Though I loved Diane's intelligence and commitment to the work, I hated her two-faced qualities. If she was overly friendly and began to kiss you on the cheeks to say hello, chances are she was trashing you behind your back.

One day I noticed that Diane was being extremely friendly to a senior producer on the show. She was asking him about his wife and family. When he left the room, she said to me disdainfully, "He is the black hole of the show. Everything goes in and nothing comes out." I remember gasping at the cold artistry of the putdown.

After *Primetime Live* and *20/20* merged, it was announced that a new magazine show would be starting at CBS, *60 Minutes II,* and it would be run by Jeff Fager. They wanted Chris Wallace as one of the correspondents. It made perfect sense—a son of Wallace joins the show that is the stepchild of the main brand. But Chris was under contract with ABC, and they weren't going to let him go.

As Chris was battling the ABC lawyers, I had entered the hospital with some severe stomach pains, and it was determined that I needed my gallbladder removed. While in the hospital, I was receiving daily calls from Chris in which he mostly spoke about his efforts to get released from his contract. He had met with David Westin, who was happy to see Chris (and his large salary) leave, but Diane was blocking it. She told Chris it would be bad for morale if he left. Chris needed Bob Iger, then the head of all television for ABC and Disney, to release him. But Iger refused, telling Chris that it was a sign of weakness in Hollywood to release someone like him from his contract. But more important, Iger didn't feel like helping the competition out.

After a week in the hospital, I was set to go into surgery when the phone rang.

"How are you doing?" Chris asked.

At the time, I was surrounded by a medical staff getting ready for the operation.

"I'm about to go into surgery," I told Chris.

"Okay, enough about you. Let's talk about me," he replied.

I hung up on him. I told the doctors I looked forward to getting knocked out.

At the end of his contract in 2003, Chris did leave ABC, going to Fox to host his own Sunday political show, the perfect job for him. Now I began to realize that maybe the perfect job for me was to return to the home of the ticking clock.

18

RETURNING TO *60 MINUTES*

Beginning in 2000, big changes were taking place at ABC News, and the direction of the broadcasts changed. *Primetime* was separated again from *20/20*, but no longer doing the serious investigations that once put *Primetime* on the map. And the change in direction resulted in a ratings collapse. In Live 1998, *Primetime* was the twenty-second highest rated show on TV. Four years later it fell to eighty-first. The audience went from 14.2 million viewers to 8.5 million. Panic set in. When that happens shows often go for quick, titillating stories that catch the viewer's eye, in the hope of jump-starting the ratings. *Primetime* did a live hour from 42nd Street on people's sex habits. And the show added a cabaret singer to compose and sing a song each week on the news; the segment was titled "That Was the Week That Was."

 20/20 was also hemorrhaging ratings, going from 15 million viewers in 1997–98 to 8.5 million in the 2004–05 season. The new executive producer of *20/20* changed the show's direction and distributed a list of story categories he wanted each producer to fill that represented what they wanted to put on the air. The "buckets," as they were called, included these categories: Moochers, Parents Behaving Badly, Losing It, Confessions, Crossing the Line, Nasty Neighbors, Strange Afflictions, and Family Secrets.

The magazine shows would later do a summer series called "Medical Mysteries," with one segment on women who are sexually aroused twenty-four hours a day. There were also stories on women who smell like fish and the werewolf syndrome—men who have hair all over their bodies.

Diane seemed to embrace the new direction of the magazine shows, as a way to counter the falling ratings. It was described as "news you can use or news that relates to people's lives." So naturally she wanted to do a story on dog bites.

"What is the story?" I asked her. "Dog bites man. End of story."

"No, dog bites are much more common than you think," she said. "In fact, I think it could be a lead."

John Quiñones ended up doing the story and it did lead the broadcast.

Then Diane wanted a broadcast on how dry cleaners are ruining clothes.

I thought the story fell into the category of "shit happens," and I did not see a reason to confront someone for ruining a blouse.

"If you don't want to do it, I will get someone else who will," Diane told me.

And she did.

She was once the champion of the groundbreaking investigations the show did and now I felt she abandoned me and those stories that made us the talk of the town. She had gone from a modern-day Nellie Bly to a local consumer reporter.

By 2004, the core that was *Primetime Live* was gone. Chris Wallace went to Fox; Sam Donaldson was slowly being retired; Judd Rose, one of the original correspondents, had died of cancer; and Jay Schadler had discovered his talent for painting and taking pictures and had begun to work less. In their place were correspondents like Chris Cuomo.

Cuomo got his start at ABC on the gritty show *20/20 Downtown*, executive-produced by David Sloan. At the time, Cuomo's office was across from mine and I would hear him yelling all day at friends, stockbrokers, and family members.

Sloan came to see Cuomo one day about doing a story on trepanation, people who get holes drilled in their heads in order to feel better.

Sloan was selling the story hard, but Cuomo, like a true politician's son, wanted something in return. He wanted to do something
more relevant than trepanation.

To drive the point home, he put his hand on Sloan's thigh and held
it there. Sloan, an openly gay man, turned red, but said nothing.

That son of a bitch Cuomo, I thought, *he is definitely going to go
far in this business.*

After Wallace left for Fox in 2003, Phyllis McGrady, now an ABC
News vice president, asked me if I would mentor Cuomo on investigative reporting. Cuomo was very smart, an attorney, and had enormous
broadcast potential, but at the time he didn't have the same journalistic
background of many other correspondents. But I reluctantly agreed.

After the meeting with McGrady, I went to see him in his office.
Cuomo greeted me at the door with "I understand that you are my new
bitch."

He thought it was funny, but I found no humor in his comment.
To paraphrase the famous line from the movie *Jerry Maguire,* "He lost
me at hello."

Later that year Cuomo finally ended up doing an hour on global
warming and became an anchor of *20/20* before leaving to lead his
own show on CNN. I was wrong about Cuomo, as he took his sarcastic
and caustic personality and made it part of his on-air identity, and he
found his voice. The same can't be said for the struggles of *Primetime,*
which would ultimately morph into another show called *What Would
You Do?* that now used hidden cameras to stage ethical dilemmas on
unsuspecting people and secretly film how they react—a very different
use of hidden cameras from what we did in the early days of *Primetime
Live.*

In 2004, I had a lunch scheduled with Mike Wallace. We were friendly
again, mostly due to the positive comments he heard about me from his
son Chris, with whom I had enjoyed working. But with Chris at Fox,

Mike knew I was unhappy at ABC and ready to leave. So Mike decided to invite Jeff Fager to the meal. Fager was running *60 Minutes II,* but he would soon take over *60 Minutes.*

Fager was an experienced newsman, who covered many international stories when he was based in London as a producer. He later joined *60 Minutes* as a producer in 1989, the year I left for ABC. He went on to executive-produce *CBS Evening News* and was now preparing to succeed Don Hewitt in what is considered the top job in TV news.

Fager was interested in hiring me back to *60 Minutes,* but I feared he might take the show in a different direction, as happened at ABC. At lunch, I asked him what kind of stories he would like to see me do. Without hesitating he said, "Iraqi contracting fraud."

"How does that help you with the 18-to-49 women demo?" I asked.

"We don't talk or think like that here," he replied.

He wanted me to work with Steve Kroft, who had a reputation as being difficult. I told him that after working with Mike and Chris Wallace, Diane, and Sam, I expected Kroft to be easy. Mike smiled approvingly.

After two more lunches alone with Fager, I was hired. My first call was to Don Hewitt, who was still running the broadcast for a few more weeks.

"Dad, I am coming home," I told him. Don was truly happy to be looped in on the news; he kept thanking me for telling him. I said I was genuinely excited to be returning to reporting and no longer being a "suit."

It wasn't hard for me to transition back to *60 Minutes,* as very little had changed in the fifteen years since I had left. The show still did mini-documentaries, with the average story now running about 12:30. Mike, Morley, and Ed were still in the same offices they occupied when I left in 1989. Andy Rooney was still walking the hallways and complaining about how his favorite football team, the New York Giants, were playing. The giant blackboard outside Don's office that listed the stories each correspondent was working on was still there, but instead of story titles written in chalk, they were now using Magic Markers. The biggest change was that Don Hewitt was being retired.

I arrived around the time of Hewitt's farewell celebrations. The first one was in the screening room at *60 Minutes*, with Mike Wallace, Lesley Stahl, Ed Bradley, and Steve Kroft all present. The staff squeezed in, with most of us forced to stand. There was an element of celebration, but more awkwardness. How do you celebrate someone who meant so much to everyone's careers being fired?

This may have been the *60 Minutes* team, but it was a gathering of rivals. Even in Don's departure, it was hard to put away old animosities. Kroft spoke first, and said, "No matter what happens in anybody's career, I think we will all remember that we worked with Don Hewitt."

It broke the ice but felt a little forced.

Mike remembered how it all began. He recounted the story of how Don talked him out of being Richard Nixon's press secretary to join him on the show that became *60 Minutes*. "I wanted to go to the White House," Wallace told the story for the umpteenth time, "but I felt sorry for Don."

Wallace then spoke about how Don made them rich and how much fun it was. "We had such a ball. For the first ten or fifteen years we worked seven days a week, twelve hours a day. It was . . ."

And Mike stopped as if he had lost his place in a speech or perhaps was too overcome with emotion. There was a certain sadness in the room, but *60 Minutes* is not a place that dwells on goodbye parties, even Don's. The gathering ended about twenty minutes after it began, and everyone went back into their offices. It was more like a study break in school. Later the producers on the show took Don out for lunch. There wasn't great camaraderie or laughter at that lunch, either. Like the correspondents, the producers are rivals and don't party well together. Aside for a few toasts and stories, that lunch ended in a whimper.

After a few weeks, Don moved directly one floor down from his old office. His new office was bigger than his old one, but it seemed a waste of space. Instead of commanding over a hundred people, he now had only one staffer, his loyal secretary, Beverly. One day Don wandered up to my office, and as he usually did, entered without knocking, and started talking.

"I don't know why they did this to me," he said, referring to getting replaced by Fager.

"Because you're old, Don," I said. Don was eighty-two.

"You are the first person to tell me that," he said. At last, he said, he finally had his answer, as he walked out of my office.

Another time Don came into my office and brought up a recent press interview where Dan Rather said he wanders the third floor of the CBS broadcast center and speaks to the ghost of Edward R. Murrow.

"Dan is going crazy," Don said. "Murrow was never on the third floor. He was always on the second floor."

"Don, if it's a ghost it can go up and down the stairways," I said.

"Murrow would never go to the third floor," Don said, and walked away.

Mike seemed to be wearing the same suits he had on when I left fifteen years ago. He still looked fit and trim, but I noticed his mental facilities were diminishing. His favorite expression had been to point to a person's belly and tell them "to stick it in." Usually a quick back-and-forth rank-out session would ensue. But now after Mike delivered his line, he would fall silent. His workload decreased and he was left with only one full-time producer. Most of his stories now were straight interviews.

In 2005, Mike began to talk openly about his depression. He wrote about his experiences and became a poster boy for the disease, doing ads and interviews on television in an effort to help remove the stigma associated with depression. Interestingly, two of his closest friends, columnist Art Buchwald and novelist William Styron, also suffered from the disease. Mike's going public with his struggles became one of the defining moments of his life.

Mike wanted his journalism to change people's lives for the better by exposing wrongdoing. Now Mike's exposure of his own personal trials would help change the public attitude toward depression. It led depression sufferers to seek treatment and gave Mike a sense that he could still make a difference.

When I went into Mike's office at that time, he would proudly display the letters he received from people thanking him for going public. Mike seemed to be in a better place emotionally. His depression medication finally seemed to be working.

But strangely, I missed the old Mike. Even though he tortured me, I felt I had learned TV from the best interviewer of our time. I had no desire to work with Mike now, but I still liked to go speak with him.

One day, after completing a major investigative story, I wanted to tell Mike all about it. But when I went down to his office, the light was off and his secretary was putting a blanket on him, getting him comfortable for his afternoon nap.

19

STARTING OVER, AGAIN

Many people would look at going back to a job they held fifteen years earlier as a sign that you are a loser or got demoted, but I put my ego and pride aside and realized that being a *60 Minutes* producer was the best reporting position in TV. Now, with the advent of computers and the internet, I could search for stories online, and I had a large Rolodex of sources and contacts who were happy to feed me ideas.

I thought back to when I first began as a producer, watching another producer who had just been fired, carrying his Emmy trophies under his arm, as he headed for the elevator to leave the building. He had produced two bad stories in a row, and despite his years of accomplishments, he was toast. The pressure to produce was still there, but the penalties under Jeff Fager for doing a less-than-stellar story were not as severe.

So I embraced the challenge of becoming a producer again. I was wiser about the ingredients for a good story, but I also still had the youthful confidence that I could out-produce anyone there.

The biggest change was going from Wallace to Kroft. He didn't have Mike's charisma, but Kroft was an established reporter with a flair for writing and explaining complicated stories.

Kroft came up through the farm leagues of CBS News, working his way from Miami to overseas assignments, where he covered conflicts in El Salvador and Northern Ireland. He traveled throughout Europe and Asia, covering terrorism and the assassination of Indian Prime Minister Indira Gandhi. He was then promoted to correspondent on the CBS newsmagazine program *West 57th,* where he fine-tuned his style and voice before making the jump to *60 Minutes.* Though Kroft was an enormously talented writer, he was insecure about the role of producers in shaping stories, and he always tried to diminish their contributions.

"Producers are like tits on a bull," he said famously at one office party at Jake's Saloon, the local bar, "an unnecessary appendage."

Kroft badgered his producers and once caused almost his entire team to quit. Kroft tended to drink excessively, stay up all night to write scripts·that he should have finished during the day, and rarely thanked the producers. On occasion, he would even use their scripts as scrap paper on which to write out his Chinese takeout orders.

I regarded all these as foibles I could handle. I'd rather work with a talented asshole than a nice person without talent. I also thought because of my seniority, experience, and accomplishments that he wouldn't treat me the way he had nearly every producer he worked with.

When I accepted the job, he was shocked. "I thought you were using us to get another offer at ABC and wouldn't take the job," Kroft told me later. "That's happened to me before."

At that moment he seemed vulnerable, not gruff, and that made me want to see if we could become a great team.

Our first story was a throwback, one that Mike Wallace would have loved to have done. I went to Canada and met with the Royal Canadian Mounted Police about a scam that they had uncovered in which con men called the elderly and told them they had won the Canadian lottery and the money would be delivered as soon as the taxes were paid on the winnings. The mark just needed to send them some money.

Amazingly, many senior citizens fell for this simple scam and lost their life savings. They looked at the lottery "win" as an opportunity to make amends to their children or family, a chance to leave an inheritance to them before they died.

The RCMP, wanting to publicize the scam, and at my urging, convinced a convicted con man to tell us how the solicitations were done. The RCMP also had the phone tapes of the con man scamming the elderly widows out of their money.

I got the scam tapes and was able to locate one of the widows who lost her money. We played the tapes separately to the con man and the widow. The elderly woman said, "Next time you see him, kick him in the knees for me." When we did the con man's interview, I made a copy of what the widow told us we should do to him and played it for him. His answer would be the final line of the story. "I am surprised that's all she wants to do to me. I deserve much worse," he said.

It was the perfect *60 Minutes* story. It had victims, a perpetrator, a scam, tapes, cops, and a great confrontation by the correspondent, Steve Kroft. The story, called "The Closer," would be the lead on the premiere show of the season.

I then decided to stretch out of my comfort zone and do a story in Pakistan. In 2004, through a friend, I had gotten to know General Jehangir Karamat, the Pakistani ambassador to the United States, who was also a former Pakistani army chief of staff. Ambassadors in Washington love to eat meals at the luxurious but overpriced Ritz-Carlton hotel, and I took Karamat there for several lunches.

I wanted to interview a recent Al-Qaeda defector, named Muhammad Naeem Noor Khan, who oversaw communications for the terrorist organization. Khan was arrested in Pakistan with plans on his computer to attack U.S. financial institutions and Heathrow Airport. Khan was educated in London, spoke perfect English, and was now cooperating with authorities, which meant he had nothing to hide and would be open to telling us how Al-Qaeda operates.

Karamat told me that they would make him available. But when I got to Islamabad, officials of the Inter-Services Intelligence (ISI), Pakistan's intelligence service, had other things on their minds.

My base in Islamabad was the Marriott, a dingy-smelling hotel located near the city's government buildings. To enter, you had to pass through two police checkpoints. Above the hotel were the flags from the countries where their guests came from. They never flew the American flag for fear of a terrorist attack. Each day I would meet with an assortment of generals, colonels, and undercover ISI agents precisely at four P.M. in a hotel conference room.

The officials would all file into the room, take their seats, and fill their glasses with water, in sync. Then the lead press representative would tell me that no decision had been made about providing me with access to Khan. At first I was respectful, thanked them for trying, and said I looked forward to our next meeting. But each day the same ritual would play out. After nearly a week of these charades, I lost my temper.

"You are conning me!" I shouted. "You have no intention of providing him to me. Why can't you be honest?"

I think the military men didn't like to be yelled at by an American Jew. They all gave me very stern, cold stares, but only the press representative spoke. "We will try again tomorrow," he said.

That night I called ambassador Karamat on a satellite phone and complained about what was happening and how I was being "fucked over."

He was sympathetic, but all he could do from Washington was to arrange meetings. After one of my nightly calls to Karamat, two ISI officials showed up the next morning at my hotel with a transcript of my conversation. "All the embassies hear what you are saying," they told me. "You must be more careful."

"I am not going to be careful when I am getting screwed. I will broadcast on my phone how untrustworthy you guys are. Every country in the world will know."

Looking back, I was pretty stupid to threaten the ISI in its own country. I don't know why the Pakistanis didn't throw me out and send me back to New York, or worse. But later that day at our next hotel meeting, a few extra people were sitting around the conference table.

I was introduced to the head of the country's counterintelligence division, who was running military raids that had led to the arrests of two hundred terrorists.

He said that it was "impossible" for me to talk with Khan. *At least he is being honest,* I thought. He talked to me while taking calls, seemingly organizing and approving raids on suspected terrorist homes throughout the country. He was doing this with the same ease of ordering a takeout pizza. I realized that this was the guy at the center of counterterrorism operations in Pakistan. "If I can't do an interview with Khan, let me interview you," I said to the man I called "the colonel."

The colonel had his own security detail and traveled different routes to and from work. He was among the top targets for an assassination by terrorists. But still he agreed to do a TV interview if we protected his identity. I now felt we had enough for a story.

Kroft arrived a few days later, and the Pakistani military, who love to create schedules for meetings and interviews, decided they needed to change things up and move our interview with President Pervez Musharraf, which was set for the third day of the visit, to the first.

Kroft and I quickly worked on questions and then went to the army garrison where Musharraf lived for his own protection. There had been several assassination attempts against the president, and these attempts weren't random shooters with a revolver.

In one, the would-be assassins spent six months digging under a road in which Musharraf's car traveled routinely. As they neared the completion of their digging, and were about to put the explosives in, they were all arrested and later hanged. Another assassination attempt was an ambush by a battalion of troops who attacked his car and protective detail; this resulted in a massive firefight. Another assassin fired a missile at his car. Somehow Musharraf survived all these attempts, and the surviving perpetrators were rounded up by General Parvez Kayani and executed.

For this loyalty, Musharraf promoted Kayani to be head of the ISI.

Still, Musharraf took no chances. He was supposed to live in a presidential palace on top of a hill near downtown Islamabad. Musharraf displaced 1,200 people living in a small village at the bottom of the hill, and he installed a radar tower there. That way his security detail could detect an airplane that was hell-bent on crashing into the palace. Still, after taking all these security precautions, Musharraf decided it best to live in an army compound surrounded by a couple of thousand troops. During our interview, Musharraf said that Osama bin Laden was more popular in Pakistan than he was as president, a not-so-subtle signal that the Pakistanis were not too keen to find him.

It was that candor and his ease in speaking English that made Musharraf a good interview. After we finished filming, Kroft went back to the hotel to sleep and I stayed and shared sports stories with the president. He told me he was a great badminton player and invited me to watch him play.

The next day I went to the Islamabad racquet club about fifteen minutes early and watched the three players Musharraf was to play with warm up. Two of them were the top-ranked players in Pakistan, and the third was also terrific. When the game began, though, Musharraf's side seemed to win every point. The reason became apparent. His opponents made sure to place the birdie squarely on his racket. If Musharraf closed his eyes, he still could hit it over the net.

After the matches ended, with Musharraf's side winning every match, he walked off the court and called me over. "See, I told you I was good," he said. The other players simply stood and stared. The president was in such a good mood he opened the trunk of his car to show me the anti-IED device the CIA had installed in his car. The device jammed any radio signals that could be sent to an explosive device within a fifty-yard radius of his vehicle. The technology was better than anything U.S. troops had at the time in Iraq, but it also signaled that the United States and the CIA wanted Musharraf to stay alive and in power.

The next morning, we took a helicopter to Wana in South Waziristan, near the Afghanistan border. The landscape there was like nothing I had ever seen—a jumble of crisscross mountains, as if they had been scrambled and thrown together in no particular order.

Waziristan is roughly the size of Vermont—10,000 square miles of peaks and valleys set against the Hindu Kush range, a landscape dotted with caves, tunnels, and walled compounds. It was here that bin Laden and several hundred of his loyal fighters escaped after the Battle of Tora Bora in 2001.

Below our helicopter were mountains and caves where bin Laden was suspected of hiding. Before staying in Wana, Waziristan's capital, we flew to a remote outpost on top of a small mountain. Only a handful of reporters had ever been allowed into the area, and only under the strict supervision of the army. When we landed, the troops looked at us like we were from Mars.

The commander at the outpost claimed to have driven Al-Qaeda from its area, but a few days before we arrived, five of their soldiers were killed. Pakistani troops stationed there looked like they had been in the sun too long or were into serious drugs.

The troops, anticipating our arrival, had slaughtered a goat for dinner in our honor. But Kroft wanted to do his on-camera stand-up with the Hindu Kush behind him and leave.

This is a vanity moment to show how far the correspondent would go for his story. But Kroft kept flubbing his words and we were about to hit our time limit on the mountaintop. A slow-moving fog was enveloping us, shrouding the valley below and making flying very dangerous. The helicopter pilot approached me and said, "If we don't leave in the next five minutes, we may be trapped here for a week."

I told that to Kroft, and the next stand-up attempt was perfect. Still, we had to beg the pilot to fly us out, as the fog had by now descended all around us. It was fortunate he did. A week after we left, that outpost was overrun by the Taliban; most of the troops were either captured or killed.

We next landed in Wana, a dusty, small town in the desert. Few people lived here, but driving from the airport to the town's military installation, we saw a few men in turbans, driving beat-up cars. These were Pashtun tribesmen, who have their own language and customs and are governed by their own tribal laws.

I was more afraid of them than of being stuck on the mountain, as each one we passed on the road gave us cold, icy death stares. We finally made it into the military base, where the tribal elders from nearby villages were brought for us to interview. They didn't seem happy to see us.

Dozens of tribal elders had already been killed for cooperating with the Pakistani military. One of the elders got up and stomped off. He obviously did not like being part of the Pakistani-created road show.

We did the interviews and watched some fairly unimpressive military exercises (the troops seemed to be constantly bumping into one another). Then the general in charge of the base served us goat for lunch. By sundown, we were in the helicopter making our way back to Islamabad, not sure of what we had seen and what it all meant.

Pakistan was trying to sell a story to the U.S. government that it was doing all it could to fight terrorism, in part because the U.S. was supplying them with military equipment and billions of dollars in aid. But the truth that eventually came out was that the Pakistanis were using the United States to fight a phony war against the Taliban.

Sensing I was unconvinced at their sell job, the Pakistani government arranged for me to interview General Parvez Kayani, head of the ISI, who had never been interviewed before. The interview would be a "backgrounder," and he would not appear on-camera for security reasons. Still, I thought I could get something out of him.

I was driven to a small house in an Islamabad suburb. The car made a quick turn into a driveway and we went into a garage. But the garage led into a courtyard of a compound. The first thing I noticed was how pretty and sweet-smelling the flowers were and how very peaceful it seemed. It was hard to believe that this was one of the most secretive and ruthless spy agencies in the world. After they took my cell phone, I was ushered into a small conference room. I knew Kayani was an avid golfer and the president of the Pakistani golf club. I decided to begin the meeting with some golf small talk. I noticed that the fairways on the private golf course were cut perfectly, better than anything I had seen in the United States. I asked how the club was able to create such great conditions.

"We have Afghani refugees cutting the grass by hand. We employ many of them and they do a very good job," he said.

I then asked if he wanted a putting tip and asked to look at his stroke. He told his aide to get him a putter and a ball, which I figured, like most U.S. CEOs, he kept in his office. Sure enough, the putter and ball materialized.

While I was fixing the putting position of the good general's shoulders, an admiral attaché looked on in a sense of complete horror, a look that said, "Who is this journalist from New York, putting his arms around the head of Pakistan's ISI?"

After the golf lesson, we spoke for two hours. Kayani was a total bore. He chain-smoked cigarettes, and every comment he made began with a history lesson dating back to the partition between Pakistan and India.

When I brought up how India had placed six consulates along the Afghanistan border, he got very animated. It was clear he regarded those as a threat. He thought India was setting up a secret front to attack Pakistan from the west. I then asked about whether he regarded the Taliban as an enemy.

"A few years ago, they were our ally, and now, because we receive some memo, we have to regard them as our enemy. In this area, our enemy one day is our friend of tomorrow," Kayani said, signaling that Pakistan continued to have a strong connection to the Taliban.

Pakistan cared only about doing the least amount of fighting possible to continue to receive the billions in aid from the United States. I decided to throw a Hail Mary. I asked if I could have the interrogation tapes of captured 9/11 mastermind Khalid Sheikh Mohammed and three other captured top Al-Qaeda terrorists. "It would show the American people you are serious about fighting this war," I said. He said he would review the matter.

A few days later, I was handed an edited disk. On it were the interrogations, conducted by the ISI, of three of the top Al-Qaeda terrorists, including KSM. There was no sound, except a little audio on the KSM interrogation. The audio was of a man with a Brooklyn accent asking KSM if he was ready to talk. The Pakistanis told me that Al-Qaeda instructed its captured terrorists to try to hold out for forty-eight hours before giving any information. The terrorists know that very few people can withstand constant torture. But forty-eight hours would give the terrorist network time to disperse. The video I received clearly showed two people watching the clock, waiting for the forty-eight hours to go by before KSM would answer questions. By releasing the audio of the CIA agent, the ISI was clearly trying to burn him.

I discovered that Pakistan was indifferent to capturing bin Laden, despite all the money the United States was pouring into the country. They told me that he was hiding somewhere along the Pakistani-Afghan border, even though he was later discovered living in Abbottabad, less than a mile from Pakistan's West Point–style complex.

Shortly before I was to leave Pakistan, a politician with ties to the extremist movement arranged for us to interview "Razi," as he was known, who had ties to Al-Qaeda in Pakistan. He lived at the Red Mosque (Lal Masjid), located not far from the ISI headquarters. The mosque, the center of radical activity in the city, was as famous in Pakistan as St. Patrick's Cathedral is in New York.

Kroft had no interest in interviewing him, as the interview was to be conducted late at night, inside the mosque. I was now beginning to see what all his other producers had experienced—a hardheaded, insecure correspondent who didn't want to give the producer any credit for a good idea.

So I conducted the interview myself. Razi spoke perfect English and blamed all the world's problems on Israel and the Jews. He believed the 9/11 attacks were carried out by the Israelis, a fairly common belief in Pakistan.

After the interview, Razi showed me around. I was lulled into liking him because he spoke English and smiled a lot, but my fixer, an old Pakistani CBS hand, had a worried look on his face. We headed to the back of the mosque, which overlooked an outdoor area with many small two-person tents, where those in the madrassa slept. Others slowly entered the space we were in, surrounding us. The CBS Pakistani fixer began to speak in rapid-fire Urdu to Razi.

I had no idea what they were talking about and was oblivious to any danger. After a minute, the fixer pulled me out of the mosque, and we ran to the car. He was sweating and heaving, almost as if he was about to vomit.

"What happened?" I asked.

"They were discussing whether they should kidnap you and make you another Daniel Pearl [the journalist who was kidnapped in Karachi and beheaded], and I told them that my brother is the police chief in Kohat [a nearby town], and he will track every member of their families down and slaughter them."

In the car I looked at him incredulously. It seemed that threat from my fixer got them to pause long enough for me to escape. I was reckless in thinking I was invulnerable. I mean, why didn't it occur to me that Islamic fundamentalists would want to kidnap an American Jew who decided to come to their madrassa stronghold?

As we drove back to the Marriott, I felt I should be scared, but I wasn't. I was more disappointed that my personal radar, which had protected me throughout my life, was not operating that night. I wanted to wake Kroft up and tell him what happened, but it would make him feel that he made the right decision by not coming. I wasn't going to give him that satisfaction.

Razi would end up being killed a few years later, in a firefight with Pakistani troops inside the mosque. After the siege, a huge weapons cache was discovered in the mosque's basement, including 50,000 rounds of ammunition, antitank weapons, and suicide belts. More than a hundred died in the raid.

I felt lucky and thankful to the CBS fixer, but I was still angry at Kroft for taking a powder on the interview. Before heading home, I had some idle time and decided to get a massage in the hotel. During the rubdown, the masseur started to stray and touch my private parts. "No extra charge," he said, with his hand brushing against my balls.

"No, I am not into this," I said. It was a very tense massage.

Afterward I ran into Kroft in the hotel lobby. I told Kroft he should get a massage from that masseur, but I left out any sordid details. Kroft went off and asked for the same masseur. When his massage was completed, he came to the dinner table at the hotel restaurant, still wearing his bathrobe.

"How was your massage?" I asked.

"That was the best massage I ever had," he said.

Who knows if he got the "special treatment," but I just couldn't help but laugh.

A few days later, I headed home. Before leaving, I ate an early dinner with my ISI handler, who was assigned to watch me throughout my visit. He was an experienced agent and didn't like the job of babysitting me. We talked about cricket and food, subjects he felt comfortable discussing. Then I brought up his surveillance on me.

"Did you listen to my phone calls while I was in Pakistan?" I asked.

"Yes, of course."

"Did you follow me around wherever I went?"

"Yes."

"Did you go into my room and go through my notes?"

He looked genuinely hurt. "My god, I would never do that," he said. "We don't act like that."

When I arrived at the airport, I was told it was about to be closed. It seemed martial law had been declared because of a terrorist threat, and all flights had been canceled except for one just about to depart. I was told the airport could be shut for days or even a week.

I headed straight to the Pakistan Air counter. "When is the next flight out?" I asked.

"There is a flight that has completed loading, but it is impossible for you to make," the ticket agent said.

"Where is it flying to?" I asked.

"Abu Dhabi," she answered.

"Print a boarding pass," I told her after giving her my credit card.

I rushed to the gate with my ticket and was told the flight was closed. I took out the business card I had received from General Parvez Kayani and showed it to the soldier at the gate.

"You do not want to piss this man off by blocking me from boarding that plane," I said.

The soldier looked at the card and quickly let me pass. He never asked me to go through any screening. The plane was held till I boarded. Once I was in Abu Dhabi, I was able to make my way back to New York.

The story we did in Pakistan would be the lead of the next season's premiere of *60 Minutes*. I think Fager liked the news we made—that one of Pakistan's most important generals didn't think it was important or necessary to capture Osama bin Laden.

"Is it that important to find him?" General Safdar Hussain had asked us, in one of the final interviews Kroft did before leaving. "Even if he is taken out tomorrow, his ideology is not going to come to an end. So I don't think that we should be overly concerned about his being dead or alive," the general candidly said.

After our story aired, General Hussain was removed from his post and "retired."

20

TOM BRADY AND KIM KARDASHIAN

A friend who runs a large New York hedge fund asked me to speak to his summer interns. The group of about thirty were all accomplished students from some of the best colleges, and I thought I had a plan for what I would say. But before I started, I asked what they wanted me to speak about. Immediately a young man smiled and asked, "Who have been the most famous people you have done stories on?"

"Tom Brady and Kim Kardashian," I said.

Even my friend who runs the hedge fund was surprised.

I met Tom Brady in 2005, at the New England Patriots stadium. He had just turned thirty, had already won three Super Bowls, and was considered a more popular athlete in Boston than Ted Williams, Larry Bird, or Carl Yastrzemski.

Our meeting took place in the basement of Patriots stadium. Brady is a gym rat, and he had just finished a two-hour workout. Naturally thin, he needed to build muscle and strength to withstand the punishment of playing a contact sport. He was drenched in sweat, as he didn't bother to change into a clean shirt before we met. But it didn't matter as he smiled and extended his hand. After a few pleasantries, he asked me about my job, and I told him about my adventures in Pakistan. At the time, Brady was thinking about going into politics when his football career ended, and he seemed to absorb my recollections and stories like a sponge. I was glad he was interested, as I believe that if you reveal something about yourself, your subject will want to open up about their lives.

Brady rarely gave interviews, except the required appearances at press conferences or on a weekly paid spot on a sports radio show, so his agreeing to do 60 *Minutes* was a big deal.

"I am honored that you would consider me," he said genuinely. He then asked me how he could make this interview special.

"Think of something you had never said or spoken about before. Not jock stuff, but something that shows the public who you are."

He stared at me, eyes wide open, mouth closed, a look of deep concentration on his face. He not only took what I said seriously, he seemed to embrace it into his psyche.

A few months later, we arrived back at the stadium with Steve Kroft. Brady wanted the entire profile shot in one day, so we hired multiple crews to be inside the film room, where we watched tape, the outside stadium, and the locker room, the location for the main sit-down interview.

He wanted us to see him practice with his favorite receiver at the time, Deion Branch, who like Brady was a Super Bowl MVP. The day we were there, Branch had food poisoning.

"Are you sure you want to do this today?" I asked him.

"Yeah, no problem. I just ran six miles anyway."

"Wait, I thought you had food poisoning?" I asked.

"I do. But there will come a game where I am not feeling well, and I want to know that I can get through it. So not feeling well is an opportunity to practice for the game when I am not in the best of shape," Branch said.

Brady listened and nodded. Branch and Brady had developed a look where they both know the pass pattern without having to say anything. That way, Brady could change the play at the line of scrimmage, seconds before the ball was snapped.

If a receiver ran the wrong route, Brady would shut them out and not throw to them for the rest of a game. "If the pattern was a ten-yard out and he ran nine yards, we don't complete the pass. It is not his fault for the wrong route, it is my fault for throwing the ball to him, so I won't," he said.

Brady seemed to have it all, but he was a reluctant star and tended not to go out much in Boston, where he would get pestered for autographs, even when gassing up his car.

"I will go out if I have the energy to put on a happy face, but sometimes I don't feel like that," Brady said. "You can't have one without the other. You can't have the football fame and not the other stuff."

In spite of his success on the field and his fame off it, he was not content or feeling fulfilled. Brady had thought long and hard about what he was going to reveal, and he didn't disappoint.

"Why do I have three Super Bowl rings and think there is something greater out there for me? Maybe a lot of people would say, 'Hey, this is what it is, I reach my goal, my dreams.' Me, I think there has got to be more than this."

"What's the answer?" Kroft asked.

"I wish I knew," came the quick reply. "I love being the quarterback for this team, but there are a lot of other parts about me that I am trying to find."

All this took place before his marriage to Brazilian supermodel Gisele Bündchen. Brady decided to open himself up, to show vulnerability. Brady's answer was honest, raw, and unpredictable—so honest that Kroft didn't want to put it into the piece.

"I don't believe him. His looks, money and fame, what is he searching for?" Kroft said.

"I have no reason not to believe him. A lot of people who have reached the top are not content or happy. You are a senior correspondent on *60 Minutes*. Are you happy and content?" I asked.

Kroft didn't answer but got the point, so the Brady quote stayed in the story.

I wanted my son Max to meet him, so I brought Max to a game

in Foxborough, Massachusetts. Unfortunately, the Patriots lost, and I thought Brady would be in a foul mood. Instead, after the game, he pulled Max, who was sixteen at the time, aside and told him that he should learn from me, as I was doing important work. He remembered my Pakistan segment, and said Max should be proud that I had the courage to do those types of stories.

"Having self-confidence is very important when you are starting out," Brady said. "Let me tell you an important lesson I learned in life. If you don't believe in yourself, then why is anyone else going to believe in you?" My son was both awed by him and appreciative of the advice.

After the story ran, Brady sent me a handwritten thank-you note. Most story subjects don't even call afterward, but Brady was raised right. "You did a great job and I have had so many compliments since," he wrote. "You have a great admirer (me!) and a huge new fan."

As for his comments about his search for meaning, after the story aired, Brady said he was sent dozens of Bibles and people offering him a path to Christ. Instead, Brady got married, had three children, and embraced a strict diet and exercise regime. I was not surprised when he left the Patriots to join the Tampa Bay Buccaneers. Brady has always been interested in new challenges; that's why he turned down the chance to do a second *60 Minutes* profile. He was also being treated by Coach Bill Belichick like he was still a rookie. Tom is considered the greatest quarterback of all time, and after fifteen years and winning six Super Bowls he resented Belichick's treatment. He wanted a new beginning, to see football life from a different perspective. Tom has always been about new experiences and new challenges, no matter how successful the old experiences were. I won't be surprised if after he retires from football, he runs his own production house and goes into acting.

I then spoke to the interns about the story I did that included Kim Kardashian; and the art of making $500 million with no apparent talent.

I told the group that my other son worked at a large consulting firm that hired a social influencer, with a few million followers, to tweet about a product that they were contracted to advertise. The influencer was flown to the location of the Super Bowl, got free tickets to the game, was invited to the best parties, and received $250,000 for three days' work.

"What talent does this person have?" I asked.

"None," my son answered.

"Then why so much money?"

"Because he has a lot of followers."

"But he doesn't do anything?"

"Doesn't matter," my son says. "He posts a lot, and people follow him."

It's the insanity of our times that the biggest social influencers are barely out of high school. Advertising agencies are falling over themselves for these people to post on Instagram or Facebook about products that they know nothing about. Some of the influencers have larger followings than most popular movies or TV shows, and they make millions of dollars wearing or using products in their posted pictures or videos.

They have figured out how to monetize the act of living—a worldwide popularity contest conducted minute by minute.

We focused on Logan Paul, whose short slapstick comedy skits are viewed by over 20 million subscribers who are attracted to his boyish charm and slapstick humor.

"I speak the language of millennials, and they respond to my content," he said, not immodestly.

His low-budget, low-quality postings, shot with a cell phone camera, earned him more than $5 million a year. Not bad for a twenty-four-year-old.

But $5 million a year is chump change for a popular social influencer like Kim Kardashian. She agreed to appear in our story, but her sisters refused, as they didn't think *60 Minutes,* with its older audience, would help expand their brands.

Kim is married to rapper Kanye West, and at the time, they were living in a five-bedroom house that was modest by superstar standards, in Bel Air. It was her temporary home while she waited for a $60 million mansion she was building to be completed. Outside the house was a white McLaren sports car, while inside, the house was also completely white, with only a few pieces of furniture, also all white. She had two housekeepers who were making fresh baby food for her two children.

Our cameras were set up outside by the pool as Kim got ready. She had a team of hair stylists and makeup specialists who took about two hours to fix her up. When she emerged, she looked simply perfect.

She is much shorter in person than I expected, and I wondered if she would be a diva. Kardashian had attracted more than 160 million followers on social media platforms by exposing her life and body in intimate detail, and I was interested in why those millions wanted to follow her.

"We've been talking to a number of young influencers," our correspondent Bill Whitaker asked. "Many of them have different talents. They do comedy, they dance, they sing. What's your talent?"

"It is a talent to have a brand that's really successful off of getting people to like you for you," Kim replied.

"You've turned you into an empire worth in excess of $100 million, I've read."

Kim was waiting for that. It is so much better to have other people cite your success numbers. She smiled, batted her eyelashes, and said, "So I would think that has to involve some kind of talent, you know?"

After the interview ended, she wanted to stay and talk, but she was pulled away by her agent and producer. I felt there was a sadness about her. Like Brady, she has fame and money but seemed to be searching for something more. She said that most people aren't made for this lifestyle of being so public and recognized. She certainly enjoys the money but has mixed feelings about the fame. It also seemed that she and her husband, Kanye, were leading separate lives.

A few months after the interview, Kim was robbed at gunpoint in Paris, tied up, and locked in the bathroom. The robbers dressed as cops and stole $7 million in jewelry. Our interview, which aired after the robbery, would make international headlines as her first comments on her lifestyle.

I worried whether including Kardashian in a *60 Minutes* story would tick off our core viewers, and it did. One viewer wrote: "I am shocked you did a story on this trash. . . . You were the one company who had a shred of dignity left in this world . . . not anymore." Another viewer wrote that they want to live on another planet because we interviewed her, while another said Kim's being on *60 Minutes* was "a sign of the apocalypse."

Still, our boss Fager loved it and asked us to add more from her interview. For me, the story was an indulgence, a chance to mix with people outside my comfort zone. She was certainly nice and spent quite a while taking pictures with us, but like Brady, she was searching for something more meaningful in her life than being a social media queen. Kim would later find it by taking law classes and helping to free the wrongfully convicted from prison—a cause we both had in common.

21

INNOCENT MAN

There have been nearly four hundred people in the United States that have been exonerated after being wrongfully convicted, including twenty-one who have served time on death row. My friend Barry Scheck, who cofounded the Innocence Project, which has helped exonerate them through the use of DNA testing, began to investigate how they got in prison in the first place. The trail led to the FBI Crime Laboratory, which provides key forensic analysis support to local and state law enforcement agencies, free of charge. But it turned out the lab was using discredited forensic tools that contributed to hundreds of convictions. The FBI never notified the defendants' lawyers or the courts that their cases may have been affected by this junk science. Remarkably, the science the FBI lab and their experts used to gain convictions in courtrooms throughout the country had been in use for forty years.

This was a big story, and I wanted to collaborate with another journalism organization that would help to expand its reach. So Fager and I traveled to Washington and met with Len Downie, who succeeded Ben Bradlee as executive editor of *The Washington Post*, and pitched him the idea. It wasn't a hard sell. Downie jumped at it and assigned one of his most prolific reporters, John Solomon, to join our story.

It was the perfect addition, as John had already done reporting on the FBI lab screw-ups and had a lot of sources he brought with him.

The FBI lab claimed to be able to match bullets in ammunition boxes to a bullet fired from a murder weapon. But then we questioned Dwight Adams, the former head of the FBI lab, and read to him cases in which his agents testified.

"*Commonwealth v. Daye*: 'Two bullet fragments found in Patricia Paglia's body came from the same box of ammunition.' Another case, *Mordenti v. State* in Florida: 'It's my opinion that all those bullets came from the same box of ammunition.' Are those testimonies supported by the science?" Kroft asked.

"The science never supported such a statement," Adams replied.

"But this was testimony that was given by people in the lab for thirty years," Kroft said.

"The science does not support that. This kind of testimony was misleading and inappropriate in criminal trials," Adams answered.

In the world of *60 Minutes*, this was a home run interview: the subject caved and admitted that our story's thesis was correct. We already had a great potential segment, but I decided to see if we could make it a classic.

Lee Wayne Hunt had been convicted of murdering two people based on the junk science and the testimony of an associate who received immunity.

His codefendant at the trial was Jerry Cashwell, who admitted to his attorney, Staples Hughes, that he alone committed the murders. Lee Wayne Hunt wasn't even there, he said. But because of attorney-client privilege, lawyer Hughes was duty-bound to keep the secret—a secret he kept for more than twenty years.

It wasn't until Cashwell committed suicide that Hughes felt free to discuss what his client told him. I went to Chapel Hill to see if Hughes would go on-camera.

He had a Vandyke beard and spoke in a clear, serious southern voice, but one that seemed burdened by the secret he was holding.

I started the conversation by asking him about where the best barbecue was, but Hughes was not into small talk and I moved on.

"I met Lee Wayne Hunt in prison a few days ago. He insisted to
me that he is innocent and didn't commit those murders," I said.

"He didn't," Hughes said.

"How do you know?"

"Because my client confessed to me that he alone did them. Hunt
wasn't even there."

"Would you say this on-camera?"

"It would be violating the attorney-client privilege and I could be
disciplined for going on-camera to discuss that," Hughes said.

I leaned across the table, my body bent toward Hughes, then in a
low voice said, "If I was in front of a jury, what position would I rather
defend—keeping quiet and causing an innocent man to spend the rest
of his life in jail for a crime he didn't commit? Or speaking out and
defending your decision to rectify a miscarriage of justice?"

Hughes thought for a moment. "I will do it."

When he spoke to Kroft on-camera, the pain of his secret was
etched on his face. He remembered vividly when Cashwell told him
what happened the night of the murder: "It was sort of one of those
moments that stops you completely still. You know my client is saying,
not only did I kill two people, but these folks didn't have anything to
do with it. The state's case is a lie, a fabrication."

But he didn't try to get Cashwell, his client, to tell the truth at the
time, as he was himself facing the death penalty. Hughes told us there
wasn't anything he could do about it. "But I knew they were trying a
guy who didn't do it.

"I'm not happy to be in this position," Hughes said. "But there is a
guy in prison for something he didn't do."

But to our surprise, instead of being complimented for telling
the truth, Hughes was reported by the judge in the trial to the North
Carolina bar for violating attorney-client privilege.

While the complaint against Hughes was eventually dismissed, the courts and the governor refused to grant Lee Wayne Hunt a new trial. In April 2019 he would die in a prison hospital, having never been freed despite not having committed the crime. After our story, the FBI reviewed the cases in which bullet lead testimony was used to gain convictions and began to inform the defendants.

The story would win the prestigious RFK Award. This is one of the cool awards—only a few are handed out and the trophy is a bust of RFK given to you by Ms. Ethel Kennedy.

I went onstage with Kroft to accept the award from Ethel. After a few smiles and handshakes, Steve began his remarks. I had been warned that he doesn't like to acknowledge the producers' contribution, but I must say I was surprised, disappointed, and a bit hurt to be quickly mentioned between the tape editor and the fact-checker.

As Kroft spoke, I watched as Ethel Kennedy mischievously grabbed his ass. Kroft never flinched. I put my snub aside and was fascinated at the onstage grope by RFK's widow. How could Kroft not feel her grab?

Later I asked him about it.

"It happens to me all the time," he said dismissively. I was speechless.

After the ceremonies we went out and celebrated. Kroft kept the Kennedy bust award close to him, and even though we were flying to Israel the next day, he insisted on taking the award, which weighed fifteen pounds, on the plane. He wasn't going to let me anywhere near it, even though I would get my statue delivered a month later.

I was excited about the trip to Israel and the story about Ashraf Marwan, who has been called the greatest spy of the twentieth century. It was a tale worthy of a John le Carré novel, involving war, deception, and murder. The question that still perplexes intelligence experts to this day is, which country was he really working for—Israel or Egypt?

Marwan was the son-in-law of former Egyptian president Gamal Abdel Nasser, who was an iconic figure in the Arab world for modernizing Egypt and taking on the Israelis in two wars. To the Israelis' amazement, in 1968 the twenty-four-year-old Marwan contacted Israeli

intelligence in London and offered to provide his country's most important secrets, in exchange for large sums of money.

Marwan spent five years stealing documents from the Egyptian
defense ministry and handing them to the Israelis at secret rendezvous
in London hotels. He demanded and was paid upward of $100,000 ev-
ery time he made a delivery, money he used to support his rich London
lifestyle of gambling and women.

According to the Israelis, aside from money, Marwan's motivation
to be a turncoat was his deep hatred of the Soviet Union, then Egypt's
major ally and chief arms supplier.

Zvi Zamir was head of the Mossad at the time and supervised the
Marwan operation, the agent he code-named "The Angel." When I met
Zamir in Tel Aviv in 2009, he was in his mid-eighties but was still quite
sharp. Zamir was at Munich when the Israeli Olympic athletes were
killed by terrorists from the Black September group, and would later
lead the Israeli assassination response, nicknamed the Wrath of God,
against terrorists and their sympathizers that was the basis of the Steven Spielberg movie *Munich*.

Zamir said Marwan's information "was pure gold. It was a bo-
nanza, a masterpiece of information." Inside the Mossad there is an
entire room of documents supplied by Marwan.

Zamir said they repeatedly tested Marwan and he never lied. But
the Mossad is a very proud organization, which might explain why it
will never publicly acknowledge that Marwan might have gotten the
better of them.

In 1973, the armies of Egypt and Syria were poised to launch a
surprise attack against Israel on Yom Kippur, the holiest day of the Jewish
year.

Marwan provided Israel with a twelve-hour warning of war at
a late-night meeting in London with Zamir, telling him that the war
would happen on two fronts and start at sundown, six P.M. But the attack took place at two P.M., which provided the Egyptians with enough
time to cross the Suez Canal with minimum loss of troops.

A top Egyptian intelligence officer told us Marwan acted as a double agent, supplying years of intelligence to the Israelis to set them up for the big moment where the Egyptians would trick them.

"How do you deceive one of the best intelligence agencies in the world? You must give them real information so they believe your ultimate deception," he said.

"We believed, with the Israelis fully mobilized and prepared, we'd lose 25,000 troops in the crossing of the Suez Canal. In order to save the army, Marwan gave us several hours before the Israelis started to mobilize. And that was enough to cross the Suez Canal with minimum casualties. And that made all the difference."

His warning did provide the Israelis with enough time to marshal their troops and save the Golan Heights, which were attacked by Syria. But the Sinai was a different story. The Egyptians were able to break through the Israeli defenses and take back part of the Sinai they had lost six years earlier in the 1967 war. That land grab by the Egyptians gave them enough leverage to work out, at Camp David, a historic peace treaty with the Israelis that has maintained the stability between the two countries for more than forty years.

In June 2007, Marwan fell or was thrown from the balcony of his fifth-floor apartment in the fashionable St. James's district in London, not far from Buckingham Palace. His death was initially ruled a suicide, but then Scotland Yard began to investigate it as a murder. The Israelis were convinced the Egyptians killed him when they discovered he was a spy for Israel.

After I left Israel, I traveled to Marwan's London apartment, where I met his oldest son, Gamal Marwan, a good-looking Egyptian media executive. Gamal said that two dark-skinned men were seen on the balcony before his father's plunge, and the memoir his father had been working on disappeared. He believed the Israelis murdered his father when they discovered he may have been a double agent working for the Egyptians. After weeks of cajoling, Marwan agreed to go on-camera for his first interview. His perspective would make the story a true international spy mystery and balance out all the interviews we did in Israel. But then Kroft almost blew the interview before it began.

As the cameramen got ready in the apartment where Ashraf Marwan was murdered, Steve sat a few feet from Gamal. He didn't bother to strike up a conversation with him, instead he was busy texting, trying to decide where to eat dinner that night with a friend. Gamal sat nervously, staring at Kroft in disbelief at his rudeness. I finally told him to put his phone away. Kroft gave me a hateful stare. I never understood why he had to act like a jerk to a producer who was trying to make him look good, but he seemed fueled by a deadly mix of narcissism and self-destruction.

"If I met him before I met you, I would never have done the interview," Marwan told me later.

"I wouldn't have either," I replied.

In the end, who was Marwan working for? Strangely he is considered a hero in both Egypt and Israel, considered by these former enemies to be their best spy ever. After months of investigating the story, I believe he set out to sell secrets to the Israelis and then his spy activities were eventually discovered by the Egyptians. Anwar Sadat, who succeeded Nasser as Egyptian president, concluded Marwan would be more useful as a double agent, rather than having a public trial which would end in Marwan's execution. So Sadat told Marwan to continue to supply Israel with information to gain their trust until the start of the Yom Kippur war. Marwan's deception allowed the Egyptians to cross the Suez and seize critical land in the Sinai. Militarily the war ended in a stalemate but in practical terms it changed the map and the politics of the Middle East and eventually led to the peace treaty at Camp David between the former enemies, Egypt and Israel.

After his death, his body was returned to Egypt for a hero's burial, and more than 100,000 people were in the funeral procession in Cairo, including the then–Egyptian president Hosni Mubarak's son, Gamal Mubarak, and the head cleric of Egypt. Ironically, I think if he had been buried in Israel, he might have received the same turnout.

22

THE CLINTONS

By the end of 2007, it was clear that the two early favorites for the Democratic nomination for president were going to be Barack Obama and Hillary Clinton. Fager wanted to profile both candidates and assigned Hillary Clinton to Katie Couric and asked me to produce the story. After Kroft, I looked at working with Couric as a welcome break.

Couric arrived at CBS in 2006 to anchor the *CBS Evening News* and to contribute stories to *60 Minutes*. Even though the public sees her as cute and perky, I had heard that Katie had a reputation in our shop for blaming producers if her stories didn't work out.

In one of her first segments for *60 Minutes,* Katie profiled tennis pro Andre Agassi. He was releasing his memoir, in which he wrote that he hated playing tennis "with a dark and secret passion" because of the constant pressure to win. But the real bombshell was his admission that he used crystal meth to deal with the stress. After the revelation, one tour player suggested that Agassi should surrender all the titles he won. But Couric, despite her producer's request, refused to even ask the tennis star about his drug use as she considered it to be "tabloidy." But the story was not going away, and Fager was not about to put it on without Agassi being asked about it. CBS then chartered a plane for Couric and her producer to return to Las Vegas, where Agassi lived, and ask him about his drug use.

Couric later blamed the producer, Harry Radliffe, who was CBS's first African-American bureau chief and one of the show's best producers, for not pushing her to ask the drug questions and after the segment aired, accused him falsely of using a reverse shot that showed some of her bra strap.

Shortly after she arrived at CBS, I asked Couric if she would record a few lines for a video I was producing for my daughter's bat mitzvah. I was told very directly by her assistant that Katie doesn't do that and wouldn't. I ended up having Mike Wallace record the lines.

But compared to the insecure and self-destructive behavior of Kroft, I welcomed the opportunity to work with her on an important interview. Besides, Katie had done some very noble work raising millions to fight colon cancer, after her first husband died from the disease. I wanted her to succeed.

The Obama and Clinton stories would appear on the same show, but team Obama had a clear advantage. Obama's campaign gave the *60 Minutes* producers almost unlimited access behind the scenes, even to watch primary returns from inside his hotel room. The Clinton staff would provide only the bare minimum to get their airtime—one main interview and a shorter one inside a Virginia classroom after a rally, and a short opportunity for some secondary video.

I met with Patti Doyle and Cheryl Mills, who were running the campaign, and they were unusually confrontational, accusing me of setting Ms. Clinton up for a hatchet piece. Mills, who defended President Bill Clinton in his 1999 impeachment trial, treated our meeting like it was a hostile deposition. I had never met Mills before and wasn't sure why she was on a war footing.

I explained that beside the interviews, we needed access and openness, which would help humanize the candidate. They were very reluctant to give any access, probably because they felt it would detract from her message.

In fact, I like Hillary Clinton. To those who get to know her privately, she can be very warm and caring, and she's whip smart. Unfortunately, because of so many hit stories done by the press against the Clintons, she and her team do not trust the media and treat most media as the enemy.

A couple of days before the main interview in a Virginia hotel room, we were permitted to shoot some secondary video at the Clintons' Chappaqua home. She was doing two-way remotes with local affiliates, each a couple of minutes long. The local hits are the preferred interviews, as Clinton's comments are broadcast live and in their entirety, leaving little room for follow-up questions. It is like providing the campaign with a free commercial.

My "holding room" at the Clinton compound was Bill Clinton's exercise studio, which contained some aerobic equipment and free weights (the pull weights were set at 35 pounds). The walls were lined with signed golf balls and pictures of him golfing with PGA pros and politicians.

When she was ready to do the two-ways, I was brought out and told specifically where to stand by Jay Carson, her aggressive press rep. I was instructed that I was not allowed to talk to the candidate. He acted like a prison guard and I was angry, first being put in a room with barbells, then being told I couldn't speak. Of course I was going to say something.

After Hillary completed her two-way remotes, I made a little small talk with her about the New York Giants, who that year were having an amazing football season, but then, sensing that her aide Huma Abedin was trying to get Hillary out of the room, I moved on to business.

"As we speak, we have another team with correspondent Steve Kroft with Obama, and they have been given extraordinary access to behind the scenes with the candidate, including going into his hotel room to watch returns come in during the last primary," I said. "Both these segments will run on the same night. And the access I am getting from your campaign pales in comparison.

"Here is one idea—my daughter's favorite show on TV is MTV's *Cribs,* which goes behind the scenes in people's homes. If we can have you show us around the house, we could have fun with it."

She gave me an icy stare, as if I had suggested she take her clothes off. "Talk to my staff about that," she said dismissively. Then she shook my hand and left.

Carson started yelling at me. "How dare you speak to the candidate about this? You need to leave right now," he ordered.

"What are you talking about? We just got here. We were told we could film around and get some pictures with both Clintons."

"No, you went around me after I turned you down," Carson said. "You are vermin."

"Because I asked to videotape her in her home?"

"I deal with the press every day and you are like the flesh-eating virus in the movies," Carson said.

Things were now getting completely out of hand. We had not even done the interview yet and we were already on the outs with the Clinton team. I was beginning to understand why parts of the press hate them.

The next few days were tense, as they wanted to cancel the interview. I said, "We have to stop having the Clinton team push us around." Hillary has always said that she has been misperceived, but judging by her staff's interaction with me, I think maybe the perceptions were correct. But Couric wanted the story, and communications director Howard Wolfson helped restore order, and we moved forward.

We agreed to do the interview with Clinton in Virginia, where she was campaigning. Fager came down and collaborated on the questions. When Couric arrived, it was clear she had her own questions and barely looked at ours. Instead, she wanted the interview to be softer, to get Clinton to laugh and smile. This was a clear diss at Fager, as they didn't like each other.

The two of them had an uneasy relationship that began almost as soon as Couric arrived, but it went completely off the rails when she went to CBS CEO Les Moonves to complain that 60 Minutes wasn't doing enough for her. Moonves told her he was not going to get involved and she should talk to Fager directly. Her complaint occurred within days after she interviewed hero pilot Chesley Sullenberger, in what became an elaborate two-part *60 Minutes* story. When Fager asked her why she went around his back to Moonves, she denied she did. He said he was incredulous at what he regarded as her bald-faced lie.

To his credit, Fager put aside his dislike of her and came down to help. He wanted a strong and serious interview, as Clinton was in the middle of a hotly contested primary fight against Obama. But Couric had a different idea. She wanted the interview to be soft.

"How do you do it? . . . I'm talking about pure stamina," Couric asked Clinton.

"Pure stamina. I have a lot of stamina and a lot of resilience," Clinton said. "I take vitamins. I drink tea, not coffee anymore. I have really stopped drinking diet drinks because I found they gave you a jolt, but they weren't good over the long run. I used to drink a lot of them. I drink a ton of water. . . . My two secrets to staying healthy: Wash your hands all the time. And if you can't, use Purell or one of the sanitizers. And the other is hot peppers. I eat a lot of hot peppers."

The interview went downhill from there. By the third question her staff realized this was going to be a puff piece, relaxed, and turned their attention to their Blackberry devices. During the breaks, Fager quietly stewed and tried his best to toughen up some of the questions. I kept thinking, *For this, they are paying Katie $15 million a year?*

After the interview, we went to a local Virginia high school where Clinton was speaking, to get some more shots and then head for the airport. There, in a small classroom, came Couric's big question. She asked if Clinton's nickname in high school had been Miss Frigidaire.

"Only with some boys," Clinton said, laughing.

On the shuttle flight back, Katie went up and down the aisle with a little minicamera, filming passengers for a webcast that she was producing. She was asking random people who they were and why they were going to New York. She was having a lot of fun filming. "This is the real me," she said, talking about her webcast, which had an audience only in the thousands.

"This is the future," she said. "CBS doesn't get it."

Over the next day or two, I put the story together with practically no input from Couric. The segment was scheduled for that Sunday. After a rough first screening—Fager wanted it to be a harder interview and wanted less of Couric smiling and trying to act cute—I stayed up all night and added whatever hard questions I could from the interview. The Saturday before air, about ten of us gathered in the screening room. Couric was not in a happy mood, as she liked the first cut, which had more of her smiles and soft questions. But Fager liked this cut; he requested only a small change and wanted the studio that opens the segment to be tweaked.

"I had nothing to do with the studio, Ira wrote it," she quickly blurted out in the screening room. I couldn't believe how quickly she played the blame game over something that could be fixed in a minute. There was a hush in the room except for one person, gasping.

"My, my, we are in high school now," Bob Anderson, who was helping to produce the story, said. Everyone laughed, except for Couric, but the joke helped break the tension and we finished the story. After it aired, I got no thank-you from Couric. I didn't need it. I was thankful I survived the process.

Couric never figured *60 Minutes* out, and her battles with Fager led to her being gradually phased out of the show. One of her surrogates told *The New York Times* that she didn't succeed at *60 Minutes* because she "never learned the secret handshake there."

The truth was that she was lazy and disengaged, and thought she was smarter than all of us who worked on the show. She wasn't.

23

HILLARY 2016

I am sometimes asked if there was ever an important story I wanted to do and didn't, and it happened when Hillary Clinton ran for president in 2016 as the Democratic nominee.

Since leaving the White House, the Clintons had managed to make nearly $250 million, and questions were being asked as to how they did it.

A researcher and author, Peter Schweizer, discovered that the Clintons had accepted large speaking fees from foreign governments and donors at a time when the State Department was considering whether to award contracts or special aid to those affiliated with the donors.

Peter had worked at the right-leaning Hoover Institution at Stanford and had accepted major funds from the conservative billionaires, the Mercers, which, in many reporters' minds, made his research suspect. But buried in his work, all carefully footnoted, were leads to potentially great stories.

One involved two speeches Bill Clinton gave in 2011 in Nigeria. The African country was ranked number three on the world list of worst human rights violators. That same year, more than two hundred people were killed and about forty thousand displaced after the Nigerian elections, which saw Goodluck Jonathan emerge as president. And the UN headquarters in Abuja, Nigeria, were blown up by a massive car bomb that killed twenty-one.

Jonathan needed to buy some legitimacy, and who better than Bill Clinton to supply it. Clinton flew in on a private jet supplied by a rich benefactor and was paid $700,000 for a speech and pictures with Goodluck Jonathan, which served to prop him up as a legitimate in front of the world.

After the Clinton speech, the State Department, run by Hillary Clinton, released discretionary funds to Nigeria that should have been withheld until the country reformed its human rights policies and combated the terrorist group Boko Haram, who claimed responsibility for the UN bombing.

The next year, Bill Clinton returned to Nigeria, again on a private jet, and delivered another speech for another $700,000. This time he awarded teachers, selected as the best in the country, individual checks for their work. But while Clinton collected his speaking fee, the teacher checks ended up bouncing. Clinton took his money and left, leaving no speech money behind, in a country where 70 percent of the citizens are living on less than a dollar a day.

In addition, the Clinton Foundation was receiving millions of dollars in donations from Nigerian billionaire Gilbert Chagoury. The former top corruption prosecutor of Nigeria alleged that Chagoury steered millions in illicit oil revenues into bank accounts in Switzerland and other countries. He would end up repaying $300 million of his own profits in exchange for legal immunity. As part of the deal, his conviction would later be expunged. There were other examples of Chagoury's ties to corruption in Nigeria. One would think that Chagoury's apparent complicity in the looting of Nigeria would deter a former U.S. president from doing business with him. Instead Bill Clinton embraced him, invited him to his sixtieth birthday party, and described him as a "close friend."

But these were the Clintons, and I knew that their staff and surrogates would try to muscle and bully any journalist who challenged them. I needed to partner with another journalism institution. I called

Jo Becker, a Pulitzer Prize–winning *New York Times* reporter, to see if she was interested in a collaboration. She loved the idea. Becker and I made a presentation to editors at the *Times* on how we would do the story and investigate some of Schweizer's findings. The one stipulation was that somewhere in our stories, we needed to mention Schweizer's name.

The *Times* managing editor and head of investigations had no problem with the arrangement, nor did Jeff Fager. But when the *Times* editor Dean Baquet heard about crediting Schweizer, he balked. When Baquet pulled out of the deal, so did Fager. I went to see him, and it was clear he didn't want to go against the Clintons without the *Times*. Fager has a death stare that warns you if you say one more word, you die. The signal was clear: we are not going to do this story. He said Kroft didn't want to do it, but it was clear Kroft didn't want to go against Fager.

I was angry that I didn't fight harder, but without the *Times* and Kroft's backing, I felt that I was in a weak position. After WikiLeaks published the Podesta emails from inside the Clinton campaign, we learned that the Clinton team was worried about our story, and rather than deal with the allegations, they planned to raise problems *60 Minutes* had in its reporting on the Benghazi story that resulted in correspondent Lara Logan being suspended. Logan was duped by a book author who falsely raised questions about the Obama administration's response to the attack on the U.S. diplomatic compound in Libya.

While we sat on the sidelines, *The Washington Post* and *The Wall Street Journal* worked with Schweizer on more Clinton revelations. Becker would later do a story that originated in Schweizer's book. Baquet finally relented and Schweizer's name was included in that article, but at *60 Minutes,* we did nothing.

24

MAFIA BOSS JOHN GOTTI JR.

There has always been a misguided romanticism about gangsters and the mob culture. The public and media see gangsters as rebels that flaunt the rules of society and live by their own code. I had that view until I saw their handiwork on the streets of Detroit, after Hoffa's disappearance—bodies discovered in car trunks, back alleys, or swamps in varying states of decay. The movie *The Godfather* emphasized their family loyalty, but the real mafia is built on a web of lies, murder, and treacheries.

Getting a mobster to spill the beans is rare, unless they become cooperators (rats), and only then do they give the public a peek at a hidden world. Certainly I was encouraged to pursue these characters by Wallace and Hewitt, who believed the public was fascinated by the secret society.

In the 1980s, I profiled former mafia godfather Joe Bonanno and his son Bill, retired gangsters living in Tucson, Arizona. The Bonannos consider themselves "men of honor" because they did not make money dealing drugs. They chose to make it the "honorable" ways—bootlegging, controlling unions, illegal gambling, loan-sharking, and providing protection to businesses that didn't know they needed it.

But the Bonanno story was done in 1985, and now twenty years later,

a new, more charismatic, and more violent gangster had emerged—
John Gotti Jr.

For two decades, the name Gotti has been synonymous with organized crime in America. Gotti was the most famous gangster of our
generation, getting more tabloid headlines than any movie star.

According to the FBI, John J. Gotti and later his son John Jr., aka
Junior, ran the Gambino crime family, the largest, most influential mob
family in the country. Gotti senior was a ruthless gangster who craved
celebrity.

Gotti made the mafia look glamorous because he looked glamorous. His suits and ties were custom-made, earning him the nickname
of "Dapper Don." He rose to power by ordering the murder of his boss
Paul Castellano, who was shot in front of Sparks Steak House in Manhattan by gunmen wearing fur hats. Gotti very much enjoyed the life of
a gangster. As Steve Kroft said, "He wanted everyone to know what he
did, as long as they couldn't prove it."

His son John Jr. says he didn't want the mafia life but felt he couldn't
refuse his father's wishes to succeed him when he went to prison. He
would end up serving as boss of the crime family longer than his father.
But he was, in his own words, a reluctant don.

John was very different from his father. He would show up with
cupcakes at parent-teacher conferences. He coached his kids' sports
teams. And when he was in prison, he would insist on having a weekly
conference call with his children's teachers. He even collaborated on a
children's book with his prison cellmate.

Junior's reluctance to enter into his father's life, and his later desire
to break away from it, made his story a much more interesting one than
that of a gangster who tells how he whacked someone. So, through a
lawyer friend, I set up a meeting with John at his home in Syosset, Long
Island, where he lived with his wife and five children. He had pleaded
guilty in 1998 to racketeering, loan-sharking, and gambling charges
and believed that after serving over six years in prison, three and a half
of those spent in solitary confinement, he could start a new life.

He was a master storyteller, a talent he learned from hanging out at the Bergin Hunt and Fish Club, a mafia social club located in Ozone Park, Queens. There, the Gotti crew would gather each day to play cards, cook, tell stories, "break balls"—Gotti's words—and have a good time. Telling a good story is part of the price of admission.

He remembered what his father told him. "That either you end up dead or in jail. There is no other choice." But John wanted to watch his children grow up and he wanted to quit the life.

He said that when he told his fellow gangsters he wanted out, they told him, "Don't let the door hit you on the way out."

But his father had a very different reaction. At that time Gotti was in prison, so Junior went to tell his father that he wanted "closure."

His father didn't understand the word. "That's a word that overeducated motherfuckers use."

But John did quit; he took a plea and went to prison for five years. When he was released, he thought his slate was clean with the government, and he could start a new life. But he was wrong. The feds came after him all over again.

He would stand trial four times in five years. Some seventeen assistant U.S. attorneys and a hundred cooperating witnesses would testify against him. If a prosecutor could convict a Gotti, it would no doubt lead to a lucrative job in the private sector.

In 2006, I went to the federal courthouse in lower Manhattan to continue to report the story. The courtroom was alive with spectators jumping up and down waving their fists. There were Gotti's enemies, like the head of the Guardian Angels, Curtis Sliwa, whispering curses as John entered the courtroom. Sliwa said Gotti tried to have him killed after Curtis criticized Gotti's dad on his radio show. Then there were Gotti's supporters, those who came over to give him two kisses on each cheek. Gotti returned the kisses with no smile.

"Are you doing okay?" he would ask each one of them. "Let me know if you need anything."

It was a strange offer for a man locked up in the basement of the U.S. federal courthouse in lower Manhattan. Standing next to Gotti was his overweight attorney Charlie Carnesi, who wore a suit that was too tight and spoke with a New York growl.

"Hey, how you doin'?" he said to me, motioning me over.

Gotti gave me a kiss on my cheeks. "How you doin'?" he asked.

"Forget how *I* am doing, how are *you* doing?" I said.

"We are going to beat this. Otherwise I fire my attorneys," he said within earshot of them. Carnesi ignored the remark, emptying the papers from his briefcase on the courtroom table.

When his associates saw Gotti kissing me, they started giving me kisses, too. My cheeks became so wet, I had to bring a handkerchief to court.

The case against Gotti resulted in another hung jury, and soon I was invited to dinners with John and his attorneys around New York and Long Island—talking, kibitzing, telling stories, and simply having a good time.

I went from being a reporter, in Gotti's mind, to being a friend.

But despite the trust I had built up with him, John still wasn't ready to commit to going on our show.

The chase to get Gotti on-camera would go on for four years. I would often drop what I was doing and drive out to Long Island for an Italian dinner with John and his attorneys. Other times, I would call to tell him a joke or gossip. I didn't want him to dread my calls, but welcome them, a chance to unburden himself and vent.

Just when I thought he agreed to go on *60 Minutes,* the feds indicted him again. I would have to wait till after that trial was over for him to even consider an interview.

Meanwhile his sister Victoria, who was the star of her own reality TV show, *Growing Up Gotti,* was telling John he should make money on the interview. Since we don't pay for interviews, that was a nonstarter. John realized that no reputable outfit would give him enough money to make it worthwhile, so he rejected Victoria's suggestion.

But during the years I pursued the interview with John, it seemed new roadblocks always appeared. One time he told me he was ready and I had booked camera crews. But the *New York Post* put John, dressed in a rat outfit, on the cover, with the headline that he was a rat and was snitching, which wasn't true. Still, John felt he had to cancel the interview again.

A few months after the *Post* story, we went to dinner at Saggio's, a small Italian restaurant in Syosset, Long Island, with his two attorneys, Charles Carnesi and a lawyer I knew at the time only as Tony. John started the dinner saying he wanted to do the interview but wasn't sure of the timing, as he was writing a book. I was ready for that. I told him we would run one story now and rerun the story at the time of the publication of his book, if it happened within a year. He accepted that.

We talked about subject areas we would cover in the interview, and I even brought up the Kennedy assassination, a subject John didn't want to discuss on the show. Bill Bonanno had written a book in which he claimed that Chicago mobster Johnny Roselli was one of the shooters in the Kennedy assassination.

"Johnny had bad eyesight. He could never make that shot,'" Gotti said. "Dellacroce [the old-time Gambino underboss, who was active in the mob in 1963] told me that it was a couple of Corsican hit men who came over and did the work. And they were later taken care of. Giancana [a Chicago mob boss] and Roselli were also taken out, Dellacroce told us," Gotti said.

This was typical of the type of banter that went on at the social club. I didn't necessarily believe it, but it became part of mafia inside lore and certainly was interesting dinner conversation.

We traded a few more stories, and at one point during the conversation, John talked about his family, telling me about each one of his kids. Tony the lawyer said only one word during dinner—*flounder,* which is what he ordered. Mostly he was just staring at me, trying to figure me out. At the end of the night John and I said our goodbyes, with a kiss on the cheek. After John left, Tony came over to me in the parking lot and said, "You're in."

"What are you talking about?" I asked.

"He will do the interview."

"John didn't say anything," I replied.

"John doesn't talk about his family unless he is comfortable with you. When he began to talk about his family, I knew he had agreed. When do you want to do this?" Tony said.

It was as simple as that. We scheduled the interview for the following week.

I had been writing questions for two years and gathering reading material for Kroft. I explained he needed to get to the house early so Gotti could get comfortable with him. I also was worried that Gotti would again change his mind.

But I never expected what would happen. Kroft overslept. All he had to do was get into his limo and arrive one hour later. It is a show of disrespect to come late to a meeting with a former mob head. The last person to come late to a meeting with John's dad ended up dead. During that half hour we waited for Kroft to arrive, Gotti was getting calls from his family and former associates, telling him not to do the interview; it could get him killed, they warned.

He told them he was committed and was going ahead with it. While we waited for Kroft, Gotti became more skeptical that the interview would produce much interest in his book he was still writing.

I told Gotti that tennis player Andre Agassi, who had appeared on *60 Minutes,* had received a $6 million book advance.

"Why so much? He never did any drive-by shootings," Gotti jokingly said.

"Yeah, but he hated tennis," I said.

"I hated the mob. That has to be worth at least three mil," John replied. Thankfully, Kroft finally arrived. Gotti teased him about being late and asked if his car had run out of gas. Kroft, as usual in his own world, ignored the comment and talked about how he had set the alarm clock for the wrong time. This was not starting well.

Gotti brought with him three lawyers, including his criminal lawyer, Charlie Carnesi; Tony, who had ordered the flounder; and another attorney who represented John in civil matters. John wanted Carnesi to sit next to him during the interview.

For the past few years, John had been thinking about what he would say in the interview, and he didn't disappoint. He spoke about how his father loved being a gangster, as he loved "the code, the action, and the chase." But his dad hated money.

"He used to say if a guy was saving money or putting money away, and he was a street guy, he would say, 'What's on his mind? What has he got planned? You know, at the end of the day, we're all going to jail. What's he gonna do with that money?'" Gotti said.

"Is that the way he looked at life?" Kroft asked.

"He felt that anybody who really truly lived in the streets, not the fringe players, not the frauds, not the pretenders, if you really, truly lived it like John did, at the end of the day, you gotta die or go to jail. That's the rules."

Gotti tried to walk a fine line between acknowledging his involvement in the mafia and not going into details about how he ran it. But he did say that when he became a made man in La Cosa Nostra, it was the proudest day in his father's life because, he said chillingly, "I was slowly becoming like him."

One subject that was taboo was asking him if he had ever killed anyone, as there is no statute of limitations on murder. Kroft still asked, and John said, "According to the federal government, who didn't I kill?" But then he pivoted, to explain why his father may have carried out killings.

GOTTI: I don't know if you can ever justify murder. I don't know if you can justify it. But I can make—I can make some type of an argument. You want to hear it?

KROFT: Sure.

GOTTI: John was a part of the streets. He swore that that was his life. He swore, "I'm gonna live and die by the rules of the streets. The code of the streets." And everybody that John's accused of killing or may have killed or wanted to kill or tried to kill was a part of that same street. That was a part of the same world, same code. And my father has always said, in his mind, "You break rules, you end up in a dumpster. If I break rules," meaning himself, "they're gonna put two in my hat and put me in a dumpster. That's the way it works." So, am I justifying it? No, I'm explaining it.

KROFT: And you were comfortable living in that world?

GOTTI: When you don't know much else, yeah. Yeah, I guess so. I guess so. When you don't know much else, I guess so.

KROFT: Did you ever worry about getting whacked?

GOTTI: Every day. Every day. That's a possibility. It's a possibility that something could happen to you every day of your life. And you know something, when you hang out in the streets you're hanging with a different type of a person. You know, you don't know what's gonna happen. You know, you can be with—Tony's here today, then Tony's doing ten years tomorrow. Billy's here today, and then you never see him again. Who knows? Anything's possible. It's a volatile existence.

The story would run in April 2010 following the Masters Tournament. Kroft would later tell Fager that it was the best interview he had ever done. Over 15 million viewers watched the broadcast that night, one of the highest rated shows of the year. The segment was twenty-six minutes, double the length of most stories, and we would later make it into a full hour.

I received calls from FBI agents and from Justice Department prosecutors, who told me that they loved the story. Even then–New York City police commissioner Ray Kelly said he found Gotti "charming and entertaining."

John began to receive a number of creative offers. One Broadway producer wanted him to do a one-man show.

"I don't want people to know where I am every night,'" Gotti told me, in rejecting the offer. Then Sly Stallone flew Gotti to Hollywood and offered him a small amount of money for the rights to his life story. Gotti rejected the offer as "an insult." Eventually he would agree to sell the rights for $500,000, with John Travolta signing up to play his father.

A few months after the segment aired, John invited me to his home to celebrate his son's graduation from high school. The backyard barbecue was lavishly catered by a friend who owned a local restaurant.

"If you want something that's not out here, Sal will go to the kitchen and cook it. If you want extra garlic or something in a dish, he will put it in," Gotti said.

I told John he looked particularly good.

"When I was in prison, I didn't want veal Parmesan sandwiches. I wanted my lawyers to bring me black powder to color my hair. That way, the feds could see they weren't getting to me," Gotti said.

He opened an expensive bottle of Opus One wine. "When I went to jail, I told my wife she needed to do three things. One, take care of the children. Two, take care of my wine. Three, take care of my cigars. She got one out of three," Gotti said.

"I had one of the finest wine collections around, but they turned to vinegar. The wine cellar where the wine was stored was like a sauna, all of them were ruined. My cigars, she put tap water into the humidors, instead of distilled water—ruined the cigars, and I had some nice Partagás ones, too."

John was having a good time. He called to the bartender and gave him a bottle of Boodles Gin. "Now we can start the party," the bartender said.

"Listen to me, no kids drink," John said, dead serious, as if he were talking to someone who owed him money. "I am going to be watching you. No hard stuff. When I am not watching you, I will have Joe watch you."

Joe was not your typical babysitter. He was allegedly a former mafia hitman. I didn't see any of the teenagers with a hard drink in hand.

While John relaxed at his house, he told the story of an Amtrak train trip he took with his father to Florida. This was not your typical train ride.

"I went up to the conductor and gave him five one-hundred-dollar bills. I said, 'Listen, my father is a degenerate gambler and needs to know the scores of the baseball games. I want you to announce them over the loudspeaker.'

"Amtrak never saw anything like it. We are pulling into Wilmington, Delaware, and over the speaker you hear, 'This is Wilmington, Delaware . . . Yankees 3, Detroit 2. Baltimore 4, Chicago 1 . . .' Each stop the conductor announces the scores.

"When we got to Florida, we ate a nice meal at Pete's in Boca Raton, and then my father wanted to go to a nightclub. We called the boys who took care of the arrangement. When we pulled up to this very fancy nightclub, it was like the parting of the Red Sea. My father was led past everyone and given a special roped-off area to sit, with bouncers guarding it.

"The problem was none of the girls at the nightclub could get near him. Suddenly, a napkin hit my dad in the face. I looked around, ready for a fight. I picked up the napkin and it said *Jill*, with a phone number, *I will do anything for you*. With the word *anything* underlined a few times. Suddenly it started raining napkins with phone numbers. Since we were roped off, the girls couldn't get near my dad, so they went to the upper balcony and were throwing their numbers at us.

"My father said, 'Let them have fun, it's okay.' Meanwhile the boys are on the floor picking up all the napkins and phone numbers and stuffing them in their pockets."

After four trials that all ended in hung juries, the feds gave up their pursuit of Gotti. But the feds were trying to "bait" him to commit a violation. John Alite, the main federal witness against Gotti in his last trial, a man whom Gotti despised, was freed from witness protection and returned to the neighborhood where Gotti lives.

During our interview, Gotti described Alite as a "garbage pail" who was chased out of the neighborhood because he was a degenerate drug dealer. During the trial he said that he had an affair with Gotti's sister Victoria, which she vehemently denied. Now Alite had returned and went to a Long Island deli. Inside was Victoria Gotti.

"I hear the tuna fish is good," Alite said as he sneaked up behind her. She reached for her keys and attacked him, while the deli owner, who was a friend of the family, jumped from behind the counter and began to go after him. Alite fled the deli, got into his car, and drove off. Victoria noticed that right behind Alite was a car with two men following, whom she said looked like FBI agents.

John Gotti understood this new phase of the game. "The FBI wants me to go after Alite and are putting him out like bait. If I throw a punch, I hit a federal witness, and go away to prison."

Gotti said that in the old days, if a member of the mob would be seen even talking to an FBI agent, he would be slaughtered. "We used to be the wolves. Today we are the sheep. And I don't know if I can be a sheep."

Gotti's movie was made. John Travolta played Gotti's father, and Kevin Connolly, of the TV show *Entourage,* directed. I brought my daughter to watch one scene shot in front of Sparks Steak House. It was the shooting of former mafia boss Paul Castellano, whom the elder Gotti succeeded as head of the crime family. The actor who played Castellano was a Jewish character actor from Brooklyn. "I am going to get shot about twenty times tonight," he said.

In fact, the movie had a lot of killings. Gotti would complain and ask why there was so much murder. I told him that's what his dad did.

"They exaggerated it," he said. "You watch this movie, you think all we did was whack people."

Gotti always worried that someone would, in his words, "put two in my hat and throw me in a Dumpster." Though he never admitted or has ever been charged with killing anyone, I did ask Gotti one night at dinner how other gangsters would go about it. He said, "Okay, hypothetically, right? Give me the circumstances."

"A restaurant."

"You never want to exit a place the same way you came into the place," he said. "The restaurant must have two ways to get out."

"How about a car?"

"Cars are easy. You want a car behind the car that you are going to do the deed. That car slows down the traffic. When the deed is done, the car behind then moves forward and lets all the traffic flood the zone. That way, everyone can escape."

Strangely, I found myself increasingly liking and trusting John. He was brilliant at describing the world he had once been part of. If he wanted to, he could have taught a course at any college of criminal justice.

Instead, John began to investigate the witness protection program, created to protect cooperating defendants who testify against criminals. More than 18,000 have participated in the program since its creation in 1971. What Gotti had discovered was that after the former criminals are relocated with new identities and clean records, where their criminal past is hidden from their new neighbors, they can keep their ill-gotten gains. And in some of those cases, they continue their life of crime.

Gotti put together a book and documentary series that would expose this so-called Witsec mafia. He was going to be the producer, and I think he was planning to be the correspondent.

"One of those in Witsec is right now running a pizzeria three miles as the crow flies from where we are sitting," he said one day at lunch in Astoria, Queens.

"'I suppose if you track him down and confront him, he will be happy it's a camera and not a gun, and may even do an interview with you," I jokingly said.

John was visibly angry at the injustice in the fact that snitches, co-operators, rats—some who have committed multiple murders—escape with little punishment. "In the old days, they wouldn't have survived sundown," Gotti said.

And you could tell, at that moment, he missed the old days.

25

"FRINGE PLAYERS, FRAUDS, AND PRETENDERS"

"Fringe players, frauds, and pretenders" are Gotti's words to describe some of the characters he met on the streets. But it also turned out to be an apt summary of some of the people I profiled. The best con men are highly entertaining and disarming, usually great storytellers who take a perverse pleasure in bilking their victims. Some con men see themselves as hunters, out for big game—using their smarts and guile to swindle victims who are often too greedy to see they are being conned.

One of the best con men I ever met was Mel Weinberg, con man who conceived and carried out the 1979 Abscam FBI sting operation, which resulted in the conviction of a senator, six congressmen, and other political figures. Weinberg and the FBI agents posed as representatives of wealthy Arab sheikhs who needed a place to invest their money, and one by one, greedy politicians fell into the trap. The FBI videotaped them taking bribes in exchange for special favors. And the congressmen were all too ready to help, with all bribe-taking caught on grainy black-and-white hidden camera videos. It was the most spectacular corruption scandal of its time.

One congressman, John Jenrette Jr. of South Carolina, said, "I got larceny in my blood—I'll take it [the bribe] in a goddamn minute."

Another, Raymond Lederer of Philadelphia, said, "I'm no boy scout" as he accepted a $50,000 payoff.

Weinberg cooperated with the FBI in exchange for all charges that were pending against him as a swindler being dropped. They also paid him $150,000 and allowed him to collaborate on a book with investigative reporter Bob Greene.

Greene was a legendary reporter for *Newsday* and we got friendly when I was a newspaper reporter investigating the disappearance of Jimmy Hoffa. I had been at *60 Minutes* less than a year when Greene told me about Weinberg and asked if I would be interested in doing a story. I didn't have to be asked twice.

For Mike Wallace's interview with Weinberg, I rented a bar on New York's West 72nd Street. Weinberg and Wallace hit it off, mainly because Weinberg was an "honest" con man—he didn't try to deny or sugarcoat his crimes.

"You needed to set a crook to catch a crook," he said. "We put the big honeypot out there and all the flies came to us. You don't think you can go up to a congressman and say I want to bribe you. You have to give them a reason why you want to bribe them . . . and we did."

Weinberg said he couldn't believe they pulled it off.

"If you knew the goof-ups that we had and the way the government tried to run it . . . it was ridiculous," Weinberg says. He recalls that an inexperienced young woman was installed as secretary. "You know how she answered the phone one day?" says Weinberg. "'FBI.'" Even the FBI agent hired to play the sheikh "was a joke" because he couldn't speak a word of Arabic.

To make matters worse, a tape recorder taped to the bottom of a coffee table fell to the floor during one of their first meetings with a target. "I spotted it and kicked it underneath the couch. How we ever got away with it was beyond me," Mel says.

After Abscam, Weinberg says he never worried for his safety. "I'm always careful," he says. "I always made a lot of left turns. If anyone's tailing you, you can always find them by making left turns."

During the interview, Mike asked him, "What do you think

the politicians of this country are really like?" Weinberg didn't hes-
itate. "I personally think they are a bunch of perverts, drunks, and
crooks. . . . .The only guilt I have was that I didn't get the rest of them.
We could have gotten half of Congress."

Weinberg died in 2018 at the age of ninety-three, but not before
he saw the movie *American Hustle,* which was loosely based on the
Abscam scandal, with actor Christian Bale portraying him.

Amazingly, many con men like Weinberg seek out a camera appearance, even if they might not come off so well. Morley Safer once
said, "A crook doesn't feel he's really made it as a crook until we've told
his story on *60 Minutes.*"

Weinberg set up a sting that exposed others, but most of the time
I was trying to find con men to reveal their own crimes on-camera and
that is much harder to do.

One scam I was investigating had to do with tax refunds. Here's
how it works: someone steals your identity, files a bogus tax return in
your name, and collects a refund from the IRS. It costs the government
billions of dollars a year, and when we came across this scam in 2015,
it had been around for years with the IRS not finding a way to stop it.

South Florida was something like the Silicon Valley for scam artists, who were drawn there by the weather, the beaches, and the opportunity to make lots of money without doing much work.

To bring a story like this to life, you need a con man who has done
the crime, can elaborate on how it's carried out, and how much money
he made doing it.

I had gotten to know Wifredo Ferrer, the U.S. attorney from Miami,
a slim, intense Cuban American who wanted to end this "tsunami of
fraud" as he called it, and agreed to help. Now I had to find the right
con man.

The perfect character is usually a crook who has accepted a plea
but hasn't yet been sentenced. That way, his attorney could say to the
sentencing judge that he has expressed remorse and has even gone on
60 Minutes to educate the public about the scam.

With Ferrer's help, I met Corey Williams, who was awaiting

sentencing for scamming the IRS out of millions. To carry out the tax refund fraud, he would first buy a list of stolen social security numbers, addresses, and dates of birth that are readily available for sale from employees in hospitals or doctors' offices. Then he would go to a tax preparation website, and using the stolen information, fill out a bogus tax return form, claiming a modest refund of a few thousand dollars. Then he would provide the IRS with an address to send the money to or would have it wired to a bank account or prepaid debit card. In seven days, the money would appear. He would fill out fifteen forms a day, and he said it worked 40 percent of the time, making about $45,000 a day. He said "a nation of people" were in on the scam, and he even set up what he said were franchises that taught others how to rip off the IRS.

Another scam we exposed involved con men who filed false insurance claims with Medicare, which has become one of the most profitable crimes in America. Medicare is the government insurance program that provides healthcare to nearly 60 million elderly Americans. But it also provides a steady income for criminals who try to steal part of the half a trillion dollars in benefits paid out each year.

To tell the story of this scam I found another great con man, named Tony, whom we had disguised by a Hollywood makeup artist. Tony told us he would make between $20,000 and $40,000 a day. "Every day, literally. It was 'Wow, I just won the lottery.'"

He ran phony medical supply companies, set up in strip malls throughout Florida, that billed Medicare for medical equipment the companies never delivered. He would invoice the government for the most expensive equipment possible, like artificial limbs, electric arms. "A regular patient, you can put them on two artificial legs, and an artificial arm, and they pay for it."

He said all you had to do was fill in some invoices and "in fifteen to thirty days you'll have a direct deposit in your bank account. It's like taking candy from a baby," he said.

As was true with the tax refund scam, there is a whole industry of people who will sell lists of patients, as many as 10,000 at a time. And then a con man like Tony would fill out the patient information and send it in. The government is required by law to pay the claims in thirty days, which doesn't give them much time to catch the scam, a reason we discovered that some of the tiny fly-by-night storefronts collect six times as much money from Medicare as the largest Walgreens in Florida.

Medicare fraud—estimated at the time to cost about $60 billion a year—had become one of the most profitable crimes in America and it exposed our government's inability to manage the medical bureaucracy.

The U.S. attorney in Miami told us that former car thieves and drug traffickers went into Medicare fraud because it was more lucrative and an easier crime to commit. Tony told us that when he operated all he needed was to "have somebody in an office answering the phone, like we're open for business. And wake up in the morning, check your bank account and see how much money you made today."

In the ten years since we did the story not much has changed. The Government Accountability Office estimated that in 2020, Medicare fraud was a $50-billion-a-year crime.

26

STEVE KROFT

I'd had a good run of stories with Kroft, but I'd been warned about his demons—not just drinking and smoking to excess, but his disrespectful treatment of producers. It seemed a year didn't go by without Kroft being "one producer short."

While shooting the Marwan story, we visited the Wailing Wall in Jerusalem. I explained to Kroft the tradition of writing a prayer on a piece of paper and placing it in one of the wall's cracks. According to tradition, there is a belief that a divine presence exists at the Wailing Wall, and your prayer request will be heard.

"Give me a piece of paper," he said and then he began to scribble on it. After he finished writing it, he stuffed it into the wall.

"What are you wishing for?" I asked.

"Another producer," he said, then quickly added, "Not to replace you, but in addition to you. Fager promised me three producers and he has only given me two."

"Steve, don't you know someone who is sick, or don't you want prosperity for your son?" I asked. "This is like having a wish from Aladdin's lamp."

"No, I want a third producer," he shot back.

He did get his third producer, but that one didn't last long, as very few producers wanted to work with him full time. Managing Kroft was, at times, more difficult than producing the segment. He would rather risk sabotaging a story than give a producer credit for coming up with a good idea. So producers had to find ways to manipulate him.

We were in Las Vegas doing a story on an internet poker cheating scandal. Steve was interviewing Greg Raymer, at the time the World Series of Poker champ. The cameras were being set up and Kroft sat next to Raymer, saying nothing. Raymer tried to strike up a conversation and Kroft wasn't interested. Any other journalist who didn't even know much about poker would have engaged Raymer in a conversation on how he won the tournament. Not Steve. Instead he noticed an attractive female card player at a nearby poker table. He left Raymer and told me to shoot him watching her play.

Afterward, Kroft wanted me to get her contact information. But I wasn't going to do that. Instead I went up to her, to make it seem that I was doing what he asked, but all I did was introduce myself and wish her good luck in the tournament.

Kroft was waiting for me. "What did she say?"

"She is a stripper at night," I said, making up a story. "And she likes you."

Steve was very happy. He didn't want to do a stand-up when the shoot began, but the idea of his new friend watching him perform suddenly got him excited.

"I will do that stand-up, if you want," he said.

Despite all his craziness, Steve and I were doing stories that were leading the broadcast, and I admired his ability to tell complicated stories and write them well. After all, that is what the job is mostly about. Maybe the most significant story we did together was an investigation into insider trading in Congress.

In 2012, it had been legal for senators and congressmen to trade stocks based on information that they had acquired in their congressional duties. Much of this information is proprietary, learned in congressional meetings or in classified briefings. Working with Hoover

Institution writer Peter Schweizer, we put together a list of senators and congressmen who had been active stock traders while key legislation was winding its way through Congress.

In the case of House Speaker Nancy Pelosi, she and her husband had participated in at least eight initial public offerings, IPOs. One of those came in 2008 when she accepted and participated in a large IPO for Visa at the same time major credit card legislation was making its way through the House. The Pelosis purchased 5,000 shares of Visa at the initial price of $44. Two days later it was trading at $64. The credit card legislation never made it to the House floor. Pelosi wouldn't sit for an interview, her press secretary Drew Hammill saying she was too busy, but he suggested Kroft attend her weekly press conference.

I warned him that was not a good idea. "That is the way I want to play it," he said. He guaranteed that Pelosi would call on Kroft. For his part, Kroft was concerned that he would be embarrassed publicly in front of the entire Washington press corps and we would get scooped on our story.

"Steve, don't worry about being scooped. This press corps is so milquetoast that they couldn't figure out what we were up to even if we xeroxed our story and distributed it," I said.

When we got to the press conference, Steve took a seat in the front row. I sat behind him. I kept jabbing his ribs to raise his hand. Pelosi was down to her final two questions. Finally he lifted his hand and she pointed to him.

For the next two minutes, Kroft peppered her with questions. He asked if her accepting an IPO from Visa with credit card reform legislation pending was a conflict of interest.

"It's only a conflict of interest if you make it a conflict of interest," was her reply.

Pelosi looked like a deer in the headlights. The other reporters present cleared a path and let Kroft have at it. She kept looking for someone else to call on, but no hands were raised. The more she tried explaining how it was not a conflict of interest, the more it looked like a conflict of interest. She and her husband had made over $100,000 on the IPO in two days.

What was described later as her "near meltdown" went viral, as it was broadcast live on CSPAN. Suddenly everyone on the Hill was interested in our story, though no one tried to scoop us.

Later, we parked ourselves outside the Capitol Building and asked congressmen on the way to vote if they had heard of the STOCK Act, a proposed bill that would have made insider trading in Congress illegal. It had garnered only twelve cosponsors.

No one we interviewed had heard of it.

We discovered that in 2007, Spencer Bachus, who chaired the House Committee on Financial Services, shorted stocks after attending a meeting with Treasury secretary Hank Paulson, who told him that the economy was cratering. Bachus posted his stock trades from his broker account in his congressional disclosure forms. All the trades were time-stamped. Paulson was meticulous in writing down his important meetings and the times they occurred, which he listed in his autobiography. I simply matched up the two documents and showed how Bachus was trading on the information he learned behind closed doors.

The story landed like a bomb in Washington and outraged and embarrassed the federal legislators who participated in it, and caused regret in those who assumed it was illegal, who had never benefited from the practice.

Nearly every House member supported the dormant bill and two U.S. senators fought over who would introduce similar legislation in the Senate. Within two weeks, 185 congressmen added their names as cosponsors. President Obama mentioned the STOCK Act in the State of the Union Address. Within a few months of that speech and our story, both the U.S. Senate and the House had passed the STOCK Act, which prohibited its members from trading on nonpublic information gathered in the course of their duties. For a do-nothing Congress, they set a record in speed and bipartisanship.

When the president signed the bill into law, I was given a front-row seat to watch the signing. I felt proud that a story I did resulted in such fast action to remedy a major ethical problem in Congress.

A few months later I saw Kroft walking the halls. I asked him what was going on.

"I am going to Washington to pick up an award," he said.

"Congratulations," I said. "What award?"

"For insider trading in Congress."

"Oh, you are going to Washington to pick up my award," I said angrily.

"Well, it is supposed to be a secret that we won," he said.

"Not from me. I produced the story. It is as much my award as yours."

"Well, it is called the Washington correspondents award. It is not the Washington producers award," he said, spitting out his words.

I looked at him with utter shock.

I told Kroft I couldn't go to the ceremony, as I was taking my family to a Yankees game, but that he had to invite the associate producer on the story.

"There may be no seats," Kroft said.

"Well then, you won't go," I said angrily.

Steve found a seat. He ended up accepting the award and thanking several people, only two who had anything to do with the story. One thank-you went to the person who arranged his car that night. That's called "watering down a thank-you" to make the producers' role less important.

As for the insider trading legislation, within six months of its passage, the House rescinded the reporting requirements of the bill by voice vote, and Washington went back to business as usual.

During the coronavirus pandemic, Republican senator Richard Burr of North Carolina dumped millions of dollars' worth of stock after receiving a nonpublic briefing about the coming horror of the coronavirus that was about to hit the United States. While dumping stock, he was actively reassuring the public about all the steps the government was doing to protect the citizenry. Then he told a private group of rich supporters about what was truly to come. At least four other senators also dumped stock after receiving the nonpublic briefings, as did twenty-four House legislators. By the way, Burr was one of only four senators to vote against the original STOCK Act.

The corruption in Congress is one of the many reasons Trump was elected in 2016 on a promise to "drain the Washington swamp." But all that seemed to happen was the corruption got worse.

While Kroft and I were doing groundbreaking work exposing the crooks in Washington, I had reached my limit and didn't want to work with him anymore. But with midterm elections looming, Fager asked if I would do one more story with him on the "broken Senate," which had the lowest public approval ratings in the history of political polling. The Senate was failing to act on many of the critical issues of the day as both parties refused to compromise, causing gridlock and dysfunction.

To research the story, I literally went door to door, showing up in Senate offices unannounced. I told the press secretaries that I worked for *60 Minutes* and was doing a story about the dysfunction of the Senate. After they told their bosses what the request was, nearly every senator made time to speak to me.

I spoke to a complete spectrum of politicos, from the most conservative senators including Richard Shelby to the most liberal ones including Ron Wyden. In all, twenty-two senators said the Senate was broken, and nearly all agreed to go on-camera.

Steve had little interest in shooting the story because it wasn't his idea. But he had to do it, so he wanted to make producing the story as difficult as he could. I felt as if I were in the reality show *Survivor,* as he kept raising ridiculous challenges.

He didn't like any of the senators I offered as interview subjects, so I became desperate.

"How about if I get the two party leaders of the Senate, Senator Mitch McConnell and Harry Reid, to sit together in their first joint interview?"

"You are on," he said.

I think I had just overpromised. McConnell and Reid had served together for twenty-five years and regularly sparred on the Senate floor. But they had never sat together for a TV interview.

I thought about it for a moment and remembered a documentary I saw on Jerry Weintraub, the Hollywood producer, who got actors Matt Damon and George Clooney to do the movie *Ocean's Eleven*.

Weintraub said he first called up Matt Damon and told him Clooney had agreed to do the movie. Then he called Clooney and told him that Damon had agreed.

In fact, neither one of them had agreed. He counted on the fact that they wouldn't call each other to see if it was true. They found out about Weintraub's scam only when they appeared on the set, first day of filming.

So I went to McConnell's staff first. "Reid has agreed to a joint interview," I said. "If the senator won't appear, we will hunt him down like a dog in the hallways while Reid will sit very comfortably in the interview chair." Then I repeated my pitch to majority leader Harry Reid's staff. I believed that neither side would talk to the other and I was right. The tricky part was getting them to agree to an interview time. But McConnell's side ended up being more accommodating.

It was a tense negotiation, but we found a common time.

Kroft then complained that the time wasn't good for him. He was shooting a story in Denver and had to fly to Washington late. When he arrived, his luggage didn't make the flight and would be on a later one. My associate producer volunteered to go to Dulles and wait for it to be delivered. She got Kroft's bag around three in the morning and found a way to get his suit pressed and dropped off in his room at 6:30 A.M.

He grumpily took them from her, wondering why she woke him up and didn't just leave them on the door.

Before the morning interview, Kroft didn't want to go over questions or even meet. He just wanted to be pissed off.

He showed up looking disheveled and was interested only in why there was no makeup person around. He didn't like any of the questions

I prepared, but he seemed not to have any of his own. We had the two Senate leaders for forty-five minutes and Steve decided to wing it. I kept breaking into the interview to instruct Steve to ask one or two essential questions, which he did. But for the most part, these two cagey senators were running out the clock, giving long answers to try to emerge from the experience in one piece.

Reid and McConnell showed up in identical red ties and blue suits. Kroft did come up with a great line to introduce them in the story. "They may wear the same uniforms, but they clearly play for different teams."

We needed more for the story, and two whistleblowing senators who were leaving the Senate, Olympia Snowe and Tom Coburn, agreed to appear.

But Kroft refused to return to Washington and arrogantly insisted the senators come to him. He was flexing his ego muscle. Still, Olympia Snowe reluctantly obliged by driving down from Maine to Boston, where Kroft was shooting another story.

But the bigger challenge was to convince the late Oklahoma Republican senator Tom Coburn to fly to New York. The Senate was in session and Coburn would come up only if there was a guarantee there would be no votes on the Senate floor.

I called majority leader Harry Reid's chief of staff, and I even surprised myself at what I asked. "Kroft is being an asshole and is insisting that Coburn fly to New York instead of doing the interview in Washington," I told him. "Coburn has agreed, but only if your guy can guarantee there won't be any votes on the floor while he is away."

"Are you completely out of your mind? You want us to stop floor votes on the Senate floor so you can do an interview?" he asked.

"Listen, we did an interview with Senator Reid, as you know, and it is terrific. We want to put this on the air soon, but I need the final interview and that's Coburn."

"I'll call you back," he said, still not believing my request.

A short time later he called and said that Senator Scott Brown was debating his challenger, Elizabeth Warren, in Massachusetts and the Democrats wanted that debate to happen, so they wouldn't hold any votes till Senator Brown returned to Washington.

"I can guarantee there won't be any votes till the afternoon," he said.

"Can you tell that to Coburn's chief of staff?"

"Sure," he said, a little annoyed.

Coburn flew to New York and did the interview, and we ended up beginning and ending the story with his comments.

Coburn laid out a devastating indictment of the broken Senate. "The best thing that could happen is that everyone [senators] lose the next election and send someone up here who cares more about the country than their political party or their position in politics.

"We are lucky we are the do-nothing Senate," he said. "We probably saved ten billion dollars on not creating programs that we don't need." After that experience, Coburn gave me a nickname, Pushy, which he used every time he saw me. We later became friends even though our political views were divergent. A week before he died of cancer in April 2020, he texted me: "I love the fact that we could have a relationship that did not depend on just politics. You have my utmost respect."

As for Kroft, the scripting process was as difficult as getting the interviews. When we finally got around to putting the story together, a hurricane was barreling along the East Coast. I live twenty-five miles outside the city, and I took a hotel room for the night.

Steve, who lives less than a mile away, decided he would rather sleep on the couch in his office, telling us he wanted to work through the night on the script.

But when I returned the next day, I discovered he had written only two paragraphs.

We somehow completed the script, and it aired two days before the November election. Old Washington hands like anchor Norah O'Donnell, who had covered Capitol Hill, knew how difficult it was to put the two Senate leaders together and invited Kroft to appear on the CBS This Morning show to discuss the story.

"How did you ever get McConnell and Reid to sit together?" she asked him.

"Well, it was like negotiating the Paris peace talks," Kroft said. He left the impression that he had done it all, with no mention of his producer. I was now done with him, and no prayer at the Wailing Wall would get me back.

When I told Fager, he couldn't have been more accommodating. "Frankly, I can't believe you lasted as long as you did with him," he said.

After I worked out a break from Kroft, I was thrilled to be teamed with Lesley Stahl. She is one of the best interviewers on TV—prepares hard, is focused on what she is after, and believes that the producer is there to help her achieve her goals. She is also a genuinely good person—taking care of her ailing husband and prioritizing time to spend with her grandchildren. Both of us loved doing Washington stories and we wanted to profile one of the most notorious and corrupt lobbyists Washington had ever seen—Jack Abramoff.

Abramoff bilked Native American casino interests out of $85 million in fees and then used the money to supply gifts to congressmen and their staffs in return for votes on legislation and tax breaks favorable to his other clients.

Abramoff's scam was simple but brilliant. At his direction, congressmen added restrictive amendments in legislation making its way through Congress that targeted individual enterprises, like Native American casinos. Then Abramoff approached the aggrieved party—in this case, the Native Americans—and said he could have the amendment lifted. The tribes hired Abramoff for a large fee, part of which went to one congressman as a campaign contribution, and the amendment would disappear. His clients were happy, not knowing they had been scammed.

Abramoff understood that legislators love freebies, so he spent over a million dollars a year on tickets to sporting events and concerts, and even rented two skyboxes at Washington Redskins games. He had two people on his staff who booked tickets full-time for the congressmen;

he even owned a fancy steakhouse so he could provide them with free meals. He also held fundraisers, which gave him "ownership rights" over them. And he was charming and fun to be with. As one congressman later said, "He could sweet-talk a dog off a meat truck."

Abramoff served over three years at a minimum security camp in Cumberland, Maryland, where he passed the time teaching screenwriting to the inmates. His one movie credit was producing *Red Scorpion,* considered one of the worst action movies ever made. But the inmates in Jack's prison loved it and packed his class. Abramoff, an orthodox Jew, instituted a movie night with a heavy emphasis on Jewish movies. And he convinced the prison warden to buy a Torah for the Jewish inmates.

When he was released from prison, he was almost unemployable and was forced to take a job at a kosher pizza parlor in Maryland. Abramoff was an observant Jew and ate only at certain restaurants, never mixing meat with dairy. I found it the height of hypocrisy that while he talked candidly about buying political influence, he was strict about maintaining the laws of kashruth. *Keeping kosher doesn't give you a pass to be a thief,* I thought.

Abramoff wanted the interview to help launch his new occupation as a reformer, a common second career for convicted criminals. After he was caught, Congress instituted some lobbying restrictions. One was that lobbyists can dine with legislators if they stand and don't sit down. Abramoff told us that "you can't take a congressman to lunch for $25 and buy him a hamburger or a steak. But you can take him to a fundraising cocktail party, and not only buy him a steak, but give him $25,000 extra and call it a fundraiser. And you have all the same access and all the same interaction with that congressman. So the people who make the reforms are the people in the system."

A few weeks after the show aired, we went to dinner at a Washington Japanese restaurant that he liked because they store his own set of kosher silverware. He thought the story we did was fair, which I found interesting, as we showed him to be a corrupt, narcissistic conniver.

Abramoff was excited to tell me that he could play golf on Saturday without breaking the Sabbath. I was dumbfounded. Orthodox Jews won't even go into an elevator if they have to push a floor button, but Abramoff figured out a way around these strict religious rules.

He explained: "I drop the clubs off the day before and pay for the round ahead of time. I can carry my own bag, as the course is fenced [which is allowed in Jewish law]. But the tricky part is to play without taking any divots or breaking tees on the drives, since you can't break wood or dig dirt on the Sabbath. So I carry a mat to hit iron shots, and when I use my driver, I build little mounds of sand that serves as the tee and put the ball on top."

He told me that he got a rabbi to sign off on golf on Saturdays. All I could think of was how much Abramoff had to contribute to the local synagogue fundraising drive. Years later, Jared Kushner, the president's son-in-law, got a Sabbath waiver to travel, because his duties were considered essential. Same rabbi?

But now Abramoff may not be playing much Saturday golf. In June 2020 he pleaded guilty to lobbying members of Congress on behalf of the marijuana industry without registering as a lobbyist, and was headed back to jail. So much for his attempt to be a reformer.

After Abramoff, Stahl and I traveled to Italy and France to shoot an old-fashioned investigative comedy—on truffles.

Truffles, the distinct-smelling fungi, grow only at the base of certain trees and only a few months a year, which has made truffles the most expensive food in the world. Black truffles sell for as much as a $1,000 a pound; the white truffles grown in Alba, Italy, can go for more than three times that amount. Stahl at first thought the story was a little soft, but then I told her that the Chinese had discovered that the cheap truffles they used to feed pigs look exactly like French Périgord truffles, but Chinese truffles sell for $20 a pound. Some bright Chinese entrepreneurs then said, "To hell with the pigs, let's sell them to France and feed the French and make a lot of money." The year we did the story, more than fifty tons of those truffles were imported from China into France.

The French then began to sell the Chinese truffles in restaurants and passed them off to tourists as real French truffles, suspecting the tourists wouldn't know the difference. Even to a mildly sophisticated palate, the Chinese truffle tastes like rubber.

Lesley loved the story. We hunted for truffles with dogs in Spoleto, Italy, in the company of Olga Urbani, the owner of Urbani Truffles, the largest seller of truffles in the world. She went truffle hunting with us in a full-length fur coat, sporting a Caribbean tan.

After finding the wild truffles, we ate a magnificent meal with the Urbanis' chef singing "O Sole Mio" and cooking a simple dish of pasta, cream, and black truffles. We then traveled to the world's largest user of truffles, Bruno's restaurant near Nice, France, for another spectacular meal.

Chef Bruno was out of central casting—overweight, secretive, yet flamboyant. He kept two large dogs inside the restaurant and had both his sons working and cooking for his patrons. Visitors throughout Europe would drop by in private helicopters for lunch. The best dish he served was a simple potato with butter and shaved black truffles.

I suppose this is what the other *60 Minutes* producers who don't do investigations enjoy most about the job—going on exotic adventures, eating well, and singing songs. Alas, as delightful as the experience was, I still found a way to make it into an international investigative story.

Bruno revealed that the mafia now controls the truffle trade, and that if anyone was to talk about it, they put their life in danger. He told us this with almost a comic flare, using his forefinger to cut across his neck, to show us that if he spoke too much, he would be killed for revealing the secrets of the truffle trade. After our interview with Bruno, we went to a local truffle market and were able to film the exchange of 40,000 euros for a large bag of truffles.

The transaction occurred quickly, with no receipts. We then confronted a man who was repurposing Chinese truffles and putting them in cans marked "Product of France," which left the impression that they were the expensive Périgord truffles and not a Chinese knock-off. After Lesley berated him for his deceit, the Frenchman yelled at our fixer, calling her a "collaborator" in French, a person lower than scum in the French vocabulary.

Before we screened the story for Fager, he sarcastically said, "So this is the story on mushrooms," as if we were about to waste his time.

"Just watch the story," Lesley instructed.

At the end, he smiled and said, "Now that's a *60 Minutes* story." That was about as high a compliment as you can get. After the story aired, even some of the more competitive producers on the show came by my office and offered compliments, a rarity. When it was posted on YouTube, it garnered more than eight million views.

While I was enjoying the stories that Lesley and I were doing, I watched as Steve's boorish behavior seemed to increase.

It all came to a head in 2014, when it was revealed in the *National Enquirer* that Kroft had carried on a three-year affair with a married female attorney he picked up at the St. Regis bar. He told her that he was trapped in a sexless marriage. He texted her: "Miss you and all that goes with it. Especially my favorite tastes and colors—pink and brown."

He said he was "old and grumpy" and wrote about drinking champagne out of her ass and his desire to "eat her pudding." The *Enquirer* even had a picture of the two of them emerging from a luxury New York hotel, a picture she set up. Clearly, Kroft did something to cause her to be so angry and vindictive that she was willing to wreck her own marriage for revenge.

Soon details emerged that she had asked Kroft to read a book she was writing, and his comment to her was that she should go back to school. That is not something you say to a woman who went to Harvard Law School, and certainly not to a woman you are having an affair with.

After all the tabloid revelations, the only part of the story Kroft denied was that he bragged to her that he was "President Obama's go-to guy." It seemed he was more concerned about his career than his marriage.

Kroft was ready to retire. In fact he said he was looking forward to it. I once asked him what he would do if he retired.

"I'd drink and play golf," he said.

"You do that now," I said.

"I can do more of it," he replied.

"How much more can you do?" I asked.

"You'd be surprised," he answered.

But then correspondent Bob Simon was killed in a livery cab crash, and all those plans for retirement changed.

27

GRUMPY OLD MEN

Fager had taken over the show just as the original correspondents were all at retirement age. It was like taking over a professional sports team with the great stars aging out. *60 Minutes* was sometimes called a "boys' club," with Lesley Stahl the only female full-time correspondent. But a more apt name for it would have been the dinosaur club.

In 2004, when I returned, Andy Rooney was eighty-five. Morley Safer was seventy-three. Bob Simon, Lesley Stahl, and Ed Bradley were all sixty-three. Steve Kroft was fifty-nine.

Fager realized that a *60 Minutes* correspondent job was the top on-air position in network news and protected the core group. In his first years as executive producer he would add only Scott Pelley, the youngster at forty-seven, to the mix.

Ed Bradley had enormous presence and was a producer favorite to work with. Besides having a great voice, he was also a master interviewer. He made over $7 million a year and enjoyed his money. He would discard all his suits every few years and buy a whole new wardrobe. He owned near-courtside seats to New York Knicks games and bought a share in NetJets, which he would use to fly privately to shoots.

He vacationed in Aspen and hung out with gonzo journalist Hunter

Thompson and actor Jack Nicholson. He also liked his women and was a chick magnet, especially when he traveled.

One time he went to one of his producers and told him that he wanted to do a story in San Diego.

"Why San Diego?" the producer asked.

"Because the best blow job I ever received was from this girl in San Francisco. And I asked her where she learned to do that, and she said from her sister in San Diego."

Every producer he worked with had a favorite story. Bradley once agreed to substitute as anchor of the *CBS Evening News* for a week. They told him that he would be on twenty-four-hour call if any news broke. Bradley didn't like that.

"We'll only call you if something really bad happens, like the president is shot," the evening news show producer told him.

The way Bradley told the story, that night at about two in the morning, he was with a woman in bed when the phone rang. . . .

Bradley shot up and said to his female companion, "The president has been shot."

It turned out to be a wrong number. Bradley loved jazz and hosted Jazz at Lincoln Center. He was a regular at the New Orleans Jazz fest and, at times, took the stage when the Neville Brothers or Jimmy Buffett performed. He would bang on a tambourine and sometimes sing the old Billy Ward and the Dominoes song "Sixty Minute Man." Sadly, he would die in 2006 from leukemia. He had been sick for about a year, and toward the end, his voice was almost too weak to record his stories.

Though it was not a surprise, his death still shook the office, leaving us all with incredible sadness. He was probably the most admired correspondent on the floor.

At his funeral, Bill Clinton spoke and Wynton Marsalis played trumpet. I had been back only two years, but I remember the looks on Mike Wallace's and Don Hewitt's faces, as if they had never considered death.

They always said they wanted to die at their desk, though neither one of them would. Andy Rooney, whom Morley said was the longest-serving curmudgeon on television, died in 2011, a month after retiring at ninety-two.

Morley would beat Rooney's mark and die a week after retiring, in 2016. In the final months of his life, Morley would tell all those who visited him that they should retire and spend more time with their families. He even said it to his talented forty-six-year-old producer, Katy Textor. She reminded him how old she was, but Morley still told her to leave and be with her children. Tragically, she would die in 2019 of cancer.

For his part Fager, amidst all these deaths, was keeping the show relevant. But losing the core correspondents was devastating. And maybe the most devastating blow was the death of Bob Simon.

Simon, like Wallace, had suffered from a bout with depression. In 1991, while covering the Iraq War for CBS, he and his camera crew wandered off to look for a road sign that would show that they had entered in Iraq. While in the desert, he was captured by Saddam Hussein's troops. He was held prisoner in an Iraqi jail for forty days, where he was starved and beaten with canes. He emerged from the experience not knowing if he would be okay.

He went into a severe depression but through intense medical treatment was able to emerge from the black state a changed correspondent. He had covered wars in Somalia, Vietnam, and Israel, but now his stories centered around music and animals, often in faraway places. He said that he found covering animals to be a healthier addiction than covering wars.

Not long after Bob was added to 60 Minutes, he made the mistake of criticizing Pelley to Jeff Fager, and as a result, he was put into the doghouse. Fager did not want the place to be run by the correspondents like it was during Hewitt's years, and he wanted everyone to get along. Also Fager had been a huge booster of Scott Pelley and his career.

The relationship between Fager and Simon deteriorated to the point that Fager considered removing him from the show. Only after the intervention of Safer, Stahl, and Kroft was his job saved. They told

Jeff if he fired Simon, it would kill him. Jeff did not want that hanging over his head.

By 2011, Simon had fully emerged from his depression and had rebuilt his relationship with Fager. He was doing extraordinary segments, and would sit in the edit room for hours, carefully reviewing all the tape that was shot before crafting the story. If you were lucky enough to walk past his office while he was there, he was always ready to tell a joke, usually off-color. He didn't care for management, particularly disliking one senior producer whom he called an "apparatchik." He was happiest on the road, finding stories and eating well. He was a brilliant writer and an underappreciated interviewer. He said that if he was to write another book, he would title it *You Should Have Been Here Yesterday,* a common remark he heard when he would cover news events a day after they happened. All the producers wanted to work with him, and the other correspondents wanted to have his talent.

In February of 2015, he left the office to meet a friend for dinner. As he was leaving, he stopped by Steve Kroft's office with a copy of that day's *New York Post.* Kroft had been on the front page of the tabloid for days, for his amorous affair.

"Do you believe in God?" Simon asked Kroft.

Steve didn't have a quick reply. "I'm not sure," he answered.

"Well, you should," Simon said, and tossed him that day's *Post.* On the cover was NBC's Brian Williams and the story of how he'd lied about being shot down in a military helicopter in Iraq. Williams's peccadilloes had bumped Kroft's adultery story off the front page.

They both laughed and Simon walked out. The next day, Simon went to meet a friend for dinner in Chinatown. He entered a livery cab, and within a mile of the office, the cab crashed on the southbound lane of the West Side Highway. The driver was a man with one usable arm and a long record of traffic suspensions. Simon wasn't wearing a seat belt, and after the crash, he was rushed in an ambulance to a hospital, where he was pronounced dead at the age of seventy-three.

There was an utter sense of disbelief at *60 Minutes.* Bradley and Rooney were old or sick, and their deaths were expected. Simon was doing some of his best work and he was accessible and funny in every interaction. And now he was dead.

Kroft wanted to retire. But now the show was one correspondent short, and Fager asked him to stay on to do eight stories a year, which he agreed to do.

Becoming a *60 Minutes* correspondent is one of the most difficult positions to attain, and even though the show was losing legendary correspondents, Fager was very careful whom he placed in that role. He occasionally allowed CBS correspondents to be contributors, almost like an audition, but rarely did they get a permanent assignment. One who desperately wanted the appointment was correspondent Byron Pitts.

Byron had dreamed to become a *60 Minutes* correspondent since he was a teenager, but he had huge stumbling blocks to overcome. He was functionally illiterate until he was twelve and had a pronounced stutter.

But Byron overcame these hardships and graduated from Ohio Wesleyan. Eventually he found himself at CBS News covering the war in Iraq. Fortuitously, he met Julie Chen in Iraq, the wife of then–CBS CEO Les Moonves. He made sure she stayed safe and in good spirits. When they returned to New York, she invited him from time to time to have dinner with her husband.

But the path to *60 Minutes* was still blocked, and Pitts got a job offer at ABC News that he was about to accept. He went to tell Moonves he was leaving. He asked Pitts what would make him stay.

"I would love to work for *60 Minutes*," he said.

Moonves picked up the phone and called Fager. "Don't you think Pitts would make a great addition to the show?" Moonves said.

Fager agreed and said he was thinking of giving Pitts a chance anyway, which was probably not true. Nevertheless, Pitts attained his dream and found himself on the broadcast.

Pitts brought tapes home of Mike Wallace and Ed Bradley stories and studied them. He wanted the job to work out, but Fager was not going to make it easy. He resented the interference in *60 Minutes*

personnel decisions from on high and assigned inexperienced producers to Pitts. His stories were weak, and some of those producers blamed
Pitts.

Pitts told Fager that with a good producer he could show Fager what
he could do. And that's how I was asked to do a story with him. I admired Byron for what he had overcome in his life, and after Ed Bradley's
death, the show was lacking a minority correspondent, and that was a
gaping hole. Byron, after Ed Bradley, was only the second black correspondent on *60 Minutes* in nearly fifty years and that was wrong. I
wanted him to work out.

We did a story on the interrogation practices of the Chicago police
and examined one case where the police forced false confessions out
of black youths who were convicted solely based on those confessions.
Byron confronted the Cook County State's Attorney, who claimed that
the five black youths convicted of the murder were guilty, despite DNA
from a convicted sex offender's being found in the body. The prosecutor
said it was possible the convicted rapist, who had been arrested thirty-
nine times, wandered by after the boys left and engaged in necrophilia,
having sex with a dead person. In his interview Byron destroyed the
prosecutor.

The story was a hit and Byron brought a unique voice and style to
the story. After we screened it, Fager called me into his office.

"You did me no favors," he said. "Byron has been saying he hasn't
succeeded here because we didn't give him any good producers."

"You should have told me to screw up the piece," I said to him
sarcastically.

"Don't be silly. I just need to figure out what to do."

Fager didn't think Pitts was *60 Minutes* material, and he eventually left CBS and became a successful anchor on *Nightline*.

Fager wanted a *60 Minutes* correspondent to have some international
experience, a strong broadcast voice, and the ability to interview, write,
and tell stories in an engaging way. One correspondent who fit that bill
was Anderson Cooper.

When Simon's office was cleared out, Anderson Cooper moved in. Cooper, a regular anchor on CNN, was already a contributor to *60 Minutes,* but now Fager asked him to increase his story count to help make up the segments that the prolific Bob Simon had turned out. Cooper was a workaholic and incredibly efficient. He could juggle multiple CNN hours, *60 Minutes* projects, intense gym workouts, and a social life with his boyfriend, and he did it all with a calmness and positive demeanor.

But unlike Simon, he did not hang out in the offices and wait for producers to come in and schmooze. He is shy and preferred to communicate by email rather than phone.

We did a few stories together. One involved Afghan teens who walked from Afghanistan across Europe to escape prosecution from the Taliban and to search for a better life. It was a 10,000-mile trek, which often brought them to Sweden, one of the few countries that welcomed them in. In Stockholm, Cooper and I enjoyed a relaxed meal and a chance to exchange stories and life experiences. We had both worked at ABC, where his talents weren't valued. He contributed to *20/20* and *World News Tonight,* but his main day job was on a reality show called *The Mole.*

Cooper is openly gay and talked about how there weren't many successful, accomplished gay men he could hang out with. One of them was Tim Cook, the CEO of Apple. He told me about a breakfast he had with Cook during which the CEO noticed that Cooper's iPhone screen was cracked. Cook asked him if he could have his phone and gave it to one of his aides, who was there.

By the time breakfast was over, Cooper's screen was fixed and his phone had additional memory space. A nice friend to have.

Cooper rarely looked at questions while he was doing interviews because he had a photographic memory. He would read them once, then listen to the interview subject and still be able to hit all questions, rarely forgetting any. As famous as he was, there was an air of loneliness around him. He joked about his sharp blue eyes as his "moneymakers," but he was one of the smartest correspondents I had ever worked with. And he usually thanked the producers after the piece aired.

Another new correspondent hire was Bill Whitaker. He was based in Los Angeles and had previously worked for three years in the Tokyo bureau. He was an experienced newsman, and like Cooper, had a calm presence. After a career of crashing last-minute stories for the evening news, Bill wasn't fazed by much of anything.

His father had been a waiter at the Cotton Club in Harlem, at the time an all-white establishment, where Bill said his dad could be an employee, but not a patron. Later, his dad became a ship welder, which provided more money for the family to live on. His example of hard work was ingrained in his son.

Bill moved in next door to me at the office and we became fast friends. He was the newcomer and I was the experienced hand, and he relied on me for advice to navigate the treacherous waters of the show. When he began at *60 Minutes,* he had been saddled with inexperienced producers, and Whitaker didn't protest, as he didn't want to cause trouble. But I told him that unless he caused trouble he wouldn't be taken seriously, and they would continue to take advantage of his friendly persona.

After Whitaker voiced his displeasure about some of the producers he was assigned, Fager asked if I would work and mentor him. Whitaker had been Fager's choice, so Fager wanted him to work out, and I was more than happy to help. Bill was a gentleman, a hard worker, and a fair newsman. He just needed to learn the art form of doing *60 Minutes.*

I passed on what I had learned from Mike Wallace: that he was the CEO of Bill Whitaker enterprises and that the public would get to know him through the stories he chose. It was important to do a cross section of stories—investigations, features, profiles, foreign reporting—in order not to be pigeonholed into one genre and to show the viewers his full range of abilities.

I said that unlike the evening news, when he would hunt for a sound bite, at *60 Minutes* the correspondents try to develop longer conversations with the subject. The way to do this is to know the answers to your questions. Then, you can prepare proper follow-ups, which are key to a successful interview. When it comes to scripting, make your point and move on. The viewers are smart and don't like to be beaten over the head with the same information.

And respect the producers. They are working to make you look good. They are not the enemy. *60 Minutes* is a collaboration, and if the correspondent screws over the producers, they'll find a way to get back at him. If he treats the producers right, they will come to him first with their best stories and help make him shine. And if he does well, he will prosper, survive, and make a lot of money.

All these seem obvious, but I can't tell you how many correspondents never understood the rules of *60 Minutes*. As for Whitaker, he absorbed these tenets like a sponge and soon became an ideal investigative correspondent. He got involved in the intricate facts of a story and was not afraid to confront the bad guys. Soon our stories were getting recognized. The first two we did together won a Sigma Delta Chi and an Emmy for investigative reporting. One involved the H-1B visa program that allowed companies to import cheaper foreign workers to replace qualified and skilled American workers' in high-tech jobs. Another story was on the biggest data leak in Swiss banking history, which we collaborated on with the International Consortium of Investigative Journalists. But our favorite story, which we did in 2015, was called "30 Years on Death Row." It was about Glenn Ford, who was wrongfully convicted and sent to Angola State Prison in Louisiana. There may be no greater miscarriage of justice than to wrongfully convict a person of murder and sentence him to death. But that is exactly what happened to Glenn Ford. He spent nearly thirty years on death row, in solitary confinement, until new evidence revealed he didn't commit the murder.

What made the story unique was the admission by Ford's prosecutor, Marty Stroud, that he railroaded him.

I heard about Stroud through attorney Barry Scheck, who said he had never known a prosecutor who had such remorse over the way he conducted himself during the case. Barry told me Stroud was going to speak at the University of Pennsylvania law school the next day and I canceled plans I had and drove down to Philadelphia.

Stroud sat alone at the back of the auditorium at the Quattrone Center. There were many judges and famous lawyers at the conference, listening to speeches on criminal justice. My first reaction in looking at Stroud was that he was an uninspiring character. He looked depressed and never smiled. I wondered if he even had teeth.

Then it was his turn to speak. He told the roomful of judges and lawyers what he would later tell us on-camera. "I ended up, without anybody's help, putting a man on death row who didn't belong there. I did something that was very, very bad. . . . I was arrogant, narcissistic, caught up in the culture of winning."

He spoke about how he took advantage of Ford's weak and inexperienced lawyers and picked a jury that had no African Americans because he said they would not vote for the death penalty when you had a black defendant and a white victim.

It took the jury less than three hours to find Glenn Ford guilty. Afterward, Stroud and his legal team celebrated sending Ford to death row.

"I had drinks. I slapped people on the back. We sang songs. That was utterly disgusting. You know, you see Mother Justice sometimes as a statue, and she has blindfolds over her eyes. Well, she was crying that night because that wasn't justice. That wasn't justice at all."

Ford would be put into solitary confinement in Angola, the maximum security prison in Louisiana with a reputation for harsh punishment and miserable conditions. Summer temperatures on death row commonly exceeded 104 degrees. He stayed in a five-by-seven cell for twenty-three hours a day, and he remained there for thirty years.

In 2014 new evidence emerged when another inmate told a prison informant that he had committed the murder. Ford was eventually released.

Stroud looked down at his notes and paused, seemingly lost in the story he had just told. Then he spoke: "It was a train to injustice, and I was the engineer. Glenn Ford will be part of me until the day I die."

The room, filled with the toughest group in the legal community, stood and gave him a standing ovation. Stroud didn't smile. He simply accepted a few congratulations and headed offstage.

I introduced myself and asked him if he wanted to get some lunch. He said he was flying back to Louisiana, so I drove him to the airport. In the car I felt the burden of a man weighed down with incredible sadness. He felt being disbarred would be one step in his punishment. The other would be carried out by God. I asked if he would go on-camera and tell his story, as this may be a cautionary tale for other young prosecutors. He agreed. Next, we located Glenn Ford. After thirty years inside Angola, all Ford was given when he was released was a twenty-dollar money card that he used to buy one meal of fried chicken, fries, and tea. He had four dollars left over.

He was living in a group home in New Orleans for released prisoners. After his exoneration, he discovered he had stage 4 lung cancer and had only weeks to live. He had ten grandchildren he'd never get to see grow up. Stroud went to visit him to ask for forgiveness but Ford refused. The utter destruction of his life by a young, ambitious prosecutor could not be easily forgiven.

But as compelling a story as we had, what made it legendary was when Dale Cox, the acting district attorney of Caddo Parish, who got Ford released when he was shown to be innocent, said the justice system worked and no one, including Marty Stroud, did anything wrong.

DALE COX: I don't know what it is he's apologizing for. I think he's wrong in that the system did not fail Mr. Ford.

BILL WHITAKER: How can you say that?

COX: Because he's not on death row. And that's how I can say it.

WHITAKER: Getting out of prison after thirty years is justice?

COX: Well, it's better than dying there and it's better than being executed—

WHITAKER: He could have been killed.

COX: Yes.

COX: If I had gotten this information too late, all of us would've been grieved beyond description. We don't want to do this to people who are not guilty of the crime they're charged with.

According to Louisiana law, Ford was entitled to $330,000, a little over $11,000 for each year of wrongful imprisonment. But the state denied him the money because they believe he knew about the robbery that led to the murder ahead of time and didn't report it.

BILL WHITAKER: That doesn't seem fair.

DALE COX: You want fairness?

WHITAKER: Isn't the law supposed to provide fairness?

COX: It is supposed to provide justice.

WHITAKER: You don't think he deserves compensations?

COX: You're trying to portray the state of Louisiana as some kind of monster. I got him out of jail as quickly as I could. That's what the obligation of the state is.

WHITAKER: What about compassion? Have you no compassion for what Mr. Ford has been through?

COX: I'm not in the compassion business; none of us as prosecutors or defense lawyers are in the compassion business. I think the ministry is in the compassion business. We're in the legal business. So, to suggest that somehow what has happened to Glenn Ford is abhorrent, yes, it's unfair. But it's not illegal. And it's not even immoral. It just doesn't fit your perception of fairness.

WHITAKER: I would say in this case many, many, many people would see this as unfair.

COX: I agree. I can't disagree with that.

Three weeks after we met Ford, he died penniless. His final months, he lived off charity. Donations covered the cost of his funeral. Stroud never got his apology, and he says that the guilt over what he did will stay with him forever.

"I've got a hole in me through which the north wind blows. It's a sense of—coldness, it's a sense of—just disgust. There's just nothing out there that can fill in that hole that says I—it's all right. Well, it's not all right. It's not all right. . . . It was a train to injustice, and I was the engineer. Glenn Ford will be part of me until the day I die."

28

NSA

In the fall of 2013, whistleblower Edward Snowden's revelations of some of the National Security Agency's most secret programs detailed the spying activities being carried out against Americans, including the gathering of millions of phone records. Facing enormous pressure from congressional investigators and the media, the NSA gave *60 Minutes* unprecedented access to its Maryland headquarters and to their employees, who had never spoken to or even met a reporter.

We got into the agency because our correspondent, John Miller, had worked at the Office of the Director of National Intelligence and the FBI. He had the trust of the intelligence community. For the NSA, the risk of letting us into one of the most secret facilities in the United States was enormous, but Snowden had turned the agency into the evil empire, and the NSA brass felt allowing *60 Minutes* to roam its hallways was a risk worth taking. Snowden's leaks raised questions about whether the NSA pried too far into the lives of Americans. One exposed program called Prism targeted the internet communications of terrorists but also had the capability to capture the emails, chats, video, and photos of millions of Americans.

John Miller got the door open, but I knew that this was a once-in-a-lifetime opportunity and I wanted to see how much we could reveal.

Mike Wallace and Don Hewitt. I learned the business from these two masters.
(Photo by Brownie Harris/Corbis via Getty Images)

At Three Mile Island Nuclear Power Plant during the accident in March 1979, while on assignment from *Rolling Stone*.

(Author collection)

Mike Wallace and I share a laugh before an interview with Abscam con man Mel Weinberg.

(Photo by Marianne Barcellona)

Discussing questions to be asked with one of the classiest correspondents in television, Bill Whitaker.

(Photo by Aaron Tomlinson)

Interviewing writer Peter Schweizer for a 2011 report on insider trading in Congress.

(Photo by Aaron Tomlinson)

Bill Bonanno and former Mafia boss Joe Bonanno look over documents at their Tucson home prior to our 1983 interview.

(Author collection)

Relaxing after our interview with John Gotti, Jr., associate producer Joel Bach, and correspondent Steve Kroft.　　　　　　　　(Author collection)

Looking on nervously as Bill Whitaker interviewed Kim Kardashian in 2016 at her Los Angeles home. Some viewers were surprised she would be on the show, but she was gracious and interesting. (Author collection)

Steven Bannon posing in front of a Lincoln portrait hanging in his bedroom.

(Author collection)

My family at Vice President Al Gore's Halloween party in 1994. Tipper and
Al Gore don't look like a happy Frankenstein couple.
(Official White House Photograph)

Vice President Al Gore and I discussing a potential story in his West Wing
office. (Official White House Photograph)

Truffle-hunting in Perugia, Italy, with Olga Urbani and Lesley Stahl. Urbani may be the only person who goes truffle-hunting in a full-length fur coat. Her company controls 70 percent of the world's truffle trade.

(Author collection)

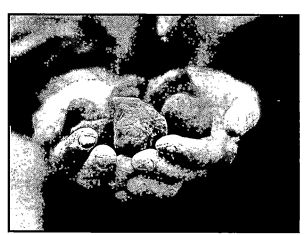

There is a reason it is one of the most expensive foods in the world. This handful of black truffles sells for $1,000.

(Author collection)

With cookbook writer Patricia Wells and associate producer Sydney Trattner in front of Julia Child's stove, which is now located in Wells's home in Provence. (Author collection)

60 Minutes producers' retirement lunch for Don Hewitt in 2004. Of the twenty-two producers here, only seven remain on the show.

(Hewitt Family Archives)

The original staff of *Primetime Live* from 1990.

(Author collection)

At the Robert F. Kennedy award ceremony with Steve Kroft, Ethel Kennedy, Jeff Fager, and associate producer Sumi Aggarwal.

(Robert F. Kennedy Library)

Accepting the Peabody Award for the opioid stories. From left: Bill Whitaker, Sam Hornblower, me, *Washington Post* reporter Lenny Bernstein, Robert Zimet, and *Washington Post* reporter Scott Higham.

(Photo by Matt Doyle/Contour/Getty Images)

Correspondents for a show I created and executive-produced titled *Strange Mysteries*. From left: Chris Connelly, Lisa Rudolph, Shari Belafonte, and Ron Reagan. It was ABC News's first foray into a nontraditional news show.

(Author collection)

Two of my favorite correspondents, Bill Whitaker and Lesley Stahl, at my retirement party. John Gotti, Jr.,delivered an unforgettable toast.

(Author collection)

Our story was going to be controversial, as the left thought the NSA was out of control and invading the privacy of everyone. While the right wanted all the terrorists locked up by any means necessary.

It was strange to deal with NSA press representatives who had never dealt with the press before. Given their druthers, they would have liked to write the story for us, but I explained politely that we would report the story ourselves and write what we believed to be the truth. I wanted to meet as many employees as I could. My purpose was twofold: an opportunity to find some new sources by handing out my business cards to everyone I met, including the cafeteria workers, and also a chance to meet some employees who were not part of the "message" the NSA was trying to put out. That message was that they were not violating the right to privacy of Americans but were protecting the country from its enemies.

It was a rainy, cold day when I arrived at the central headquarters of the NSA in Fort Meade, Maryland. My phone was taken from me and I went through a double screening before being allowed in. I was brought to a small auditorium, where an assemblage of NSA staff waited.

It was clear the thirty people assembled were specially handpicked by the NSA PR department. They certainly were aware of my arrival.

"I really enjoyed your book on baseball stadiums," one NSA intelligence officer said. I was a bit puzzled but smiled and shook his hand. Then another person came up to me and said the same thing. When the third person complimented me on the baseball book I never wrote, I asked that person where he got the information that I had written a book about baseball stadiums.

"I looked it up on the internet," he said.

Later, when I got my phone back, I looked up my name. There was indeed an Ira Rosen who had written a book on baseball stadiums. But even a very casual reader would have discovered that this was not the Ira Rosen who worked for *60 Minutes*. He did not even look like me. If these were our frontline intelligence operatives, I was, so far, not impressed.

I went around the room and asked for each person's name and job title. Some of those present looked like fashion models. They all spoke about the long hours they worked and the importance of their mission, as if they were reading from a script. One woman I hadn't called on seemed to be jumping out of her skin to talk with me.

Before the meeting ended, I called on her. She gave me her name and then added with much enthusiasm, "I am a lesbian." It was such an obvious attempt to spin me that. . . . I shot the PR team a glance, and they quickly broke up the meeting. I was looking for old, tired white men with bad eyesight. They offered employees who looked like they just stepped out of *GQ*. Not a good start.

The NSA headquarters resembles a large office building, with small conference rooms linked to every dozen offices. The most interesting rooms are the ones resembling giant bank vaults, with special codes, badges, and fingerprints needed to gain access. In one room there was a satellite video feed that was being watched by five men. Their eyes were glued to a screen in which a car was being driven down a mountain road somewhere in what looked like Afghanistan. It looked like a scene from the TV show *24*. They then explained what I was seeing.

"This is a Russian ex-military person who is trying to sell a nuclear device to what he believes is a terrorist organization," they said, describing the ghostly figures captured live by a surveillance satellite. The intelligence agencies had infiltrated the operation and were watching the transaction take place in real time. Posing as terrorists, they were waiting for the Russians with what the Russians believed to be millions of dollars. The intelligence agents were able to thwart the purchase.

I was impressed by the number of undercover operations going on at the same time—operatives planting bugs in diplomats' cars, and their high-tech people being able to turn on phones remotely and listen to conversations. U.S. intelligence even got into the nuclear business, selling nuclear hardware to countries like North Korea. The components all had slight defects that would prevent the targeted countries from attaining their goals. It was also a way to keep track of the progress those countries were making in their nuclear program.

We interviewed four-star General Keith Alexander, who ran the agency. He explained that America's phone records should sit in bulk, with the NSA being able to access them on a case-by-case basis. "If you don't have the data someplace, you can't search it. And the phone companies have a different set of records. So by putting all the records together, we can view them essentially at one time." Only a few records from Americans are ever accessed, and each one is cleared through court orders, he added.

We also met the "defense team," NSA staffers who are geared toward preventing infiltration from foreign hackers trying to steal money or manipulate an election. Hacker groups exploit tools that can help them break into a network and steal information. One such tool, called the Black Hole exploit kit, can be purchased for twenty dollars.

But the most interesting news we made came from Richard Ledgett, the deputy director of the NSA, who assessed the damage of the Snowden leak. He told us that Snowden took over 1.7 million documents from the agency, including the information about U.S. capabilities and U.S. gaps in information on targeted countries—Russia, China, and Iran.

He said that if those documents fell into the wrong hands, they would provide a road map of what we know and what we don't know and give the targets a way to protect information from the U.S. intelligence community.

Miller asked, "It sounds like a gold mine?" And Ledgett responded, "It's the key to the kingdom."

The codebreakers work in a separate building on the NSA complex. Before computers could be used to crack secret messages, there were the codebreakers. The NSA was born out of the codebreakers of World War II. And even today, the most secret room, inside the most secret building in the NSA, is called the black chamber. This is where the nation's top codebreakers work. Outside the black chamber is an ordinary-looking file cabinet that can be opened only with a code known by a handful of people. In it is the record of every code America has broken over the last sixty-five years.

Each summer 10,000 high school students apply for a few openings to be codebreakers. They get security clearance and full access to the problems that the NSA couldn't solve. And each summer they solve some of those problems. Chris Inglis, the number two person in charge of the agency at the time, told us that the students bring "a perspective and audacity to the work that they hadn't thought about in all the years of experience that they have brought to bear. We are always pleasantly surprised."

The story came under attack within minutes of its airing. Journalists who had written critically about the NSA thought we were conned by the organization, and we were trashed all over Twitter. The story was called "embarrassing," "a whitewash," and "a puff piece."

It didn't help that in our car ride back to New York, Miller surprised me by saying he had accepted an offer to leave CBS and head the NYPD's counterterrorism office. I felt that whatever criticism would result from Miller accepting a job in intelligence, while reporting on the country's most secret intelligence agency, would be outweighed by the extraordinary access we were given. We disclosed his new appointment at the beginning of our story, but that only gave the critics another talking point to tear us apart.

The most critical high-profile attack came from the *New York Times* media critic David Carr, who said it was a "friendly infomercial" for the NSA. After his article appeared, Carr had the audacity to ask if Miller could help get his son a job in the New York City police department.

While we took our hits, Fager thought the story was perfect and took the team to Campagnola, an East Side Italian restaurant frequented by cops and some gangsters, where he toasted our work.

I never did make it back to the NSA, as the agency would once again shut down media access. But my opinion of the agency shifted. I never saw any invasion of privacy against U.S. citizens that resulted in harm or injury. The Snowden revelations disclosed secret programs to gather personal data, but no one showed me any examples of how it was being used nefariously.

The NSA did fire one worker who would use a satellite to eavesdrop on an ex-girlfriend, but that was all we discovered. Of course, to say that the NSA was doing its job and keeping America safe was not an opinion popular in the media or even in the *60 Minutes* hallways. Our story was important because it didn't embrace the conventional media narrative. Some of my "friends" in the media and even a couple of *60 Minutes* producers stopped talking to me for a while. But that was okay. The story helped people understand a misunderstood agency that was the demon of the moment. I learned a valuable lesson—that you will be punished if you buck the established narrative of mainstream media. But the NSA revelations quickly fell into the background with the election of Donald Trump as president.

29

TRUMP

It seems everyone in New York has a Trump story. The first time I met him, he had just purchased the golf course that I was a member of, Briar Hall Country Club. It was a very modest club that catered to the middle class. It was a fun, short track that made you feel good about your golf game. Trump took it over and immediately began to put sand traps, waterfalls, and lakes everywhere. The waterfall he built, he told people, cost $6 million and was created mainly for promotional pictures of the place.

Oh yes, and he decided to raise the membership fee by over $125,000. After he took over, he golfed there regularly and would often ride in a golf cart with his then-wife Marla Maples. Once my wife and I were about to tee off on the first hole, a short par four. He drove his cart practically onto the tee box and wanted to convince us to become members of the new club. He pointed to the hole we were about to play and said, "I am going to make this hole longer and bigger."

"What is it with you men who think longer and bigger is better?" my wife said.

It was the only time I ever saw him speechless, but it didn't last long. He kept trying to sell us a membership.

After Trump priced me out of that course, I joined Branton Woods, a beautiful course in Dutchess County. I thought I was safe from him. But sure enough, one day he flew his helicopter over the course and ended up buying it. Once again, he made certain holes longer, but he was smart enough to keep the rates the same, as Dutchess County does not have the same rich patrons as Westchester.

He visited the course by helicopter, landing it near the eighteenth green. A golf cart waited to pick him up.

Then he entered the club's restaurant, now with a new wife, Melania, and he gorged on a filet mignon cooked well done. After eating, he played a quick eighteen, speeding through all the members as if he were on a Disney FastPass, and then he'd fly away on his chopper. Melania and their son, Barron, waited inside the clubhouse for hours until he finished golfing.

The members hated that he parked his helicopter near the green, so they started "missing" their shots and hitting it. Trump then stationed a guard to watch the chopper while he played.

After his rounds, he walked around the dining room and asked the members if he should run for president. It was four years before he ran for president, but no one ever thought he was a politician. They viewed him as a nut.

60 Minutes had done a couple of profiles and interviews with Trump in the 1990s, and it never crossed my mind he would now be particularly newsworthy until I got a call from Bo Dietl in 2015 who said Trump was going to run for president. Bo is one of the great characters in the city. He has a thick New York accent and has appeared in a couple of Martin Scorsese movies, including a large speaking part in The Irishman. Bo is a private detective, but I think he is more comfortable being a schmoozer and media celebrity. He frequents the exclusive restaurant Rao's, where he has a regular table, every Thursday.

Dinner with Bo at Rao's is theater and gluttony—sharing the eight-person table with assorted real estate people, Chinese businessmen, hedge fund operators, and of course, their girlfriends. The food comes out in platters of meatballs, lemon chicken, fresh mozzarella, and pasta done three ways, with the dinner ending with plates of cakes and ice cream. Bo generously pays for it all, as he always does, in cash.

So imagine my surprise when he said Trump would run for president and that he was part of Trump's "kitchen cabinet."

"Trump is leaning on me for advice, along with Steve Bannon and Roger Stone, and we have been coaching him on a presidential run," Bo said.

Stone was a leftover from the Richard Nixon dirty tricks group, and even had a tattoo of Nixon on his back. I knew Bannon from the previous story I had done on insider trading in Congress. He was anti-Washington and wanted the political swamp drained of all lobbyists and influence peddlers. Bannon's heroes were Sarah Palin, the former Alaska governor who was John McCain's vice-presidential candidate, and Michele Bachmann, the erstwhile congresswoman and flamethrower. Bannon tended to like feisty and beautiful female politicians. He was also a big fan of the attractive congressional representative from Hawaii, Tulsi Gabbard, who ran for president. Even Bannon's financial support came from an attractive donor, Rebekah Mercer, the conservative billionaire and, at the time, a part owner of Breitbart News, the right-wing website.

Before Trump was a candidate, Bannon was a world-beater—taking on liberals, hanging out with then–Fox News president Roger Ailes, and talking about one day running a media empire. He had done a few documentaries, the most notable one on the coming destruction of the world.

He wore nicely tailored suits and had wildly unkept hair that he would toss back every few minutes as he railed on about the global elites, the rise of nationalism, and how China was "eating our lunch," causing factories and jobs to disappear, while the Chinese smuggled opioids into the United States. He spoke in theatrics and extremes that would turn off most journalists but attracted a fellow bullshitter like Trump.

When Bannon and I would get together, we discussed Washington corruption, a subject that crossed all party lines. His New York visits often involved meeting with Ailes, and I wanted to connect afterward to see if I could pick up any gossip. Bannon always showed up late and talked a mile a minute.

He'd call me dude or brother, never Ira, and encouraged me to do stories about the Washington swamp, while I enlisted his help in trying to get Roger Ailes to sit for a *60 Minutes* profile.

Though Bannon operated the Breitbart news site and had a daily radio show, he was mostly unknown by the mainstream media. It was the end of 2015, and I hadn't seen him for a while, but Bo Dietl's "kitchen cabinet" remark piqued my interest. I called him up to grab a drink. Bannon doesn't drink alcohol, but chain-drinks Coca-Cola, a reason he was thirty pounds overweight. We agreed to meet at the bar at Ted Turner's restaurant. I showed up at the appointed time, but after waiting about half an hour, I left.

Later that night he called and told me he was at the bar. I didn't believe him, but we agreed to get breakfast the next morning.

The next day, I understood why I didn't recognize him. He had long hair, a beard, and an army flak jacket. He looked like a homeless person. I paused when he came over to the table, but I immediately recognized that voice.

"I am going to run the Trump campaign," he said.

I looked at him like he was crazy. There was so much wrong with the scene, I was shocked. Here was this disheveled mess that was telling me he was about to take over a presidential campaign. And it was for Trump, who, like Bannon, had no idea what he was doing.

Bannon was not a political operative but viewed himself as a documentary filmmaker, and his film work brought him in contact with right-winger Andrew Breitbart, founder of the website that bears his name. After Breitbart's sudden death at forty-three, Bannon took the helm at Breitbart News. Under Bannon's stewardship, the website pushed conspiracy theories and a virulently anti-immigration agenda. He had interviewed Trump on his radio show a few times, and liked his anti-government, in-your-face approach to conflict resolution.

The truth, Bannon said, was that Trump really had no core belief except for advancing himself and making money. Trump understood mass market thinking and believed he could destroy any of his opponents by identifying weaknesses in an adversary and creating a two-word moniker to describe them. Bannon said Trump never wanted to be vetted, as it would leave him open to political attacks from his opponents. He told Bannon the vetting report would end up being leaked.

"What are you going to do about the fact that he paid for abortions for girls he had knocked up?" I said, fishing for him to confirm a long-held rumor. "That won't go over well with the Republican conservatives."

"They won't care," Bannon predicted. "With jobs being lost to China, they won't care about what he did twenty years ago."

Within a couple of months of our breakfast, Bannon took over the campaign from Paul Manafort. Over the course of the next year, we exchanged more than a thousand text messages. He trusted me in a way he never trusted any reporter. I acted at times as a therapist-friend, keeping our conversations at the time between us. But all the conversations were on the record, except when he would type *OTR* (off the record) on the text.

The texts revealed a man who was conflicted about Trump. Bannon admired Trump's no-bullshit style, but was troubled that Trump, was not smart, and in his words, "never read a book in his life."

In August 2016, three months before the election, Bannon was running the campaign as chairman from Trump Tower.

"Do you want to get a drink tonight?" I texted.

He responded, "Tomorrow after I shove DJT off to a rally. Trump Tower . . . name will be at security."

When I arrived at the campaign headquarters on a Saturday, it was a hot August day, and there were a few protesters outside. Inside, there was no one at reception, and the headquarters contained large, empty boardrooms left over from the sets of *The Apprentice*. After Trump won the nomination, he raised the rent on his own campaign headquarters, thinking that if he was not going to win, he might as well make some money out of it. There were no "Trump for President" signs on the walls, because, Bannon joked, Trump didn't want to ruin the paint.

Bannon had the corner office. Kellyanne Conway, the campaign manager, was next door. When I arrived, she was talking with Maggie Haberman of *The New York Times,* who would later lead the *Times* Trump coverage. They said they liked Haberman because she once worked at the *New York Post,* Trump's favorite paper.

That day in August, less than three months before the election, Bannon was flying high.

It was Rebekah and Bob Mercer, who were the principal money behind Trump, who suggested that Bannon and Conway be brought in to run the campaign.

Manafort was proving to be a disaster, and once Trump started to tell people he had "low energy," the end was near.

Bannon had to fire the man he was to replace. He went to visit Manafort and to ask him about a story *The New York Times* was about to report, that he had taken $13 million from the Ukraine government.

Bannon went to Manafort's luxury apartment in Trump Tower. When he asked about the money, Manafort's wife, who was lying on the couch, suddenly sat up. As Bannon tells it, when she heard how much money he got, she gave him a look that could kill.

Afterward Bannon told Trump about the meeting. "Who would give him $13 million?" Trump said. "I wouldn't pay him two cents."

Bannon showed me the nerve center of the operation, a room with five televisions on the wall and four staffers who looked like they were waiting to get takeout pizza. "This is where I will run the campaign from," he said. There were more TVs on the wall than people. I asked if he would let me be an embed and document the campaign the way D. A. Pennebaker did in his 1993 documentary, *The War Room,* on the Clinton campaign. Bannon, who saw himself as a filmmaker, readily agreed. "We will debut it at Sundance and Trump will come," he said.

"He will be president. He won't have time," I said.

"Dude, it's about him. He will love it."

In the end, Jared Kushner shot down the idea.

Bannon took over the campaign and ran it while traveling on the Trump plane. "I've been on the plane for two months," he texted. Their campaign strategy, he said, was to sweep through the entire South. "Sherman's march to the sea," he wrote, referencing the North's Civil War general.

While Hillary Clinton was already building her White House staff by having sub-cabinet meetings in Brooklyn a month before the election, Trump barnstormed the country, being directed by astute polling data provided by Cambridge Analytica, a company owned by Bob Mercer.

On the night before the election Trump made a last-minute decision to hustle to Michigan for a midnight rally. There was no planning, only a few emails that announced his surprise rally.

More than 10,000 showed up to hear him promise that Mexico was going to pay for the wall he wanted built along the border. Trump ended up winning the state by a few thousand votes.

Later I asked Bannon for a play-by-play of election night. And he did it, by describing the first meeting, a week after the election, between Obama and Trump in the White House. The media speculated that they talked about Obamacare. In fact, they discussed election night, as seen from two different camps.

Obama said that the "geniuses in Brooklyn" wanted him to campaign only in Pennsylvania and North Carolina.

"Back and forth between those states, I asked what happened to expanding our base?" Obama said. "What about going to Arizona and Utah? I told them I was available the last week before the election. They only used me on the last day. On election night, I kept calling Brooklyn as I watched the returns. I asked, 'What about North Carolina?' They told me, we feel good about it, Raleigh hasn't been counted. Next thing I know, CNN declares North Carolina for Trump.

"Then I called the geniuses in Brooklyn again. I asked about Florida. They said don't worry, Broward hasn't been counted. Next thing I know CNN declares Florida for Trump. Then I stopped calling Brooklyn and they stopped calling me," Obama told Trump.

As for Trump, he said, "Let me tell you what I did. I told my staff, 'We left it all on the battlefield, nothing to be ashamed about.' I went upstairs to my apartment to watch the returns. Then we won Georgia and Florida.

"I came down and asked Jared why the media was saying we were still behind. He said he had just talked to Matt Drudge, who said ignore all the TV media guys. It's all a bunch of psyops. Hillary was not getting the vote out."

Bannon said that they had a team of computer geeks in a windowless room at Trump Tower who were focused on certain key cities like Green Bay and Akron, and when we saw low turnout, we knew we could win. "All the network embeds should be fired," Bannon said. "They were always discounting Trump's big crowds, who waited in line to hear him speak. Trump supporters were going to vote, while Hillary's were indifferent. Sanders could have beaten Trump, but the Democrats rigged it for her. Even when [Deborah] Wasserman [Schultz] was thrown out as head of the Democratic National Committee for working against Sanders, Hillary allowed her back into the campaign. That was noticed by the Sanders people. They didn't get their people out."

After Bannon's appointment as chief strategist and senior adviser to Trump, the second most powerful staff position at the White House, we met for a dinner in New York. At the table was Alex Marlow, who ran Breitbart, and Peter Schweizer, who wrote the book *Clinton Cash*. Peter and Alex brought their wives. Steve joined us late, but he was filled with stories from inside the Trump Tower, which had become the new administration's job center.

Bannon said, "Governor [Nikki] Haley of South Carolina came in looking hot, wore a tight dress, smelled good, and told Trump how she made all these business deals to ensure businesses remain in South

Carolina. Trump got hard. He loved hearing her stories. He offered her a job to be UN ambassador on the spot."

Knowing they needed to add women to the cabinet, they tried to convince Democratic congresswoman Tulsi Gabbard to join the administration. "She is a rising star in the Democratic Party, and we would love to poach her," he said about Gabbard, who would later run for the Democratic nomination for president. They also tried to get Sarah Palin for secretary of interior and Michelle Rhee as secretary of education. Both women would turn down the positions.

He said that Rudy Giuliani was in the running to take over State, but Rex Tillerson of ExxonMobil was coming in. "He knows everyone in the world but may have too many conflicts. He was leaving Exxon to run the Boy Scouts of America, but he could end up taking it." Bannon said that Trump thought Tillerson, with his erect posture and gray hair, looked like a secretary of state, while Rudy didn't. Tillerson would get the job, while Rudy decided he could make more money and even be more influential outside of a cabinet position.

Bannon said no one wanted homeland security. "It's a career-ender; everyone has been turning it down, including Rudy. All those who took it ended up as dead-enders. Ridge, Napolitano. So we got General Kelly to take it."

"Governor Chris Christie of New Jersey was begging for any job. He was asking Rebekah Mercer to help him land him one. But Christie abandoned Trump the weekend that the Billy Bush story broke and he was getting no appointment."

Peter Schweizer mentioned that he went to Trump Tower and ran into Trump's attorney Michael Cohen, who bragged that Trump was now getting offers for hotels and business projects all over the world. He said that business opportunities had never been better. Bannon said that Cohen looked at the future presidency as a good moneymaking opportunity. That was, of course, before he went to jail.

Bannon was already laying the groundwork for his war against Senator Mitch McConnell, whom he regarded as part of the "Washington swamp" that Trump ran against. He said the senator asked him,

"What is all this shit with draining the swamp? I can't get a Coke bought for me in this town without filling out paperwork."

During the dinner, Trump called Bannon. He got up from the table and went outside and came back and smiled. "Trump was being attacked for taking a call from the Taiwan president, a sign to the Chinese that he recognizes Taiwan, a clear no-no in U.S.-Chinese relations."

Bannon told him that Trump wanted to send out a tweet that said, "We are selling Taiwan two billion dollars in arms. Why can't I accept a call from a good customer?"

"I told him not to send it, but he did and then he was watching CNN and in seconds, they reported it as breaking news."

Trump loved it. He was discovering the power of a tweet.

Bannon referred to the group that won the election—Jared, Reince Priebus, Ivanka—as a gang of misfit toys. They knew nothing about running a government and soon had to turn to the establishment for staffing and advice. I asked Mike Morell, who was going to be Hillary's CIA director had she won, if he would brief Bannon on what each intelligence agency's mission is. Bannon was clueless about the functions of each intelligence agency, and as a good citizen, I thought it was important for a new president to have a working knowledge of the intelligence community.

Morell reluctantly agreed to talk with him, even though he was worried that he would be "used" for PR purposes by the group.

Over the next few months, I traveled to the White House on weekends. My goal was to get Bannon to do an interview when Trump fired him, as he does with most people who are not family. At the time, he didn't trust media people, but he trusted me, as I had not yet reported any of the inside stories. He told me some things that would have been front-page news, but he asked that I not divulge them at the time. I honored those requests, though there weren't many of them. When Bannon decided to go on-camera for his first interview, I believed he would choose me to tell his story. I was playing the long game.

I would usually get to Washington on a Saturday afternoon and wait in a local bar for Bannon's assistant to call. Jared was off observing the Sabbath and Priebus left to have a date night with his wife. Bannon and I would grab a couple of Cokes and hang out in Priebus's large chief of staff office.

The first time I went was on January 29, 2017, shortly after Trump was sworn in. There were protesters surrounding the White House. Some of the signs tarred Bannon, who was the face of the anti-immigration policies of the administration.

Bannon had just been placed on the National Security Council and was full of "deep state" conspiracies. He said Obama's national security advisor Susan Rice and her deputy Ben Rhodes were personally selecting the targets for drone strikes from inside the White House. He accused the Obama administration of conducting a huge wiretapping operation against the Republicans (not true) and how they needed to make the media the enemy to discount everything they said. Bannon believed Trump needed a foil, since he considered the Democratic Party too weak and boring to be an effective sparring partner and the media was a perfect opponent.

Trump put Bannon on the NSC to keep an eye on the national security advisor, Mike Flynn. "He wanted me to prevent World War III and said to watch him," Bannon said Trump told him.

Bannon's office in the White House was between Jared Kushner and Priebus. His wall didn't go up to the ceiling, and when you sat in it, he asked you to whisper, as people walking by could hear the conversations. Kushner's office was also open at the ceiling. I found it strange that in the West Wing of the White House, the two most important staffers didn't have enclosed offices.

After a while Bannon didn't want me to go to the White House but to his home on Capitol Hill; the Breitbart news staff is housed in his basement. He calls the place "the embassy."

Bannon, a disheveled mess on his good days, looked particularly bad three months into his White House job. His house was dark, and it seemed like it had been abandoned. The only sign of life was a bunch of clean shirts on hangers in the living room.

I visited on April 13, the day after Trump excoriated Bannon for being on the cover of *Time* magazine, with the caption "The Great Manipulator," and taking credit for the Trump victory. Bannon was also engaged in a very public spat with Jared Kushner, trying to advance his personal agenda by backstabbing Kushner to anyone who would listen. Trump chose family.

"I like Steve, but you have to remember he was not involved in my campaign until very late," Trump said. "I had already beaten all the senators and all the governors, and I didn't know Steve. I'm my own strategist, and it wasn't like I was going to change strategies because I was facing crooked Hillary."

He ended by saying, "Steve is a good guy, but I told them to straighten it out or I will."

Steve had just been kicked off the National Security Council, but in his mind, he had accomplished what he had set out to do. In a text he wrote: "Went there to baby sit Flynn, get focus and deoperationalize."

Flynn later pled guilty for lying to the FBI but had his case dismissed by the Justice Department.

I asked about stopping "nation building," the euphemism that the military-industrial complex employs when it is building roads and schools in war zones.

"First, I have to stop incompetents from running wars . . . also, to find [out] about surveillance," he wrote back.

So when I saw him that day, Bannon looked like he had been run over by a lawn mower. This dispute between Bannon and the president was more than a bad day at the office. It was taking a toll on him.

"[Stephen] Schwarzman was hitting at Trump that Bannon won the election and it was burning in his craw, so he lashed out," he said. Schwarzman, the billionaire head of the Blackstone Group, was kibitzing with Trump at Bannon's expense.

Bannon's true feelings about Trump began to come out. He was sitting at the head of the table at his house, angry. "Trump needs constant reinforcement about how great he is. His family is most concerned with their brand, and they worry that nationalism will damage it forever," he said.

He particularly dislikes Ivanka, who he says is a spoiled and entitled rich kid. "She doesn't like to be scorned in New York, so if she can move her father more to the center, she thinks she would be more accepted by the high society circles.

"Her clothing line took a hit during the travel ban rollout," Bannon said happily.

Jared was more concerned about making contacts for the future. "His head is so far up Tim Cook's [Apple CEO] ass," Bannon said. "Trump tells Jared he has too much on his plate but won't do anything about it."

Bannon said that Jared tried to leverage the Chinese insurance giant Anbang to bail his family out of the disastrous investment purchase of the 666 Fifth Avenue building in New York. Jared's family was also trying to sell them a $400 million stake in the building rights— terms that were unusually favorable to the Kushners—right before the Chinese arrived for a summit. The White House counsel told Bannon anyone else would have had his security badge pulled and have been escorted out of the building. "The problem here is nepotism, and all the sins done by the family are forgiven.")

He said the infighting at the White House was so intense because Trump had no core beliefs and they changed depending on whom he had last spoken to. Which was the reason, Bannon said, he spent so much time in the Oval Office. He worried that if he left Trump alone, someone else could slip in and change his mind on a crucial decision.

Bannon's anger built. "Trump has never read a book in his life, not even the book he wrote. And he is jealous that I was influenced by books." In particular, Bannon is influenced by *The Fourth Turning,* a book that maintains that every eighty years the old order is destroyed and a new one is created.

He was angry that the White House was overrun by ex–Goldman Sachs staffers and that the then-chairman of Goldman Sachs, Lloyd Blankfein, was a regular. Blankfein tried to get his old cronies to help him get the Aramco account from Saudi Arabia. Aramco was set to be the largest IPO in history, and Blankfein was trying to steal it from JPMorgan and was leveraging his friendships inside the White House to get it for his company.

"Goldman would never loan Trump money, and now Trump gets satisfaction because they all want to kiss his ass."

He then went after then–national security advisor H. R. McMaster, who succeeded Flynn. He said McMaster has a contingency plan to carry out a preemptive strike on North Korea.

"He wanted to present a plan to bomb and invade the country. I told him you can't. He said the president should have all options available to him. And I told him not this president. He will negotiate with you and then compromise, and we will bomb and not invade. You can't do that."

He said McMaster ignored him.

"The generals want to build a road or schoolhouse in Iraq for every dead ISIS person they kill. They even discussed sending in 150,000 troops to the Al-Faw Peninsula in Iraq, where the oil and shipping is. They want to get us involved in another war," Bannon said.

He hated every minute inside the White House. It was a den of thieves that he said was eating away at his soul. As much as he hated it, he understood that this was a once-in-a-lifetime opportunity to push through his ideas, which was why the media described him as "the shadow president."

Before he left, I told him how important it was to say this on-camera.

I waited a month before visiting him again. This time I went with Peter Schweizer, who was a partner with Bannon at the Government Accountability Institute, which investigates political corruption.

Bannon was in a much better mood, having engineered the rejection by Trump of the Paris global warming accords.

"I got Pruitt [the former EPA director] to give him the legal basis for rejecting it. He told Trump the accord was nonbinding and that China and India would take advantage and violate it and handcuff the

U.S. We got twenty-two senators to call for its rejection, to give him political cover, and then I stayed away.

"Ivanka and Jared got Tim Cook and Mark Zuckerberg to call him and that didn't get anywhere. Tillerson and McMaster were begging him to stay in it, but he blew them away. It was a campaign promise and he followed it."

For Bannon it was a good day. He was now in a storytelling mood. He told about the day Trump went to Rome to meet the pope. Channeling Trump, he relayed the story the way Trump told it, sounding like a gangster.

"The pope posed for a picture and he couldn't even smile. Then he gave me a book on the fuckin' environment. What do I need a book on the fuckin' environment for? Besides, the pope is a communist.

"Then when we posed for the picture, Ivanka gets the position next to the pope. Melania was pissed. She [Ivanka] converted to Judaism, she told me, why was she standing next to the pope?

"Then Melania said out loud, 'I'm a Catholic. . . .'"

Bannon said it was intended as a slap at Ivanka, but the pope didn't know what was going on. "What am I supposed to do, there was one spot next to him and they both want it."

After the visit to the pope, Trump went to NATO headquarters. He said he looked around the glass building and asked, "Wasn't this supposed to withstand a war? Like the way NORAD is built at Cheyenne Mountain? A hand grenade could take this place out."

Talking about the Russian investigation, Bannon said the person who could bring the whole place down would be Michael Cohen, Trump's attorney at the company. This was months before Cohen became a household name.

"He knew where all the bodies were buried and who threw the dirt on the bodies," Bannon said.

He said the president at first liked having Gary Cohn (former president of Goldman Sachs) around, but then Cohn said that he was trying to make the president smarter. "Trump already thought he was the smartest guy in the room. That didn't go over well," Bannon said.

He talked about Mika Brzezinski and Joe Scarborough, who criticize Trump on TV but asked him to officiate at their wedding. They visited Trump at Mar-a-Lago, right after Mika had some plastic surgery done.

"She had bandages from her facelift." Trump said that "'she had better not bleed all over my carpets.'"

Bannon despised Jared and Ivanka. "They wanted to fly a gay-lesbian flag over all U.S. embassies on gay pride day. I said are you crazy? Our followers would go crazy and it wouldn't have converted one person to our cause. Trump's base would have killed him."

Russia, he said, wanted to get the convicted arms dealer Viktor Bout back. They were offering him to be exchanged for a list of thirteen Americans being held. Putin wanted Bout back, Bannon said, because he knew where Putin keeps his stolen money.

Bannon liked Trump's blunt style when it came to foreign policy. He believed there is too much coddling of governments. He gave an example with South Korea and the THAAD antiballistic missile defense system. It is the most advanced interceptor in the world, designed to shoot down a ballistic missile. The Koreans complained that they received two less than they were told they were getting. Trump's reply?

"Fuck them. Let them get overrun."

Bannon said the Koreans stopped complaining.

As I was leaving that day in April, I asked him, "Have you figured out what you want to say in the interview? Do you want to kill him [Trump] or kiss him?"

"I haven't figured it out yet."

"You need to do that before we sit down," I said.

Bannon was fired in mid-August 2017, exactly one year after he joined the campaign. He finally agreed to do the interview at his house, located a block from the Supreme Court.

"You think this will be epic?" he asked about the interview.

"Absolutely," I said.

Charlie Rose and I hadn't worked together on *60 Minutes*. We had several stories we had been about to do, but the interview subjects, as sometimes happens, changed their minds. Many people agreed to appear with Rose on his PBS show, such as golfer Tiger Woods, but don't want to appear on *60 Minutes,* fearing its tough reputation. They prefer the longer and mostly unedited format of Charlie's PBS show to get their opinions out.

The advantage Bannon saw in doing the interview with Rose was that he would reach a large audience and the fuller interview would appear the next day on Rose's PBS show. This protected him, he said, from some quote being taken out of context.

I wrote about a hundred questions based on my many conversations with Bannon. Executive producer Jeff Fager and Rose edited them down, and then Rose fashioned them into his own voice.

It was September 2017 and Rose was at the top of his game. He had won a Peabody the previous year for his interview with Syrian president Bashar al-Assad. It seemed every week he was getting and accepting another award. He had a heart operation that February which put him on the sidelines for a couple of months, but now he was recovered and had lost about twenty pounds. He returned to his crazy schedule—doing a two-hour CBS broadcast in the morning and then later in the day taping his PBS show. At night, he often hit the town, going to high-powered dinners and parties.

Though he was seventy-six, he loved the action and would take two naps a day to fit it all in. We didn't know it at the time, but the Bannon interview was his last major story before the sexual harassment revelations destroyed his reputation and career. I had known Rose since the 1980s when both of us were in Washington. He had a middle-of-the-night interview show where he learned the art of interviewing, without a large audience seeing his mistakes. He honed his craft and built an impressive Rolodex that would serve him in the years ahead. We would occasionally go out to bars in Washington, and I was happy to be his wingman. Charlie was dashing, handsome, and not shy, and had no trouble meeting women.

But Charlie was now in his mid-seventies. His body was thin, and he was beginning to walk with a stoop. In his mind he was still that same handsome cleft-chinned young man who had dated some of the most glamorous women in the world.

While waiting for Bannon to finally commit to the interview, Charlie asked me to meet actor Warren Beatty, who was about to release his movie *Rules Don't Apply,* a fictional version of Howard Hughes's story. I went out to California and met Beatty at a small screening room located in a Santa Monica office building.

The screening was set up for me and one of the film's producers. Beatty sat directly behind me and I felt he watched every move I made—when I scratched my nose or cleared my throat. It was intimidating, and I dared not get up to go to the bathroom. At the end of the screening he moved to the front and asked what I thought of his first movie in nearly twenty years.

"Brilliant," I said, and then I looked over to the producer who screened it with me and said, "This is going to do very well."

The movie was perfectly shot, with a great cast, but it was a boring story. But I didn't have the heart to tell Beatty.

Afterward, we went to the Beverly Glen Deli, a regular spot for movie folks. Beatty was eighty, but still mentally sharp. He desperately wanted a *60 Minutes* profile to help launch the movie, but I had my doubts. Aside from the movie being dull, Beatty was known for being a boring interview subject. He was known for dissecting an interviewer's questions before answering or playing coy, to get by without answering the question.

"As interesting as you are over deli sandwiches, you and I know you won't speak candidly once the cameras are rolling," I said.

"Listen, we can do the interview over six hours. I will put a pot of coffee on and we will stay there until we get it right," he said.

For the next several hours over lunch, he regaled me with stories of many of the famous women he had affairs with, from Brigitte Bardot to Carly Simon.

One of them was with actress Julie Christie. He said shortly after they first met, they sat on a park bench in San Francisco, when a cat wandered by.

"Christie started calling for the cat. "Come here, pussy, pussy," Beatty said. "So I said, 'I will be saying that to you later.'"

They ended up becoming one of the most famous Hollywood couples of the 1970s. But when I asked him if he would talk about all these affairs on-camera, he demurred.

"You know there have been several books about me, and I haven't cooperated with a single one of them," he said.

Aside from his good looks and seductiveness, Beatty is incredibly persistent. I had no doubt some women slept with him just to have him stop bothering them. As much as I enjoyed our lunch, I didn't think it would make a good *60 Minutes* story.

When I returned to New York, I told Charlie.

He took it all in and didn't act surprised. "You know what Beatty and I have in common," Charlie said. "We both know how to satisfy women."

"That was like me saying, 'Do you know what Roger Federer and I have in common? We both know how to hit forehands,'" I said.

Charlie had always talked about how great his interviews were, and who complimented him. He even had an assistant put together a binder of all the complimentary emails he received following one of his stories—a source of ego stroking. But I had not seen him express his grand view of himself as a ladies' man.

"Charlie, would you sleep with a woman who was sixty years old?" I asked.

"Are you crazy?"

"That is a woman who is fifteen years younger than you," I replied.

"You have no idea what my life is like," he said.

Charlie clearly hadn't looked in the mirror for a while.

"Charlie, you are seventy-five. You are old enough to be some of these younger women's grandfather. They want to hang out with you, talk to you, go to parties with you. They don't want to fuck you."

He got up and left my office.

The day before the Bannon interview was set to happen, the White House was pressuring him not to appear. Schweizer, who prepped him, said that Bannon wanted to have his own crew film the interview and to limit the interview to one hour, so that the entire interview would run on the Rose show, nearly unedited.

I told him that wouldn't happen. Peter suggested I go to the embassy, Bannon's home, and talk with him. When I arrived, he was upstairs in his bedroom. It was a large room with a fireplace, and the only artwork was a giant portrait of Abraham Lincoln.

I greeted him and said simply, "Cut out this bullshit with filming us. We own the copyright and I am not going to have another copy floating out there."

"Okay," he replied.

"And we will go as long as we need to get this interview right. If that means three hours, it will go three hours. You want this to be epic, right?"

"I do," he said. "But, dude, all these White House people are saying this is a bad idea. That you are going to fuck me."

"I promise, I will not fuck you."

"Okay, we are good then," he said. All the hours and months of building trust had finally paid off.

I went to dinner later with Schweizer. He made it clear that Bannon would not throw Trump under the bus but instead would say he was going to be his supporter outside the White House.

I was disappointed, but also understood. This was Bannon's opening gambit—down the road, he could turn on Trump, but he wasn't ready to do that now.

The next morning Charlie arrived on Amtrak. Charlie spent a lot of time preparing and it showed. He is a brilliant counterpuncher, and he was at his best during the interview.

ROSE: You will not be attacking Donald Trump?

BANNON: No, our—our purpose is to support Donald
            Trump. By the way—

ROSE: —And destroy his enemies?

BANNON: To make sure his enemies know that there's no
            free shot on goal. By the way, after the Char-
            lottesville situation, that's what I told [White
            House chief of staff] General [John] Kelly, I was
            the only guy that came out and tried to defend
            him. I was the only guy that said, "He's talking
            about something, taking it up to a higher level."
            Where does it all go? Where does this end? Does
            it end—does it end in taking down the Washing-
            ton Monument? Does it end in taking down—

ROSE: I tell you where many people suggest it should
            have gone, it should have gone in terms of de-
            nouncing specifically from the very beginning
            neo-Nazis and white supremacists and people of
            that political view. . . . And you didn't at first in-
            stinct. In fact, you seemed to be doubling down
            in terms of a moral equivalency.

BANNON: What he was trying to say is that people that
            support the monument staying there peacefully
            and people that oppose that, that's the normal
            course of—of First Amendment. But he's talking
            about the neo-Nazis and neo-Confederates and
            the Klan, who, by the way, are absolutely awful—
            there's no room in American politics for that.
            There's no room in American society for that. . . .
            And all Donald Trump was saying is, "Where
            does it end? Does it end in taking down the
            Washington Monument? Does it end in taking
            down Mount Rushmore? Does it end at taking
            Churchill's bust out of the Oval Office?" My

problem—my problem, and I told General Kelly
this—when you side with a man, you side with
him. I was proud to come out and try to defend
President Trump in the media that day.

ROSE: And no exceptions in terms of siding with someone?

BANNON: You can tell him, "Hey, maybe you can do it a better way." But if you're gonna break, then resign. If
you're going to break with him, resign. The stuff
that was leaked out that week by certain members
of the White House I thought was unacceptable. If
you find it unacceptable, you should resign.

ROSE: So, who are you talking about?

BANNON: I'm talking—obviously, about Gary Cohn and
some other people. That if you don't like what
he's doing and you don't agree with it, you have
an obligation to resign.

ROSE: So Gary Cohn should have resigned?

BANNON: Absolutely.

The interview ran almost three hours, with Fager in the New York office listening in. It was scheduled for the week before the official opening of the show, of the fiftieth season of *60 Minutes*. Fager wanted it to
run two segments.

Within minutes after the interview aired, it caused a sensation.
CBS played excerpts on every news show. CNN wrote an article on
their website: "48 of the Most Revealing Lines of Steve Bannon's *60
Minutes* Interview." Then CBS president Les Moonves called Fager and
said it was the best interview he had ever seen on TV. Trump watched
it and called Bannon that night. "I spoke to him for an hour. Trump
loved it," Bannon texted.

Trump told Bannon: "u r a piece of work and a very special guy; it
was not normal TV but so amazingly entertaining—he watched it multiple times—we had a detailed discussion of the entire thing."

The Charlie Rose show played the entire three-hour interview spread over five nights. A year of meetings, late-night calls, and honoring his confidences had paid off. It was, in Bannon's word, epic. But the story created a monster. Bannon took the interview momentum and began to speak and act like a presidential candidate. A narcissist, he told me that he wanted to run for president if Trump decided he didn't want a second term. He ticked off the rich right-wing money people who would fund his campaign—the Mercers, Sheldon Adelson, the Koch brothers.

His criticism of Trump privately to me took on a different tone. He believed Trump was suffering from early stage dementia and that there was a real possibility he would be removed from office by the Twenty-Fifth Amendment, where the cabinet could vote that the president was no longer mentally capable of carrying out his duties. Bannon began to push that story hard.

Bannon said that the president had no attention span, didn't read, and now doesn't listen. He said Trump repeats himself a lot, telling the same story minutes after he told it before.

I sent him part of a David Brooks column from *The New York Times*: "The Republican senators went to the White House and saw a president so repetitive and rambling, some thought he might be suffering from early Alzheimer's. But they knew which way the wind is blowing. They gave him a standing ovation."

"You need to do the 25th amendment piece . . . BTW brother I never steer u wrong," he texted back.

But Bannon began to push removing Trump via the Twenty-Fifth Amendment to some of his friends and biggest Trump backers. In the summer of 2017, he went to the Long Island home of Bob Mercer and briefed him on his trying to build up a consensus to remove Trump from office. He mentioned a Sunday prayer service some cabinet officials attended, along with Vice President Pence, as a place where the conspiracy to remove Trump could begin. Mercer dismissed the talk and began to have serious doubts about Bannon. But the fact that Bannon tried to build support to have Trump removed, after having served as his most senior adviser in the White House, was astonishing.

After he left the White House, Trump, and then the Mercers, cut Bannon off. His disloyalty and fickleness were too much for them to deal with. So he found a new backer, Guo Wengui, also known as Miles Kwok, a Chinese billionaire.

Bannon heard about Kwok while in the White House. Trump had spoken to Steve Schwarzman, the head of the Blackstone Group who urged Trump to send Kwok back to China to face charges of bribery, kidnapping, money laundering, and rape. "It would buy a lot of good-will," he told Trump.

Bannon said he told the president that before they repatriated Kwok, he wanted to check him out.

As Bannon's story went, he spoke to the FBI and found that Kwok was providing very valuable intelligence on China. The FBI was ana-lyzing documents Kwok provided that helped identify Chinese sleeper cells in the United States. Bannon said he told Trump about this and he agreed to block Kwok's extradition.

Kwok was an outspoken critic of the Chinese ruling class, who he believed wanted to kill him. Bannon thought he would make a good *60 Minutes* profile. We met at the Sherry-Netherland, where Kwok owned a $68-million apartment that had five balconies wrapped around an entire floor of the building. Inside he had numerous living rooms, bed-rooms, and at least a dozen bathrooms, all made of gold and marble.

Kwok told us that a small group of "kleptocrats" associated with the Communist Party were running China and stealing billions, and the group included the head of the anti-corruption campaign in China.

He said that China has launched "thousands upon thousands" of sleeper agents into the United States for the coming war with the West, which he said would happen within five years. And the $17 billion he said he had was now all frozen by the Chinese government—though from the looks of the apartment, it was apparent he still had a few bucks left.

Now Bannon and Kwok were besties. I invited Charlie Rose, who lived in the same building, to join us for dinner. Rose came up to the apart-ment to see if Kwok would make an interesting story, but when he heard Kwok's poor English, he realized he would make a bad interview subject and tried to leave. But Kwok's wife had been cooking a nine-course "authentic" Chinese meal and he wanted Rose to stay. Kwok pulled Rose into the kitchen and took a soup spoon loaded with beluga caviar and shoved it into Rose's mouth. Rose swallowed the caviar in one bite.

Rose wanted no more caviar and said he needed to go to bed to rest for the morning show. But Kwok tried again to serve Charlie with another spoon of caviar. Charlie tried to escape.

So here was the scene. Chinese billionaire trying to stuff beluga caviar down the throat of Charlie Rose in a $68-million Fifth Avenue apartment with Steve Bannon looking on. Finally I said to Kwok, "Stop being a Jewish mother. Leave the man alone."

Kwok smiled and pulled back the spoon. Charlie quickly left, and Bannon and his cousin, who served as his new aide-de-camp, and my associate producer Sam Hornblower joined Kwok in the dining room. Bannon sat to my right. Bannon bragged that he had lost fifteen pounds on a new juice diet, but you couldn't tell from that night. He ate *his* pork dumplings, then *my* dumplings. The food served that night was spectacular: chicken, beef, fish, vegetables . . . all washed down with magnums of Opus One and Mouton Rothschild wine. No rice, just food. Kwok barely ate. He sat at the table talking about Chinese corruption and after dinner showed us some videos he had made that he posted on YouTube.

The whole night was truly bizarre, and it occurred to me why Bannon was part of it. Bannon was looking to Kwok as his new sugar daddy. In July 2020 it was revealed that the FBI had begun a probe of media companies the Chinese billionaire was funding in the U.S. that were linked to a one-million-dollar consulting deal he gave Bannon.

After our crazy dinner, Bannon declared war against certain GOP candidates and began to set the foundations for his own political movement, to take on what he calls the "Party of Davos." The Democrats were ecstatic and said nothing, as they knew this would create a fissure in the Republican Party.

The next time I saw him, Bannon was at the Bryant Park Hotel, a place known on Wall Street to go for discreet affairs, before catching a train at Grand Central. Bannon was occupying a small room and being guarded by a security person who looked like he had just come from the Hells Angels. That day Bannon had given an off-the-record speech on China to a small group at the Council on Foreign Relations. His topic was mostly the same and can best be summarized as "the Chinese are going to clean our clocks unless we do something about it."

Later that day, Bannon wanted me to meet his new girlfriend at a small French restaurant on the East Side called Le Veau d'Or. He entered the restaurant with a small security force and an attractive brunette.

His girlfriend was about twenty years younger than Steve and he was smitten. He had already bought her a car and a house and later texted me that "She could be the next ex Mrs. Bannon she is very very cool—first time I've enjoyed anything outside of work in 30 years."

Bannon tried to support the president as a way of building up his own brand, but it conflicted with his true feelings about Trump's family. I had read an early version of Michael Wolff's book, *Fire and Fury*, and it quoted Bannon as saying Trump Jr.'s meeting with the Russians at Trump Tower before the election "was treasonous." It was apparent that Bannon believed he could throw Trump's kids under the bus and still be a Trump loyalist.

The day after the Wolff revelations came out, Bannon said on his radio show that he still supported Trump. Five hours after he said that, he emailed me a story from *Politico* on the Twenty-Fifth Amendment: how it can be used to remove Trump from office. The article he sent claimed a psychiatrist had briefed U.S. senators as to Trump's mental incapacity.

Bannon was living in an alternate reality.

He supported Trump while pushing stories to get him removed. Maybe the most accurate thing Trump said all year was in response to Bannon's comments about his son's "treasonous" activities: "Steve not only lost his job; he lost his mind."

30

THE MERCERS

It seemed that with the election of Trump the characters I began to hang out with were outliers who were ruling the world. None fit that definition more than Rebekah Mercer. In the world of eccentric, reclusive conservative billionaires, the Mercers, Rebekah and her dad Bob, were near the top of every list. The press has portrayed her as a right-wing wacko, who became the principal backer of the Donald Trump candidacy and helped convince him to hire Bannon and Kellyanne Conway to run his campaign. Those hirings laid the groundwork for Trump's 2016 victory. Besides advice, the Mercers offered money, donating $23 million in the 2016 election cycle to Republican candidates, including more than $2.5 million to Trump. I had gotten to know Rebekah through Peter Schweizer and found her to be endlessly interesting and full of surprises. In 2019, she went to the Burning Man festival in Nevada, a pop-up metropolis of radical self-reliance and free expression, where people tend to dress more in tribal garb. Not exactly the look of conservative Republicans.

Her father, a computer scientist, was an early developer of artificial intelligence, who made his billions picking the right stocks for his hedge fund by using advanced mathematics. He invested in a data mining firm called Cambridge Analytica, which claimed it developed psychological profiles of more than a hundred million voters. The company became one of the most important data collection groups the Trump campaign employed in 2016 to target voters.

Rebekah ran the Mercer Family Foundation, often donating to groups that helped expose government corruption and crony capitalism. And she funded alternate right-wing media like the website Breitbart, which gave Steve Bannon a platform for his "America first" ideas. But what father and daughter also shared was a hatred for the mainstream media. They never did any press interviews. I took it as a challenge to get her to do a profile on *60 Minutes.*

The first time we met was in her $60-million apartment on 72nd Street and Riverside in New York. I was invited to a book party she had for Schweizer. Her apartment is two entire floors of one of the Trump buildings, beautifully decorated but with lots of open space, perfect for parties.

She has four brilliant children. One of them loves complicated 1,200-piece puzzles, one of which was laid out on their dining room table. At the time, the kids were homeschooled in a separate multi-million-dollar condo that functioned as their schoolhouse.

Guests at Rebekah's parties and get-togethers probably assume that all attending have been prescreened to be ideologically pure— Republican, anti-tax, mostly pro-Trump, and certainly believers that global warming is a hoax.

She took a liking to me, in part, because of the exposés I did about Congress. I also was not a leftist ideologue like some of my colleagues. I certainly believe global warming is real, and left unchecked, will devastate the planet, but I am willing to listen to how those who don't believe in it got there. As a result, those who frequented her condo opened up to me, the stranger in their midst.

One such person was Bob Cohen, a famous New York matrimonial lawyer. He had represented the ex-Trump wives, Ivana and Marla Maples. After Rebekah introduced me to him, the eighty-year-old, former marathon-running attorney felt like bragging. He said that he now represented Melania Trump.

"But she is not divorced," I said, a bit puzzled.

"I had gotten her a postnup agreement."

I was puzzled again. "What is a postnup?" I asked.

"You know what a prenup is?"

"Sure."

"Well, a postnup is after you have a prenup. After Donald got elected, he said I can't be president without a first lady, so he added four years to her existing agreement," Cohen said with a big smile. "I got her millions more added to her deal."

It was implied from Cohen that had Trump lost, he might have separated from Melania. But it is not good optics to be a president without a wife, so Trump renegotiated his agreement to ensure she had a financial incentive to remain. It was clear that if Trump won in 2020, there would be yet another renegotiation.

Rebekah was a great hostess and I enjoyed listening to her ideas. Both of us want to change the world, though we have different ways of getting there. She began to invite me to parties and lunches, giving me a chance to meet rich Trump supporters who seem bonded over their hatred of Hillary Clinton.

One party she invited me to attend was the twentieth-anniversary gala for Encounter Books, an ultraconservative publishing house, in Washington, D.C. Rebekah was being honored as "an individual who has fostered the intellectual and moral resources that nurture liberty and the pursuit of truth." She placed me at a table which included Bob Mercer's security guard and Larry Solov, publisher of Breitbart.

Her acceptance speech was an attack on progressives and what she says they are doing to education. "The progressives have remodeled the American education system to churn out wave after wave of ovine zombies steeped in the anti-American myths of the radical left, ignorant of basic civics, economics, and history, and unfit for critical thinking."

She went on to call out universities for pushing silly courses like tree climbing to students. She quoted a statement Huey Long, the governor of Louisiana, made in response to the question "Do you ever think we will ever have fascism in America?" He replied, "Sure, only we'll call it anti-fascism."

I wonder if she was thinking of Trump when she said that.

I was told that Bob Mercer, who sat a few feet away from me, rarely spoke, so I took it as a challenge to get him to talk. I went over and told him about the Washington corruption stories that I had done with Peter Schweizer, whose investigative foundation they financially support.

Bob Mercer has an easy smile but said little. He didn't have to, as he was the richest person in the room. I learned that he has a large mansion on the North Fork of Long Island. Visitors who have been there say that as you first enter the property, there is a large house. But this is the phony house for people who may want to do him harm. That is where they would think he lived. In fact, his real mansion is a quarter mile down the road.

Bannon described it as Xanadu, complete with an underground bunker better than the one in the White House. Mercer invested in a gun factory and had a huge supply of weapons, with a particular fondness for machine guns. His mansion also had anti-drone technology, to block or shoot down any unwanted flying machines.

The underground bunker was built to withstand a direct nuclear bomb strike. It also has an indoor pool in the sub-basement and a food supply to last for years.

Mercer loved billiards. He once invited the top billiard players in the world to his Long Island mansion. He offered them large prize money to compete in a weekend tournament. He was the only spectator.

Rebekah has two sisters. Both were quite amazed that I was hanging out at the dinner with her. One is a top attorney and the other had been a professional poker player who married her bodyguard. They didn't understand why a 60 Minutes producer was in their orbit.

But Rebekah brought me into her confidences and introduced me to her children, Nikolas, Christian, Alexandra, and Josephine, who

were prodigies. One of them was interested in World War II stories, so
I gave him my collection of videos, like *The Longest Day* and *A Bridge
Too Far*. I think her kids regarded me as a curiosity.

Rebekah had direct access to Trump before the 2016 election and
advised on his cabinet picks. But 2020 was different. She had withdrawn her financial support of Trump because he didn't deliver on his
promise to take on the entrenched corruption on both sides of the aisle.
The political swamp had only grown during the Trump presidency. She
also was offended that Trump's campaign manager Brad Parscale had
been spending millions on fancy cars and expensive real estate and he
and his company were being paid millions by the campaign. She didn't
want her contributions to benefit his lifestyle.

If she had her misgivings about Trump, I was surprised she didn't
support Vice President Pence as a second choice to Trump.

She gave me a look. "You know he talks to G-d," she said.

"A lot of people talk to G-d. What's wrong with that?" I asked.

"G-d answers," she said.

"Like the burning bush?" I asked.

"Yeah."

I realized it is very hard to disagree with someone who says he got
his orders from G-d.

Rebekah is an active member of the Gatestone Institute, a mostly
old-moneyed conservative group that meets regularly for lunch at Le
Bernardin, one of New York's best restaurants. Rebekah invited me a
few times a year. I found it fascinating to hang out with those who have
beachfront property on Long Island and Palm Beach but believe global
warming is a hoax. In October 2019, Ken Langone, the billionaire who
cofounded Home Depot, gave a short address to the gathering on a
book he had just completed and about his love of capitalism. As rich
and philanthropic as he was, he was aware that income disparity was
one of the most significant issues of our time.

At the time, the top 1 percent had gained $21 trillion in wealth
since 1989, while the bottom half had lost $900 billion. The top 1 per-
cent owned nearly $30 trillion in assets, while the bottom half owned

less than nothing, meaning they were in debt. And the world's richest 2,100 people controlled more money than the poorest 4.6 billion combined in 2019.

Langone spoke about this and Rebekah seemed angry. She didn't believe in handouts to the poor or in attempts to make things equal. "That's socialism," she scolded him in a question. But those at the lunch were a little surprised at her taking on a conservative legend like Langone and calling attention to what those present understood—they like their rich and privileged life and don't want anything to disrupt it.

Langone defused the tension by saying he agreed with Rebekah, though I doubt he did, and the lunch ended. Before most of us got up from our chairs, Langone was in his limo.

Rebekah has become a lightning rod for the conservative movement and has had death threats against her family. Every year the Mercers held a very fashionable Halloween costume party at their Long Island estate. Kellyanne Conway came one year as Superwoman; Trump flew in for it dressed as—you guessed it—himself. The following year they discovered that one of those involved in the event had the intention of poisoning the guests and the Mercers have since canceled the party.

While pursuing Rebekah for an interview, I was also meeting with Dylan Howard, then the chief content editor of the *National Enquirer*.

When I first met Howard at a New York party, he was brimming with self-confidence and seemed to be on the make for juicy gossip or rumors of scandal. An Australian entertainment journalist, he spoke in low conspiratorial tones, trying to ferret out any bit of dirt he could use or trade. He is in his late thirties, overweight, with stylish glasses. He fancies himself as an investigative reporter because of his scoops on Mel Gibson's anti-Semitic comments, Charlie Sheen's being HIV positive, and Natalie Wood's mysterious murder. He also was the editor who supervised the story on Steve Kroft's affair.

Drink in hand, he said they offered significant money to Kroft's mistress, but she turned it down. She wanted to get back at Kroft for free. He said there were more love note texts from Kroft to his mistress that had not surfaced, but a high-level CBS executive had reached out to the *Enquirer*'s publisher, David Pecker, and had the stories stopped. You could tell he was disappointed. At first, I was a little worried even to be talking to Howard, knowing that these tabloid editors would sell out their mothers if it meant a good headline. But the ways of the planet are that people like Howard will eventually find themselves at the center of a major story, and I was not about to be disappointed.

Howard became paymaster to porn star Stormy Daniels and *Playboy* playmate Karen McDougal to keep quiet about their affairs with Trump. Facing a possible federal indictment, Howard hired multiple lawyers and entered into an agreement to cooperate with New York's U.S. attorney's office, which was looking into the hush payments made by Trump attorney Michael Cohen.

Howard and I began a series of meetings over drinks, lunches, and dinners spread across New York's finest sushi bars and steakhouses; my goal was to convince him to go on *60 Minutes*. With each drink, Howard revealed his bitterness in helping get Trump elected.

"I was a patsy," he told me early on about supplying the hush money payments to McDougal and Daniels.

"You were not a patsy," I said. "Lee Harvey Oswald was a patsy. You were an ambitious young man who was making a lot of money, was commanding a large staff, and was king of the hill. You loved it."

"I did, but I should have known better," he said. "It may have impacted the presidential election."

"Listen, when you wrote those headlines and stories that Hillary Clinton was about to die or Ted Cruz's father was involved in the JFK assassination, you knew they were false, and it would affect the election. But you didn't care," I said.

He smiled. "We also did UFOs landing in America. We are a tabloid publication."

I was treading a thin line. I wanted to push back gently so he knew I was not trying to totally suck up to him, but I also didn't want to scare him off. The goal was to get him to sit for an interview.

Tabloid reporters like Howard have great bullshit meters. If you tell them the interview will make them look good, chances are they will run for the hills, knowing you are lying. If you say that TV has a way of making charismatic and articulate characters come off as sympathetic, that strikes them as being more believable. They want to believe in redemption, even if they are borderline incorrigible. So how did the tabloid editor find himself hanging out with Trump in the White House?

Trump had invited Howard and *National Enquirer* publisher David Pecker for dinner on July 12, 2017. Howard told me that while touring the Executive residence of the White House, when he was just outside the Lincoln Bedroom, the president said to him, "Editor man, I'm glad I've been good for business."

He then asked if the former *Playboy* model Karen McDougal still loved him. "Of course she does," Howard said. Trump seemed pleased.

Trump then told Howard the secret nickname he had for her, "the Hoover Dam," Trump said, "because she was always so wet." Howard smiled and said he couldn't help but notice a copy of the Emancipation Proclamation on display, a few feet away, when Trump spoke.

At a dinner of chicken and risotto, he asked Howard which celebrity sold the most newsstand covers.

"Brad Pitt and Angelina Jolie. They increase sales by twenty-five percent. You increase it by fifteen."

Trump thought about it for a moment.

"Make mine thirty," the president said, according to Howard.

It seemed that Trump and Howard were simpatico. They were both ruthless and would do what was needed to win, even if it sometimes skirted every rule of decency. The difference is one of them ran the country and the other ran the country's most famous tabloid. After months of courtship, Howard agreed to take the next step and come to a lunch with me and correspondent Bill Whitaker. Howard was nervous, not at all sure he was ready to go on-camera. He repeated his story of how he became one of the main players in the Trump hush money scandal, and revealed that he was the one who leaked the story to *The Wall Street Journal,* which was his attempt at redemption for his role in the cover-up.

Whitaker did his best to persuade him to go on the show. Howard called me later to say that his lawyers cautioned him to remain quiet, but that he was contemplating doing a tell-all book and would certainly then go public. But in February 2019, while we were still in discussions, the Jeff Bezos story would put Howard once again in the public crosshairs.

Howard discovered that Amazon founder Jeff Bezos was cheating on his wife with entertainment reporter Lauren Sánchez. Howard said that the story about Bezos was "the biggest investigation in *Enquirer* history" and he had sent their reporters traveling over 40,000 miles to observe Bezos and his girlfriend Lauren Sánchez boarding private jets, entering limousines, and staying in five-star hotels. And the potential story had photos of Bezos and his girlfriend at what the tabloid called "a beachfront love-nest in Santa Monica."

Over a lunch with Howard at the Blue Ribbon Sushi bar in New York, he said he was worried that the *Enquirer* lawyers wouldn't let him publish the story. "If they kill it, I will quit," he said. With all the legal scrutiny he and the paper were under, he was worried that the Bezos story would be looked at as a hit piece ordered by publisher David Pecker because of Bezos's friendship with the president.

To insulate themselves from that attack, the *Enquirer* wanted Bezos to say that their coverage of him was not politically motivated. In an email sent to Bezos's attorneys, Howard said that the *National Enquirer* had obtained below-the-belt selfies [shots of Bezos's penis] and pictures of Bezos, "with a full length body selfie" of Bezos in his underwear, and messages and photos exchanged between Bezos and his girlfriend Lauren Sánchez.

"It would give no editor pleasure to send this email. I hope common sense can prevail—and quickly," Howard wrote.

The *Enquirer* was willing not to release the shots of the Amazon founder's penis if Bezos would not attack them. Instead Bezos went public with what he said was an extortion demand and became perceived as a victim, a brilliant PR move.

Howard said he should have left the "negotiations" about not revealing the pictures to the *Enquirer* attorneys. Instead, he ended up doing the negotiations himself. A big mistake.

Besides paying off the Trump women, Howard also reportedly helped cover up the sexual harassment behavior of Harvey Weinstein. He allegedly tried to intimidate actress Rose McGowan, who was trying to blow the whistle on Weinstein, telling his staff that "he wanted dirt on that bitch."

I found it humorous that with all Howard has done and exposed he still described himself as "one of the world's foremost investigative journalists on celebrity, pop culture, and true crime."

Howard wanted his story told, but he had a hard time trying to spin what he did was for the good of the country. And even after our lunch with Whitaker, I was not getting too many positive vibes at work about putting him on. He had hit a weird trifecta of sleaze. He was accused of intimidating women for Harvey Weinstein, covering up the philandering of Donald Trump, and trying to blackmail one of the richest men in the world, Jeff Bezos. Howard might have been a tabloid prodigy, but he got caught and that is a no-no in that business. He eventually lost his editor's job.

After being removed from the *National Enquirer,* Howard returned to subjects that are tabloid's bread and butter: books on the death of Princess Di, the Kennedy assassination, and the life and death of pedophile Jeffrey Epstein.

I knew a little about Epstein, as I had met Ghislaine Maxwell at a book party at the Four Seasons in April 2014. She was the youngest daughter of deceased British press magnate Robert Maxwell, who either committed suicide or was killed by falling off his yacht in the Mediterranean Sea. At the time, little was known about her role in procuring underage girls for sex with Epstein and his friends. She was mostly running an ocean conservancy nonprofit to clean up the high seas.

She had gotten interested in the oceans by watching oceanographer Jacques Cousteau's documentaries. Later she learned how to pilot a small sub. When she went down to the ocean bottom in one of her first dives, she expected to see fish but instead saw a plastic hanger. At that moment she says she decided to focus her professional efforts on preserving the deep seas.

At the book party she wore a sexy red dress. After talking to me for a few minutes about the stories I covered, she asked if I could give her a lift home to her East Side townhouse. Once there, she turned to me in the front seat with an offer.

"If you come in and fuck me, I will tell you the secrets of my father," she said coolly.

I was stunned and speechless, my mind racing. I was not about to sleep with her, but the reporter in me still wondered if her information would make a good *60 Minutes* piece. Her father had reportedly worked with the Mossad in helping Israel secure key components to build nuclear devices. But that story was known, and it was dated. Her father was also a criminal who raided his company's pension funds to pay his debts. Of course all that was a long way back. Who cared about Robert Maxwell now?

"What a great offer," I said. "But I left my dog home alone and I really need to get back to her."

It was a lame excuse and she knew it. She smiled weakly and said good night. Before she left the car, I got her card and said I would give her a call.

But as I would later learn, the upfront sell job was not only a Maxwell trait but was also used by Epstein. Writer Jesse Kornbluth wrote that the night before his wedding to his current wife, Epstein called her and said, "It's your last free night. Why don't you come over and fuck me?" It turns out that Maxwell said to Kornbluth at a party a few years later, "If you lose ten pounds, I will fuck you." His wife was standing next to him.

As more sordid details began to emerge about Epstein and Maxwell's role in pimping for him, I called her a few months before the 2016 presidential election and asked if she would join me for a drink. She immediately said yes.

She thought I was following up on her previous seduction offer, but I was more interested in what she knew about Trump's visits to

Epstein's Palm Beach house and any interactions he may have had with underage women. One lawsuit filed that year named Trump as the person who allegedly had sex with a thirteen-year-old at Epstein's place, a suit that was dismissed.

But because I had a sense of who Epstein was, I surmised that he had wired his homes with security cameras that videotaped his guests having sex, a fact later confirmed by one of the underage women he seduced. So I played a hunch.

"I want the tapes," I told Maxwell at a table at the Regency Bar. "I know he was videotaping everyone, and I want the tapes of Trump with the girls."

She didn't deny the existence of the tapes but said, "I don't know where they are."

"Ask Epstein. The fate of the country is at stake. Trump could be elected president, and how would you feel if those tapes emerged after he was in office?"

She gave me a stern look and pointed a finger in my face. "I am the daughter of a press baron. I know the way you people think. If you do one side, you must do the other. If you get tapes on Trump, you have to do Clinton," she said.

"I will," I said. "I will go wherever the story goes."

Former President Bill Clinton had taken at least twenty-six trips abroad on Epstein's private jet, the "Lolita Express"—even flying without his Secret Service detail. He has said that it was all for Clinton Foundation business, but flight logs showed there were unidentified women on the flights, including one who was later identified as giving Epstein "massages."

Maxwell didn't want Trump elected but said that Hillary Clinton was comfortably ahead and there was no need for the story to come out. Besides, she said, Epstein never shared with her the location of the tapes.

At the end of the night, I hailed her a cab. She asked if I was going to go back to her place.

"Get me the tapes, and I will go back to your place," I said.

She seemed to expect that answer. She gave me a kiss on the cheek and was gone.

It was the last time I would see her. After Epstein's death she went on the lam. Reporters and detectives claimed she was seen in London, Los Angeles, Manchester-by-the-Sea in Massachusetts, and even Brazil when it turned out she was living in a million-dollar home in rural New Hampshire. I believe she wasn't scared of testifying or being indicted. She was afraid of being killed. She told me that Epstein spent millions trying to find a medical fountain of youth. He wanted to remain forever young and even explored preserving his body cryogenically, so he could be brought back to life in the future, when he believed living forever was possible. Why would someone who believes in that want to kill himself?

Even if she didn't know all his secrets—which celebrities were involved with underage girls—she worried that those who had the means to kill Epstein could do the same to her.

She knew the scene in Palm Beach, a playground for rich men loaded up on Viagra, trying to make up for missed chances when they were younger. They invested with Epstein, I believe, after being extorted with pictures from nights of debauchery. Maxwell was the procurer, enabler, and occasionally a participant in the sexcapades.

As one friend, a prominent Palm Beach therapist, cynically told me, "There is nothing in Palm Beach but closet gays and druggies living in mansions waiting to die."

The Palm Beach culture was never more evident than when Patriots owner Robert Kraft got busted, along with other wealthy people, for going to a low-rent massage parlor to get a hand job. I had gotten to know Dave Aronberg, a young, ambitious Palm Beach County prosecutor who had made a name for himself aggressively prosecuting doctors who recklessly prescribed insane amounts of opioids to patients.

Aronberg's team got a tip that Chinese massage parlors, which had taken the place of the pain management clinics that once dotted South Florida strip malls, were now engaged in sex for pay. The local police set up cameras inside one called the Orchids of Asia Day Spa after they noticed eight men in golf carts showing up and acting, in the words of the police, "as if they were about to score."

One of those who would later go was Kraft. He claimed that he couldn't get a massage at the Breakers, a fancy upscale hotel-condo complex in Palm Beach, so a friend volunteered to drive him to the place for a massage.

Kraft was at the location twice and was caught on surveillance, getting masturbated by a Chinese female and anally stimulated. It was not a good look for the Super Bowl–winning owner, who stopped by the location on the way to his private plane, to travel to a Patriots playoff game.

Kraft's high-powered legal team fought the charges aggressively, knowing a conviction could result in a suspension from the NFL. Pressure was soon put on the local judge and the prosecutors to drop the case. It seems that is the Palm Beach way of doing things. Even though Jeffrey Epstein was convicted in 2007 of having sex with minors, he would go to jail only to sleep.

Epstein's private army of detectives, lawyers, and hired guns muscled local prosecutors, harassing them with late-night calls and even reportedly, running their cars off the road. The U.S. attorney, in part fearing for his staff, caved to Epstein's demands of no twenty-four-hour jail time.

Now Kraft's team was working from a similar playbook. They filed a lawsuit against Aronberg that would hold him liable personally. They got his top donor to ask Aronberg to drop the case. And they worked the local judge to agree to suppress the damaging undercover tape of Kraft in the massage parlor, effectively eliminating the evidence. The case against Kraft was eventually dropped.

But then the outrage over the terms of Epstein's sentence became public and the state attorney general was forced to appeal the local judge's verdict. As for the patrons, I was told if the police had kept up the surveillance, they would have busted half the male members of Mar-a-Lago.

At some point, after Trump won the nomination in 2016, I noticed that the stories I was involved in had taken a seedier turn. Bannon, Howard, Cohen, Kraft, Ghislaine Maxwell. Even the correspondent I was working with, Charlie Rose, acted in a way worse than those whom we wanted to profile. The world was now being run or manipulated by crazies and I found myself chasing all of them. I needed to go back to an old-fashioned investigation that exposed corporate greed and a corrupt Congress. While I didn't realize it at the time, I was about to embark on the most significant investigation of my career.

31

THE WHISTLEBLOWER

More than 200,000 Americans have already died in the worst drug epidemic in U.S. history. Their deaths were triggered by the billions of opioid pills that made their way to crooked pharmacies and doctors' offices, giving easy access to people who had no legitimate need for the drugs.

If those pills are taken around the clock, a person can quickly become tolerant of their pain-relieving effects. Then to continue to get relief, the person needs higher and higher doses. As the doses grow, the risk of death increases, and eventually victims asphyxiate.

The largest maker of OxyContin, Purdue Pharma, run by the Sackler family, and the largest drug distributor, the McKesson Corporation, made fortunes pushing pills while their high-priced lawyers kept their executives out of prison. If the companies got caught misleading the public about Oxycontin's risks of addiction, they paid relatively small fines, a price of doing business.

The drug companies, through campaign contributions and influential lobbyists, had Congress in their pockets. It was like Al Capone owning the city of Chicago during Prohibition. Meanwhile, the death toll kept climbing. More Americans have already died from opioids than were killed in the U.S. in the coronavirus pandemic.

And there was one man who tried to prevent this genocide on American soil and who took on the whole system of lawyers, doctors, congressmen, and corporate heads—Joe Rannazzisi.

There is no hiding the rough edges of Joe Rannazzisi. He is a tough, blunt-talking, former DEA deputy assistant administrator, who supervised six hundred federal investigators responsible for cracking down on the drug companies that do not follow the prescription drug laws. He believed that if these companies did not follow the law, people die. And they were not following the law.

Before he was forced to resign, Joe discovered that the big drug distributors, who were supposed to stop suspiciously large orders, were instead shipping them to rogue pharmacies and pain clinics in small towns, which provided the rocket fuel for the opioid epidemic. But rather than going to war against the drugmakers and distributors, Joe said the DEA stopped their enforcement efforts. "There is no doubt that at the height of the opioid epidemic, when the addiction rate was rising, we at the DEA slowed down."

The story was so important that I went back to *The Washington Post*, partners of mine in the past, and they readily agreed to a collaboration. They had done some stellar reporting on the opioid epidemic, but the stories came out right before the 2016 election and received scant attention. Our collaboration, if it worked, would attract more visibility than any previous reporting effort. And we were confident in what we would find. You don't cause the death of 400,000 people and not leave a paper trail.

We felt lucky that two of the *Post*'s best reporters were assigned to the project. Scott Higham is a badass Pulitzer Prize–winning journalist who is relentless in holding scoundrels' feet to the fire. Lenny Bernstein, a former *Post* editor, has an encyclopedic mind and covered medicine and health as part of his beat. Bernstein wanted everyone to get along, even the targets of our investigation, which was helpful. Since Scott and I share the same doggedness, we needed someone whose phone calls would get returned.

Rounding out our team was my associate producer Sam Hornblower, who was a vacuum cleaner of facts. Sam would interview someone on the phone or in person for five hours or spend a week in a small courthouse in West Virginia, going through court records. That, to Sam, is a perfect week. And we had the best correspondent on *60 Minutes,* Bill Whitaker, who brought all his energy and wisdom to the interviews.

Before we all launched, I set up a phone call between *Post* executive editor Marty Baron and Jeff Fager. For this to succeed, we needed their backing. Fager was full of enthusiasm and excitement and had encouraged us to do this investigation. Baron, the definition of understated, has a great newsman's nose for right and wrong and is a strong advocate of investigative reporting. He understood, as did Fager, that the collaboration of two great institutions will result in a better story, combining our sources and reach to have the greatest impact.

Bernstein had gotten to know Rannazzisi by covering his not-infrequent testimony in front of congressional committees. These small backwater hearing rooms were often breeding grounds for great stories, and Bernstein was expert at mining them. Rannazzisi warned Congress for years about the opioid epidemic and pleaded with members to do something about it. His testimony fell on deaf ears, which only led to Joe's becoming more discouraged and eventually being forced to resign from the DEA.

Hornblower and I flew down from New York and went directly to our lunch with Joe at an out-of-the-way Greek restaurant in Arlington, Virginia. Joe came in pissed off; he regarded the meeting as a waste of time, but agreed to show up as a favor to Scott.

Dealing with pissed-off people is my sweet spot, after working with TV prima donnas. Joe's brusqueness was almost soothing. He was a no-nonsense, principled man who saw the coming epidemic and tried to stop it. As smart as he was—he held degrees in law and pharmacy—his solution for ending the opioid crisis was to send drug company executives to jail, and he didn't think our potential story would accomplish that.

"Nothing matters until *60 Minutes* does the story," I said. "The *Post*'s work was comprehensive but didn't get an emotional reaction. Ours will."

Joe was skeptical but was listening. He wanted to believe.

"Whitaker is a rock star interviewer and I know how to tell a story to get viewers angry. And you have two great institutions that are now prepared to invest in your story. This is a no-brainer. And it also might be your last chance to do something that can save lives."

Joe wanted to save lives and agreed to the interview. A week later, he came up to New York, and with three cameras and a well-prepared correspondent, Joe carefully and angrily began to tell his tale.

In the late 1990s opioids like oxycodone were used routinely for issues of chronic pain. The drug companies assured doctors they were safe. One Purdue medical expert even testified in Congress that addiction is rare for users of opioids. Joe said that because many doctors were convinced the drugs posed few risks, prescriptions skyrocketed, and so did the mass distribution of the opioids through pain centers located off highway exit ramps and on busy thoroughfares in big cities.

"It made the crack epidemic look like nothing," Joe said. "These weren't kids slinging crack on the corner. There were professionals who were doing it. They were just drug dealers in lab coats."

The interview would last for nearly four hours, with Whitaker leaning forward, almost touching Joe's knees. Our *Post* colleagues watched, mesmerized. They had spent dozens of hours alone with Joe and had never gotten him to open up like he did with Whitaker. I explained to Lenny and Scott that the magic of TV lights sometimes gets interview subjects to go to places they never had gone before. And Joe certainly went there.

Joe's strategy of prosecuting crooked doctors was not making a dent in the drug trade, so he decided to move up the food chain and went after the distributors. These distributors are multinational corporations like McKesson, whose CEO, John Hammergren, was the third highest paid corporate head in the United States, behind Apple's Tim Cook and Netflix's Reed Hastings. In one ten-year period, Hammergren made more than $700 million.

Hammergren owned multiple homes on both coasts, including one outside Berkeley, with a tennis court, a squash court, and a four-car garage filled with Ferraris. The home also had its own waterfall.

McKesson made a fortune on the opioid epidemic, shipping thousands of suspicious drug orders when they had a legal obligation to stop them. One example was a small town in West Virginia, with under 400 people receiving 9 million hydrocodone pills over a two-year period.

As a result of Joe's investigations, the drug distributors were eventually fined over $300 million but no executive from the companies went to jail. Those companies didn't want to pay large fines, or risk going to prison, so their lawyers and lobbyists began to work the Justice Department and Congress to change the law to make it impossible for them to ever be prosecuted. They had money and influence, and it worked.

The top echelons of the Justice Department believed that the drug industry was not foreign drug cartel operators but U.S. corporations that employ thousands of Americans, and so they wanted to work out any differences around a conference table, and not in courtrooms. But Joe felt differently and began to push back against his own bosses inside the Justice Department. He declared war against his own Justice Department and increased the temperature on the drug industry. "We were going to go after these people and not stop."

But lower-level Justice Department lawyers working cases against distributors began to experience roadblocks.

Agents who had put together major cases against drug distributors were stalled. "I spent a year working on this case and I sent it down and it's never good enough," one agent told us. "At this point you know they just don't want the case."

After strong-arming the DEA, the drug industry lobbyists and lawyers turned to Congress to create legislation that would take away the authority of the DEA to enforce the regulations of the Controlled

Substances Act, the DEA's most effective tool to fight the spread of the narcotics.

The bill was written by a drug lobbyist who had previously worked as chief counsel in the DEA. It was introduced by Pennsylvania congressman Tom Marino and the then–Tennessee congresswoman, now senator, Marsha Blackburn, and it was promoted as ensuring that patients have access to pain medication. But what it really did was to defang the DEA of its enforcement abilities.

The drug industry spent $106 million lobbying Congress to pass the bill, an extraordinary sum of money even by lobbying standards.

But for the drug industry to succeed, they needed to eliminate Rannazzisi. And when Joe publicly attacked Marino and Blackburn for creating legislation that would, in his words, "protect criminals," they had their opening. The legislators wrote the inspector general of the DEA demanding that Rannazzisi get investigated for trying to "intimidate Congress."

Pressure was exerted on the DEA to have Joe removed. The DEA stripped him of his responsibilities, and he went from supervising six hundred agents to supervising no one. So he resigned.

With Joe out of the way, Congress passed the legislation on a voice vote and President Barack Obama signed it into law without the usual bill-signing photo op. The "do-nothing Congress" had finally done something, and no one wanted to call attention to it.

No one except for Congressman Marino, who issued a press release claiming credit for its passage. The DEA chief administrative judge told us that the new law now makes it impossible to prosecute unscrupulous distributors.

"Why would Congress pass a bill that strips us of our authority in the height of the opioid epidemic, when people in their backyards are dying from drugs that are coming from the same people that these bills are protecting?" Joe asked.

He was going to answer his own question. "Because the drug industry has an influence over Congress that has never been seen before. They came in with their influence and money and got a whole statute changed because they didn't like it."

Joe resigned before he was able to accomplish his ultimate mission: "The one thing I wanted to do was lock up and arrest one of these corporate officers. You arrest a corporate officer, you arrest someone involved in the decision process, then everybody sits up and takes notice, because three-piece-suit guys just don't do well in prison. They don't."

But the biggest surprise was that after Marino created the legislation that neutered the DEA, he was named Donald Trump's new drug czar.

Marino had refused an interview with us, so we went to his congressional office to ambush him for comment. His aide said he wasn't there, so we decided to wait. After only a few minutes, the Capitol Hill police came, and at the congressman's request, asked us to leave.

As we prepared to go, we saw the congressman leave through a side door. Whitaker gave chase, as did our cameraman.

"Why did you vote for a bill that the lobbyist wrote?" Whitaker asked.

"A lot of lobbyists write legislation," he answered.

"Did you know what was in the bill before you voted on it?"

"You don't always know what's in the bill before you vote on it," came the reply.

"This is a bill that takes the powers away from the DEA to enforce the law against big drug corporations that are causing the opioid epidemic. Don't you think you should know about it before voting on it?"

"I will look into it," the congressman said.

Whitaker had chased him to the elevators, where the congressman entered and disappeared. Whitaker was ecstatic. It was his first run-and-gun ambush and it couldn't have turned out better.

Except for the fact that it was the wrong congressman. It was Louis Gohmert, a Republican from Texas, who must have felt guilty about something and ran away from us.

Gohmert looks a little like Marino, as both are bald, white, and about the same height. But we didn't find out until we examined the video later that day that we had the wrong congressman. Still, we found Gohmert's admissions interesting. As for Marino, we never got him on-camera, as he went into hiding.

Our stories would run on the same day, The stories would run on the same Sunday. The *Post*'s was on the front page with a banner headline with multiple full pages inside the paper. Our story was a double segment later that day on *60 Minutes.*

Mike Morell, a former acting CIA director and a consultant to CBS news, called me the night of the broadcast and said he got so emotional watching that he threw a shoe at the TV. Senator Chuck Schumer took to the floor of the Senate and said Marino as drug czar was like the fox guarding the henhouse. But more important, Trump saw the broadcast and said the next day, "We are going to look into the report, and we are going to take it seriously."

He also added that Marino "was a good man." In Trump world, that means you are toast. Marino would withdraw his name for consideration for the drug czar position the next day. Our stories would become the most award-winning series in the history of *60 Minutes,* garnering eight major awards, including a Peabody, a duPont, and an Emmy. The *Post* was equally in awe of the power of the partnership and invited me to speak to a *Post* lunch gathering of reporters and a meeting with their national staff about future collaborations. We felt that the power of the partnership would conquer all worlds and would do what reporters love to do: help make the world a better place through our stories. But then a *Post* editor quietly came up to me and told me of an active investigation the paper had against one of the anchors of CBS News and *60 Minutes,* and all the goodwill we had developed would disappear.

32

CHARLIE ROSE AND #ME TOO

The *Post* editor took me into his office and told me that two of their reporters had a story about Charlie Rose's harassing the women he worked with. The story would say that Rose either touched or exposed himself to them. There were eight women making the claim, and I found out later that CBS management was aware of the coming story but didn't know any details.

Charlie had always been a ladies' man, but I never thought he would cross the line and use his position and standing to take advantage of his coworkers. At CBS, everyone was waiting for the story to drop.

A few weeks went by after my *Post* sidebar conversation. I happened to be on the phone one afternoon with Norah O'Donnell discussing a story idea. Norah worked with Charlie every day as co-anchor of the CBS morning show before she became the *CBS Evening News* anchor; she seemed to have a sense of what was about to be reported. As we talked, the article appeared online. We skimmed it quickly and I said instinctively, "This is horrible. I feel so bad for Charlie."

And she answered appropriately: "I feel sorry for the women." Her response was from her gut and gave me an inkling of what it may have been like for women, even Norah, to work with him.

Within a few hours of the article being posted, Rose was fired. I had dinner that night with former New York City police commissioner Bill Bratton and his wife, Rikki Klieman. All of us knew Charlie, but we had a hard time reconciling the Charlie we knew and the one described in the article. At the end of the dinner, Bratton thought it would be a good idea to check in on him, to make sure he wasn't suicidal.

I got in my car and called. "Charlie, Ira. Are you okay? Do you need some company? I can come over," I said as soon as he answered.

"I am fine, Amanda [Burden, his longtime companion] is on her way here. I am fine. Don't believe everything you read."

"Charlie, I know you are fine now, but you may not be in ten minutes. I would be happy to babysit you tonight."

"I am telling you everything is fine. There is no truth to any of these stories," he said.

But unfortunately there was. The level of detail from so many women could not be dismissed, and more stories of his groping and harassment would surface. In the ensuing weeks he consulted with his friends, many who would cut him out of their lives. A few stayed in touch, including Oprah Winfrey, Gayle King, Warren Buffett, and actor Jeremy Irons, whom Rose said wrote him a warm and heartfelt note.

A month after the story appeared, he sounded more upbeat. He said he was now helping people on his staff find jobs and that he was working out every day and playing tennis.

"I had five assistants at the shows, and they have all said that I never harassed them," he said. However, I pointed out that he worked with many more females than just his personal assistants. I was angry at him for being an asshole, but I didn't want to lecture him. I wanted to try to understand his thinking.

"The Smithsonian was going to give me an award they rarely give out. It was going to be a special award for me. They canceled it," he said somewhat sadly. He said he now found more solace talking to priests and therapists than to big-time celebrities.

"I cannot go in public with a woman alone. Someone would see me, take a picture, and post it. 'Charlie Rose out again with women having a good time,'" he said, imagining the headline.

Meanwhile, no one at CBS would admit to having any idea about Rose's abusive behavior toward his female subordinates, which included groping and taking showers in front of them. But male and female supervisors who might have suspected his inappropriate behavior chose to look the other way, as "Charlie is being Charlie." And that was wrong.

After the initial article was published the *Post* reporters began to investigate who at CBS was aware of or covered up his behavior, and whether there were larger cultural issues at the network that allowed him to act like a harasser. And their main target became *60 Minutes* executive producer Jeff Fager.

Jeff had risen from a producer on the evening news to becoming chairman of CBS News and executive producer of *60 Minutes*. At CBS, everyone wanted to live in "Fager World," where all stories work out, and every few years you would get promoted and rise up the ladder of success. It also meant parking spots always seemed to be open, right in front of the restaurant. "Fager World" became the definition of living a charmed life.

He had managed to keep the show on track after the death of the founding correspondents, and now Oprah Winfrey volunteered to do stories for the show. That is how Fager World works.

But after the fiftieth-anniversary celebrations of *60 Minutes,* Fager World began to fall apart. Oprah Winfrey did a few stories for *60 Minutes* in the 2017–18 season, but they didn't showcase her talents.

When she went to record her stories, she said she was told to slow down her delivery and practice saying her name over and over, as there was too much emotion when she did her enunciation. She felt those directives were pulling her down and flattening out her personality, which is not what you want if you have Oprah Winfrey. Ultimately, she decided to leave *60 Minutes* to focus on her projects for Apple TV.

Around the same time the two *Post* reporters who reported the Rose stories focused on whether Fager was guilty of harassment.

Over four months, nearly every female member of *60 Minutes* received a call from the *Post* reporters, asking if they had ever been groped by Rose or Fager. One female producer was asked if she was promoted because she was pretty. Another female producer was ridiculed by the reporters when she told them she had never been groped by Charlie Rose. "Well, you are too old for him anyway," they told the forty-six-year-old producer. At the time of that call she was in the midst of getting chemotherapy to treat a cancer that would later claim her life.

In their search for harassers, the *Post* reporters became harassers themselves. Ultimately, the editors at *The Washington Post* said, their story on Fager "did not meet our standards for publication," and when it ran, it didn't include any harassment allegations against him.

So the *Post* reporters leaked their rejected story to Ronan Farrow of *The New Yorker,* who printed allegations of harassment by Fager, including that he touched women inappropriately at office parties. Fager's story appeared linked with the shocking revelations against CBS CEO Les Moonves, in which he was accused by multiple women of serious sexual assault.

Having two of the most important figures at CBS linked together in one article forced the CBS board to hire two law firms to investigate the charges.

It would be a fateful decision. The firms the board chose happened to be the law firms that were defending the principal corporate entities accused of causing the opioid epidemic, the ones that we exposed in several *60 Minutes* stories.

Covington & Burling, a large international thousand-person law firm that once defended the tobacco industry, was now the main firm for McKesson. The firm settled substantial litigation claims against the company with the Justice Department, which was run by their past and future law partner, Attorney General Eric Holder. The drug distributor paid a fine of $150 million for their illegalities, but the law firm kept all their executives out of jail.

And then there was Mary Jo White of Debevoise & Plimpton. She has represented the executives and interests of Purdue Pharma for more than fifteen years. In 2007, she described the Purdue's general counsel Howard Udell as a "moral compass." That's how she described the man who would plead guilty to helping mislead the public as to the danger of opioids. The company would pay $634 million in fines, but none of their executives went to jail.

Purdue and the Sacklers would continue to make billions selling opioids. And Mary Jo White would continue to represent them.

So imagine my surprise when these two law firms were hired by the CBS board to investigate not only the sordid stories around Moonves but the culture at CBS News and *60 Minutes*. Leading the investigation of *60 Minutes* was none other than Mary Jo White.

To do their investigative work, CBS would provide the law firms with complete access to our emails, essentially giving them an open look at the sources and methods we used to expose the opioid industry.

I called the CBS associate general counsel, who worked with us on our opioid stories, and expressed my concern and outrage about the hirings. She said that she didn't hire the law firms, the board did.

CBS corporate had in fact hired a reputable attorney, Betsy Plevan with Proskauer Rose LLP, but the board felt Plevan had done work for CBS in the past and her investigation therefore might be called into question. So the board hired the opioid law firms to investigate the TV show that had done the most to expose their well-paying drug company clients.

While the law firm's investigation was going on, a second article appeared by Farrow that alleged that Fager, while inebriated at company parties, touched employees in a way that made them uncomfortable. In September 2018, CBS reporter Jericka Duncan sought a response from Fager on the allegation, and he sent her a threatening text: "there are people that have lost their jobs trying to harm me."

The day after he sent that text, CBS president David Rhodes fired him.

"My language was harsh and despite the fact journalists receive harsh demands for fairness all the time, CBS did not like it," Fager wrote. "One such note should not result in termination after 36 years, but it did."

Before the Fager text surfaced, the staff was devastated at losing

Fager and felt he was being treated unfairly. After the text, there was a different vibe, and nearly all felt Fager was crazy to send that text to a reporter, much less one who works for CBS News.

A few months later, the law firms leaked a copy of a draft of their final investigation to *The New York Times*, breaking every confidence they had promised me and all the CBS News employees who agreed to cooperate. More than 250 CBS news and corporate people cooperated in their investigations, but the only part they leaked had to do with Moonves and *60 Minutes*.

To my astonishment, they included my name in a paragraph, in their leak, as having "encouraged women to use their sex appeal to secure information from sources."

In fact I gave a lecture in 2012 at the Investigative Reporters and Editors conference on the art of source development. I said that reporters should be charming, make themselves an interesting person, and show emotions so people will know you care about their plight or story. And as I told the men and women attending, flirting (not sex appeal) is a tool in a journalist toolbox to use, something I witnessed Mike Wallace and others use to great effectiveness.

Now this advice was being twisted as an example to make me look like a sexist. This item was rejected and never published by the *Post*, and CBS HR cleared me a year before, saying I need no remedial work. But the two law firms had an opportunity for payback, a chance to dirty up the lead producer against their corporate clients, and it seemed that they took their shot.

Mary Jo White would take responsibility for the leak and apologized to the CBS board. And that was it. No disciplinary action was taken against the law firms, and they certainly didn't give a break on any of their billable hours.

It was later revealed in a bankruptcy proceeding that Mary Jo White's firm was paid more than $11 million by the Sackler family during the same time period she and her firm were investigating harassment at *60 Minutes* and leaking stories about us.

Our collaboration with the *Post* ended. And after Mary Jo White's investigation of CBS concluded, she continued to defend and promote the Sackler family.

And there was a lot to defend. It was revealed that the Sackler family had withdrawn $10.4 billion from Purdue Pharma over the last decade. The withdrawals came as Purdue's OxyContin was fueling the opioid epidemic and as they were about to begin settlement talks that could cost the company tens of billions, money that was to go for treatment of the thousands of addicts their drugs created.

A few months after her investigation and leak, Mary Jo White's office contacted *60 Minutes* and pitched us a story. They wanted Bill Whitaker, the correspondent who has led the show's effort to expose the opioid companies' role in creating the epidemic, to do a story on the positive contributions the Sackler family has made to society, including all the art they donated to museums.

"I can't make this up," he said to me in his office. "Needless to say, I rejected the offer."

33

NO HAPPY ENDINGS

It occurred to me, after nearly forty years in TV, that there are few graceful exits. Most of the time the high-level TV stars are forced to resign, are fired, or are gently pushed out, usually when viewership numbers inevitably decline. There is an old adage in how to fix a broken TV show—first you change the set, then you change the executive producer, then you fire the talent.

After the embarrassing and false Dan Rather *60 Minutes II* report that alleged that George Bush received preferential treatment in his military service, several major television careers were in jeopardy. They included Mary Mapes, the award-winning producer, who dug up the story; Josh Howard, the show's executive producer, who was at one point second-in-command at *60 Minutes*; Betsy West, the senior vice president of CBS News, who had also been a top senior producer at *Nightline* and *Primetime Live*; Andrew Heyward, the longtime president of CBS News; and of course the anchor of the network, Dan Rather.

As is typical of some of these fiascoes, everyone in the senior management of the show was fired, except for Heyward.

Heyward later was seen at a restaurant with Gil Schwartz, the senior vice president in charge of public relations for CBS corporate, talking about how they cleaned up the mess. But these large media disasters always have an afterlife, and ultimately *60 Minutes II* was canceled and Heyward left CBS a few months after he fired everyone.

In 2014, Heyward applied to be the executive producer of the *CBS Evening News* with Scott Pelley. Some would regard this as a demotion, but Heyward wanted to be back in the action, as a show producer. He didn't get the job, as it ended up going to Steve Capus, who had himself been fired as president of NBC News.

Rick Kaplan may have set the record for being fired from top network jobs. He was president of CNN, MSNBC, executive producer of *Primetime Live* at ABC, executive producer of the *CBS Evening News* with Katie Couric, and finally back to ABC, where he was hired and fired from his job running political coverage and the Sunday news talk show. After a brilliant career, in his last network job, he was escorted out of the building by security. They allowed him to return later to collect family pictures.

In 2005, Ted Koppel announced he wanted to leave *Nightline*. This of course was not entirely his choice. The show's numbers had been in decline, and it was not the moneymaker it had been in the past. Koppel was offered a contract, but for much less money than his reported salary of $10 million a year.

A reporter for *The New York Times* asked Koppel what he would do next. He replied, "There are some very interesting prospects out there, let's put it that way."

In fact they were far less interesting than the job he once had. He joined BBC America as an occasional commentator, and then he and his former executive producer Tom Bettag did stories in 2012 for *Rock Center,* the failed NBC newsmagazine show. Koppel became one of at least twelve correspondents, and he seemed out of place to be sharing a rostrum with correspondents like Chelsea Clinton. I tried and failed to have *60 Minutes* hire him as a contributing correspondent, but he did find a home as a contributor to the CBS show *Sunday Morning,* where he continued to do stellar work.

When Sam Donaldson was being phased out at ABC, he was given a daily internet show. But as Donaldson neared eighty, he divorced his wife of twenty-nine years, Jan Smith Donaldson, and was arrested on DWI charges in Maryland, charges that were later dismissed.

He would then in 2009 quietly retire to a horse ranch in New Mexico, with a new woman, and finally accepted that at eighty, he'd reached the right time to leave the stage.

Barbara Walters had a harder time with retirement. One week after she had been celebrated in one retirement event after another, ending with a street being named for her outside the ABC News building, she was back on the air, at the age of eighty-four. Today Walters rarely leaves her home, and according to some of her former producers, she is suffering from the early stages of dementia.

Charlie Gibson retired from the anchor chair at ABC News when he turned sixty-five. Gibson told anyone who asked that he wanted to leave when he could still travel and enjoy life.

Gibson did travel, to Paris for a cooking class. He took a long cruise and enjoyed ski vacations in Utah and summers at the Cape. He also had to battle throat cancer, which he was able to beat.

Gibson, his voice softer now since his cancer bout, seems to miss the action, though he will not acknowledge that he retired too early. He returned in 2017 to visit *Good Morning America* and told the anchors that in his nineteen years on the show, his favorite interview subject was Kermit the Frog. That tells you a lot about what Charlie thought of politicians and actors.

For his part, Rather's final days at CBS News weren't pretty. After his report on *60 Minutes II* was discredited, he was taken off the news as anchor and assigned to do occasional stories as a *60 Minutes* contributor, though he was there playing out his contract.

One time he wandered down the hall near my office and asked one of the secretaries what the soup of the day was. Seemingly reflecting on the moment, he said, "I used to be anchor of the *CBS Evening News,* and now I am asking what the soup of the day is."

A short time later, he would be fired from the only network for which he had ever worked. He would end up suing CBS for breach of contract. Rather would be one of the lucky ones, as he discovered a second act interviewing aging rock stars on cable.

As for Mike Wallace, the way his career ended was quite painful to watch. One of his last stories he did was an interview in 2006 with the Iranian leader Mahmoud Ahmadinejad. Mike was stuck in an Iranian hotel for seven days without air conditioning. As Mike sweated, he changed the direction of the interview to be more about the crazy leader's lifestyle than about Iranian policies. Mike didn't even question Ahmadinejad about some of the incendiary comments he made regarding Israel and America. Afterward, he called Ahmadinejad "an impressive fellow." But the story Mike did on veterans of the war in Afghanistan is the one that would end his career.

Mike thought it was worth two parts, while his producer, Bob Anderson, thought it should be one. They decided to screen two parts and let Fager rule. Jeff decided it should be a single segment, which did not sit well with Mike. He said to Jeff what he sometimes said to Hewitt whenever they disagreed: "Go fuck yourself."

"What did you say?" Fager asked.

"You heard me, go fuck yourself," Mike said.

Fager was not Hewitt and didn't tolerate that language or that insubordination in a screening.

"You're done," Fager said and got up and went back to his office.

Mike was not quite sure what had happened, but those in the screening room certainly understood. Fager had just fired Mike Wallace.

Fager immediately called Sean McManus, the president of CBS News, and told him what occurred.

"I totally support you," McManus said.

Mike was in a state of bewilderment. He had talked that way his entire career and thought he had developed immunity. But being a prick, as Safer had called him, had finally caught up to him, and Fager was not going to put up with it. He went across the street and McManus told him he supported Fager's decision.

The Mike Wallace era at CBS was drawing to a close. Meantime, Richard Leibner, Mike's agent, got an offer from NBC News that they were willing to hire him. While the details were being negotiated, Wallace agreed to give a speech in front of the staff at ESPN, in Bristol, Connecticut. Leibner drove with him there and gave him a copy of the contract that called on Mike to give a half-hour speech for $20,000.

When Mike began his address, he told those assembled that he really had nothing to say, and he took the contract out of his pocket and began to read it out loud. After that, Leibner realized he couldn't move Mike, in good faith, to NBC. When Leibner returned to New York, he called CBS and told them that they should figure out an accommodation to allow Mike to stay, in some capacity, until he decided to retire.

CBS agreed, but said they would remove Mike from his office and give him one that wasn't on correspondents' row at *60 Minutes*. They found some space in a back office near the editing suites. Mike never set foot in that office. It was a great diminishment of Mike, and one in which Fager sent a clear message to the other correspondents: I am not someone you fuck with.

The correspondents understood. And there was very little dissension after that. As Lesley Stahl later said to me, "My career goal now is to survive." Mike began to spend a longer time in his Martha's Vineyard house, which he loved. He could no longer play tennis and spent his time reading and entertaining his friends and grandchildren. Having lost his job, Mike was a bit out of sorts. He never wanted to "reflect on his life," as he once told Morley Safer. He wanted to die on assignment, covering a big story.

But I realized he had accepted retirement when he dropped by my office after the summer break in 2006. He wanted to show me his hair.

His hair was always black and perfectly combed, and Mike always maintained that he never dyed it.

But in fact he did. We were once in Geneva, Switzerland, doing a spy story when I was in Mike's hotel room going over that day's schedule. I went to the bathroom and found bottles of hair dye. In my best Mike Wallace moment, I walked out of his bathroom and asked, "What is this for?" holding up one of the bottles.

"What the hell are you doing going through my stuff? Get out of here," he said.

Now back from the Vineyard, he walked into my office wearing sandals, no socks, and a baseball hat. He had a slight beard.

"Kid, take a look," he said. And with that he lifted his hat to reveal a mostly gray head of hair.

"I don't give a shit anymore," he said, and with that, he put his hat back on and left my room.

Mike was getting reflective as he neared his eighty-eighth birthday. He told one interviewer, "I am a demanding guy. I can demean people when I get under pressure, when stories aren't going well, when I'm feeling bad. Sometimes I can be excessively acerbic, occasionally I have done it in public, and I deplore what I have done. . . . I've been mean. But the stuff I have turned out has been first-rate."

Many of the producers who worked with Mike did not forgive him for the way they were treated and stopped talking to him. All the pain and abuse he dished out could not be forgiven simply by saying, "but the stuff I turned out was first-rate." And yet as mean and exasperating as he could be, I wanted more moments to be with him.

The last time I saw Mike and Don together was in Mike's office in October 2007. A tribute was being prepared for Mike at the University of Illinois, and Mike and Don were watching old shows to select clips of stories that would be played at the event.

When I walked in, they were watching a *60 Minutes* story on the Muppets, who were playing the role of certain *60 Minutes* correspondents. You could tell Mike and Don both loved this TV medium that they'd helped popularize, and they laughed at the Muppets portrayals.

Mike would occasionally interrupt Don's enthusiasm to point at Don's stomach and say, "Stick it in," something I had heard Mike say to me since the first time I worked with him. Even today, when I take a family picture, I hold my stomach in to make myself seem thinner.

I looked over to the corner of Mike's office and there sitting in a glass case was the old tennis ball Art Buchwald had given Mike. My career was due in part to that tennis ball. When I saw the tennis display during my job interview in 1980, I told Mike I played college tennis, and that's why he offered me the job. I reminded Mike and Don of the story of how they hired me.

"I had to lose to you, otherwise the shoot would go horribly," I reminded Wallace. "It was part of my job description." Mike would even announce our scores over the office loudspeaker.

"You couldn't handle the pressure," Mike said. "I would love to drop-shot you and watch you scamper to the net and fall on your face. It made me so happy."

When it came to stories, Don could always top anyone's. "I remember calling your house and your mother answered. I told her I wanted to give you a job and she said you have a job already," Don said, remembering the conversation as if it had happened yesterday, not twenty-seven years earlier.

I enjoyed staying in that room. I wanted to save that moment forever. These two men gave me a career, a professional life. They were both American originals. And I was sad that it would soon be over for them.

Morley Safer, who occupied an office next to Mike, did Mike's TV exit interview. It was an ironic moment that Morley, who spent much of his career competing with Mike, would be the one conducting the final interview.

Mike looked at Morley and started to talk off-camera. "You know I was always jealous of you," Mike said.

"You were jealous of me? You dominated this place," Morley said.

"You could write, and I couldn't," Mike said. "And I always wished I could."

Morley would later tell me that Mike was an incredibly insecure man, and it affected his personal and professional business relationships. "He was always envious, always looking over his shoulders," Morley said.

As for Don Hewitt, he continued coming to his office, which was now directly one floor below his old *60 Minutes* office, almost till the end of his life. The last project he worked on was a documentary on the Radio City Rockettes. He would die of pancreatic cancer in 2009.

Mike eventually began to have health problems. A heart procedure left him with a diminished mental capacity that was later identified as the early stages of dementia. He lay in bed most of the day, wearing nothing but a bathrobe. He stayed in his room surrounded by tapes of his old stories, as if they were put there to jar his memory.

Once when I visited him with his producer Bob Anderson and a former female associate producer, Mike spent part of the visit pretending to look up her dress. He said little that visit except "that's absolutely correct," in responding to conversation.

As Mike began to lose more of his memory, he stopped seeing people. He stayed in a dark room in his large Park Avenue apartment and would walk around unshaven, hair uncombed, and in his underwear.

His wife, Mary, let me visit him. She thought I might cheer him up. I reminded him of some of our adventures together, but all he did was give me baffled looks. All he seemed to remember was how he used to drop-shot me in tennis and how happy it made him.

Later that day, I wondered what the meaning of all this was, if the only thing he remembered from his long, celebrated life was playing a few sets of tennis with a producer. I remembered what the great actress Katharine Hepburn said on *60 Minutes*: "Well, all my contemporaries have died off, so I'm all that's left. I'm in a safe group. I haven't gotten this romantic feeling about age. I think we rot away, and it's too goddamn bad we do."

I would tell Chris about the visit I had with his father, and he said that Mike had lost so much of his memory, that he had asked Chris if he had any children, Mike's grandchildren. Chris has four.

My last visit with Mike occurred at a Connecticut nursing home in 2012. Mike at this point had full-blown dementia and spoke very little. His stepdaughter Pauline looked after him with great love. Mike was in his own room, which was covered with pictures from his career. He stayed most of the time in a wheelchair.

We rolled him to dinner, where a lovely woman, almost Mike's age, waited for him. When he arrived, she put her hand on top of his and said, "Mike, I want you to know that I am available to you anytime." Mike didn't respond.

After dinner, back in his room, I tried reminding him of some of the stories we did together. He kept saying "yep" or "absolutely," but he seemed to remember nothing.

It was sad to see Mike in this state. He had even forgotten he worked at *60 Minutes*. "He spends most of the time in a fog, but there are moments when the fog lifts and you get a glimpse of the man that was," Chris Wallace told me before I went.

Sure enough, as I was about to leave, Mike asked me about a particular female TV correspondent we both knew. I told him that as far as I knew she was doing well.

He looked at me with a mischievous look and said, "She's a lousy lay."

And those were Mike's final words to me. He said nothing for the rest of the visit. He would die a month later.

34

TIME TO GO

Watching the great comedians perform in the Catskills taught me the life lesson to leave the stage with the audience wanting more. After our series on the opioid epidemic, I felt I had done my best work. The stories, as the CBS press release declared, won more awards than any series in the fifty-two-year history of the show. It was a perfect and fitting end to a career.

I was also losing interest in working at *60 Minutes*. I am not quite sure when my blind and total dedication to the job began to wane. When I first arrived at *60 Minutes* in the 1980s, there was a sense of mission, a calling—we felt we were doing the work of the Lord. But as time went by, I felt that the stories we produced were getting softer, the producers younger and more inexperienced, and the sense that each show we did should make a difference no longer seemed to matter.

Now I would stand outside my corner office, located at the nexus of correspondents' and producers' rows, and listen for the shouting and laughter that was once commonplace but is now gone. It felt like I was working in a library. I simply didn't want to be there anymore.

The new order from management was that people should be polite and treat one another with respect. There was to be no more drinking or smoking in the office, a clear dig at the behavior of Steve Kroft and

Morley Safer. All these were needed changes, but the crazy recklessness of a bygone era had disappeared. And with it, the magic energy that created programs that were iconoclastic also seemed to disappear.

The Me Too reckoning was needed, as it left too many women in tatters. And even if Wallace and Hewitt were geniuses, it didn't excuse their Neanderthal behavior toward women. If I had been a twenty-six-year-old woman working for Wallace in 1980, I doubt I would have survived the experience. I wonder how many women decided to leave journalism because they didn't want to put up with Mike Wallace snapping their bra strap in the office.

For a short time in 2019, there was someone from HR hanging out at *60 Minutes* on a regular basis. Unfortunately, he came thirty years too late.

When I cleaned out my office, I left thirty-two small producer book jackets, the ones that are shown on the screen each week behind the correspondent. They were from the stories I did while working with Wallace. They were the same ones about which a rival producer once complained that the font size of my name was bigger than hers. She is now dead, and I am leaving them for the janitor to throw away. Why clog up my garage.

I again looked up and down the hallways. I looked for ghosts— Wallace, Hewitt, Safer, Bradley, Simon, Rooney—but I didn't see or hear anything. There was only a deafening silence left.

Even Steve Kroft had finally retired. I turned off my office lights and didn't look back. It was the right time to go.

A little while after I left, Bill Whitaker, Lesley Stahl, and producers Ruth Streeter and Sam Hornblower organized a retirement party for me at the Harvard Club. I chose the guests to invite and included only one non-CBS-connected person, John Gotti. John has been described as a gangster poet, and I wanted him there, as he was a testament to the work and effort needed to be a successful *60 Minutes* producer. He told the story of our first meeting in the federal courthouse in New York City, when he was on trial.

"I come out to the courtroom, shackled and chained, and I turn to the spectators in the courtroom and this guy is winking at me. I turned to Charlie [Carnesi, Gotti's late attorney] and ask him, 'Who is that guy winking? I haven't been in jail that long that some guy would make a pass at me.'"

"He is that *60 Minutes* guy. He wants to interview you," Charlie told him. ·

"I ain't doing any interviews," Gotti replied. "I certainly am not doing interviews with someone who winks at me.

"Ira stopped winking, and he began to 'court me like a bride,'" Gotti said. "He kept coming to the courtroom, where we became friends, and eventually, four years later, we did the interview."

Bill Whitaker then gave me credit for teaching him how to be a *60 Minutes* man. "I owe my career at *60 Minutes* to you," he said, smiling.

Producer Ruth Streeter, whom I have known for thirty-eight years, recited some of the stories I did in my career.

"Ira did stories about con men, gangsters, fraud artists, tax cheats."

Gotti then interrupted. "It sounds like the people at my last Sunday barbecue," he said with a laugh.

Everyone cracked up. It was a special and warm night of celebrating *60 Minutes* past, and a shared camaraderie that usually surfaces only at funerals. It was nice to hear the tributes while I was still alive.

As the night was nearing an end, Gotti stood and told a story about his father, the most notorious gangster New York had ever known. "My father said life is about creating memories. At the end, that is all that matters. And as a tribute to you, with all the people here, you have made some amazing memories tonight. Love you, my friend."

It was a great send-off. It took a former gangster like Gotti to remind all the ambitious producers and correspondents in the room about how special and important their mission is. For me, it has been a great memory.

ACKNOWLEDGMENTS

I have been working on this book for more than twenty years—stealing moments to jot notes, on planes, in the office, or during boring meetings. I was guided by a quote from oceanographer and filmmaker Jacques Cousteau, "When one man, for whatever reason, has the opportunity to lead an extraordinary life, he has no right to keep it to himself." I wanted to leave this for my three amazing children, Max, Jake, and Johanna, and for the many dedicated journalists I have mentored over forty years. I am indebted to former St. Martin's Press editors Stephen Powers and Thomas Dunne, who believed in the memoir and pushed it forward, and to Charles Spicer who saw it to the finish line.

I owe special thanks to my friends and readers, Bob Reiss, Carol Darr, Caren Neile, my wife Iris Schneider, and especially to Antonio Mora, who possessed the rare combination of being a former network news anchor and Harvard lawyer. His meticulous notes made me look smarter. I also want to thank the three executive editors who hired me—Don Hewitt, Phyllis McGrady, and Jeff Fager. Because they took a chance, I was employed in TV for forty years. Thanks, too, to Mike Feldman, Barry Scheck, Daniel Alterman, Meryl Kaynard, and Buck Briggs, who provided wise counsel during stretches of choppy seas. And to my friends and colleagues who have enriched my life and work.

ACKNOWLEDGMENTS

There are too many to mention but special shoutouts go to Bill Whitaker, Lesley Stahl, Ruth Streeter, Sam Hornblower, Peter Schweizer, John Miller, Mike Gray, Byron Pitts, Anderson Cooper, David Rosen, Charles Gibson, Margaret Fox, Tim Grajek, and my colleagues from my Nieman years, a thirty-seven-year friendship that keeps growing.

And finally to the memory of my parents, Leo and Ethel Rosen, who taught me to always trust my instincts.

ABOUT THE AUTHOR

For nearly twenty-five years, IRA ROSEN has produced some of the most memorable, important, and groundbreaking stories for *60 Minutes*. He has won every major award in broadcast journalism, including twenty-four national Emmy Awards, placing him among the top all-time news Emmy winners in broadcast history. His report with *The Washington Post* on the opioid epidemic won more awards for *60 Minutes* than any series in the show's fifty-two-year history. A former Nieman Fellow at Harvard University, Rosen was a senior producer and one of the creators of *Primetime Live* at ABC, a show hosted by Diane Sawyer and Sam Donaldson.

Rosen pioneered the use of hidden cameras for *Primetime Live* investigations that became the signature stories for the show. At *60 Minutes*, his investigations often focused on corruption in Washington, including one that exposed the practice of legislators trading stocks on insider information that they learned in closed-door hearings. That led to a major ethics reform bill that was passed by Congress and signed into law by President Obama.

In addition to his Emmys, he has won four duPont Awards, two Peabodys, six Investigative Reporters and Editors awards (IRE), two RFK awards, a Hillman Prize, and an Edward R. Murrow Award. He has served on the advisory board of Meetup and the Stony Brook School of Journalism. Rosen has lectured at over thirty colleges and institutions, including Harvard Law and Business schools, and the Aspen Institute.

Ira Rosen is the coauthor of *The Warning: Accident at Three Mile Island.*